SELLING AIR POWER

Number 124: Williams-Ford Texas A&M University
Miliary History Series

SELLING AIR POWER

Military Aviation and American Popular Culture after World War II

STEVE CALL

Texas A&M University Press • College Station

Library of Congress Cataloging-in-Publication Data

Call, Steve, 1956–
  Selling air power : military aviation and American popular culture after
World War II / Steve Call. — 1st ed.
        p. cm. — (Williams-Ford Texas A&M University military history series :
no. 124)
  Includes bibliographical references and index.
  ISBN-13: 978-1-60344-091-2 (cloth : alk. paper)
  ISBN-10: 1-60344-091-7 (cloth : alk. paper)
  ISBN-13: 978-1-60344-100-1 (pbk. : alk. paper)
  ISBN-10: 1-60344-100-X (pbk. : alk. paper)   1. Air power in popular culture—
United States. 2. Air power in mass media—United States. 3. Air power—Public
opinion—United States. 4. Air power—United States—History—20th century.
5. Air warfare in popular culture—United States. 6. Air warfare in mass media—
United States. 7. Air warfare—Public opinion—United States. 8. Air warfare—
United States—History—20th century. 9. Propaganda, American—History—
20th century.   I. Title.
  UG633.S374   2009
  358.4′030973—dc22
                                                              2008036833

To my friend, Major Kirk L. Cakerice, USAF, November 3, 1954–September 19, 1997. He died in service to his country. He was loved and respected by all who knew him, and his memory will live in our hearts forever.

Contents

Illustrations

Acknowledgments

In the course of this study I received considerable help from numerous people, and I take great pride in documenting that assistance. First and foremost has been the help in shaping and refining my ideas from colleagues who are also my friends. Dr. Pete Maslowski, Dr. Dennis Showalter, Col. Phil Meilinger, Ph.D., Col. Rob Owen, Ph.D., Lt. Col. Mark Clodfelter, Ph.D., and Lt. Col. Mark Conversino, Ph.D., all listened to my first vague groping or read outlines and offered invaluable advice, pointed critiques, and, most important, encouragement. For this I am truly grateful.

I also wish to thank those unsung heroes of historical research, the archivists who helped me find material that proved so critical to my research. The staff of the Air Force Historical Research Agency was very helpful and provided a research stipend at a critical stage of my research, but I especially want to thank archivists Joe Caver and Micky Russell. Their assistance made my work there far more productive than it otherwise would have been, and they maintain by far the most "researcher-friendly" working environment of any archive I have ever visited. At the National Archives David Giordano was truly a godsend. He single-handedly turned one inadequate citation into a wealth of invaluable material that unlocked the inner workings of Air Force–Hollywood co-operation. At the Library of Congress Bill Barry in the Motion Picture section went the extra mile in identifying and locating material, and his help allowed me to make advanced arrangements so that my research in Washington would be most productive.

This work started as a dissertation at Ohio State, and for that stage of the project I wish to thank all the professors who provided help and advice, especially the members of my dissertation committee. I also owe a big debt of thanks to all the people of the interlibrary loan office at the OSU library and Karen Pitcher at Broome Community College. The nature of this study meant many requests for obscure articles and pamphlets, and many people at interlibrary loan went above and beyond the call of duty in tracking down my numerous requests. I would also like to thank two archivists at Texas Women's University—Dawn Letson and Tonya Hartline—for their help. Numerous fellow graduate students provided comments and patiently listened as I bounced my ideas off them. While the list is far too long for inclusion, I wish specifically to mention Kelly Jordan and Bill Roberts and thank them for their thoughtful input. Both David Mets and Harry Borowski graciously answered innumerable questions and gave me their thoughts on the general topic of my research, and I am deeply appreciative of their kindness.

Last, but certainly not least, I wish to thank my family. I have been blessed with a large cheering section of kids, parents, siblings, aunts, uncles, and cousins, all of whom kept up a steady stream of encouragement and concern that meant more to me than words can convey. They all supported me even if they did not understand my curious interest in this subject, and I only hope I can repay them in kind for their constant faith and affection.

SELLING AIR POWER

CHAPTER I

Introduction

In the closing scene of *The Court-Martial of Billy Mitchell,* a 1955 movie attempting to redeem the memory of one of America's leading air power visionaries, the lead character, having just been convicted and sentenced, walks out onto the street after bidding an emotional farewell to his faithful supporters—America's early airmen. The scene is loaded with romantic imagery but also revealing symbolism. As he steps out, the Air Force Song is playing in the background, slow and restrained; while still on the steps, though, he looks up at a formation of biplanes, and as that image morphs into a formation of F-86 Sabre jets flying a starburst maneuver, the song swells into triumphant glory. More than just Hollywood schmaltz, this scene is emblematic of both the heroic image of air power in the United States after World War II and the effort of postwar air power advocates to foster that heroic image and shape the public's understanding of air power through popular culture. Believing that World War II air power had proven its revolutionary capabilities, those who espoused that revolutionary vision sought to shape public attitudes toward the "proper" use of air power, but moreover, they sought to convert average Americans to the air power gospel. They enjoyed great success in getting their message into such unlikely venues as movies, radio shows, and popular magazine articles—even a Broadway play and a popular comic strip. Before long, however, air power's critics turned the tables and employed similar means in an attempt to depict air power as sinister and a grave threat. Both efforts offer revealing insights into attitudes and images of air power in Cold War America.

For centuries humans had imagined they could obtain great advantage by attacking their enemies from the air—mythology and folklore around the world are littered with images of powerful beings striking helpless victims from the air. When the flying machine first burst onto the scene it captured popular imagination to an extent perhaps unparalleled in history. Human reason had shattered one of the most fundamental and age-old limitations of human experience: gravity. Science had opened a whole new dimension, both literally and figuratively. Popular imagination did not just revel in the new physical freedom, though; it also celebrated a spiritual release as well, for contemporaries felt the technological breakthrough was as much an aesthetic experience as it was a physical one. Just as the body could now soar into the heavens and dance among the clouds, so too could the human spirit and imagination.

It is perhaps difficult for modern readers to appreciate how deeply the dawn of flight moved Western imagination in the first few decades of the air age. We have grown up with the commonplace reality of aviation, and during our lifetime science has moved on to new wonders, such as space travel and quantum physics. But historians who have studied the impact of aviation on Western imagination are unanimous in their amazement at the full magnitude of cultural forces sweeping Western society and unlocking primordial yearnings and passions as a result of the advent of human flight. This fascination is most clearly evident through its reflection in popular culture, for the fantastic visions soon found voice through thousands of novels, poems, movies, and works of art, each extolling the virtues of flight and awakening expectations of deliverance from all manner of ills plaguing the human race. Moreover, these works were very popular, and that popularity hints at a public eager for such images. Those who tell the story of Western society's response to the airplane are remarkably similar in their accounts: human flight unlocked ancient passions that filled popular culture with stirring rhapsodies and eschatological visions. As Joseph Corn and others have shown, the American public embraced the airplane as fervently as any other nation.[1]

Most of these studies, however, focus primarily on the public's response to aviation in general and redemption of a universal nature, not necessarily how the public saw military uses of aviation.[2] As in other Western nations, though, America's fascination soon extended to those military uses for the airplane, and eschatological expectations followed there too. As Michael Sherry illustrates, those fanciful expectations colored how air power was shaped by its early adherents and contributed directly to how they employed the new weapon.[3] As public enthusiasm continued and media images proliferated, air power gained a growing hold on American popular culture throughout the interwar period and into the 1950s. Many Americans saw air power as an integral part of what they believed was a glorious new air age. Within the context of enthusiasm for aviation and cultural themes proclaiming the arrival of a brave new air age, it is not surprising that some members of American society would imagine a revolutionary role for air power just as others were imagining a revolutionary role for other forms of flight. Often the same individuals prophesied of a great future for both aviation and air power, for they saw the two as part of the same movement, the same force for change.

Air power advocates did not create the fascination with air power in popular imagination; rather, public fascination with the flying machine and the reveries inspired by aviation helped to create and sustain exaggerated expectations for air power in the minds of both its proponents and the U.S. public. What air power advocates did do was to appeal to the public's fascination with aviation and air power in an effort to nurture the public's expectations for air power and guide those expectations in directions envisioned by the air power advocates themselves. This they did primarily through the medium of popular culture. Having been influenced by popular imagination themselves, they returned to the realm of popular culture to share their dream of revolutionary air power and try to get the public to share that dream as well. In short, they sought to make the United States a nation of air power advocates.

Many scholars have examined the development of air power in the United States, and several have commented on air power advocates' attempts to win support for their cause, but none have specifically studied the postwar air power advocates' use of popular culture to build that support. Nor have they explained America's fascination with air power as reflected in popular culture.[4] Those who do consider popular culture focus particularly on the years before World War II, and they fit the popular culture campaign into the political-bureaucratic struggle for air power. According to this view, air power proponents, stymied by government and military authorities, turned to popular culture to appeal directly to the American people. In short, they were "going over the heads" of military and congressional leaders in an effort to generate favorable public opinion that would then force Congress to vote greater air power appropriations. While this is true on the surface, a closer look reveals that there was more to the popular culture crusade than a public relations campaign—air power advocates were evangelists trying to win over millions to their new faith.

More specific treatments of some areas of popular culture have at times touched on air power themes, but none consider the air power advocates' crusade in its entirety or approach the subject within the context of the imagined air power revolution. For example, Michael Paris has written perhaps the most penetrating study of aviation films, and while he fits the popularity of air power films into the context of nationalism and the fascination with aviation in popular imagination, he does not identify a campaign to convert the American public to the air power revolution through cinema. H. Bruce Franklin's *War Stars* identifies a cultural fascination with air power in the context of exploring America's historic fixation with "superweapons" and explores air power advocates' interwar efforts to sell America on air power through popular culture. Written under the obvious influence of the Strategic Defense Initiative—or "Star Wars"—debate, however, and somewhat polemical in nature, the book largely ignores the postwar air power crusade and focuses instead on the debate over nuclear weapons. Laurence Goldstein's *The Flying Machine and Modern Literature* adds many unique insights into how aviation and space flight are reflected in fiction and poetry, but its interwar themes echo Corn and Sherry, while its narrower focus on the postwar period examines only a small group of authors and does not touch on the effort to advance air power through popular culture.[5] Air power themes in other areas, such as radio and television, have remained largely unexplored.

The image air power advocates presented through popular culture is a critical chapter in understanding the rise of American air power. Early air power proponents were caught up in the eschatological visions that burst forth in America's popular imagination at the dawn of flight, and these visions spawned a revolutionary dream for air power in the imagination of its advocates, the ramifications of which can be traced right up to today. While Michael Sherry has described the air power proponents' agitation in the interwar period and its effects on the use of air power in World War II, that chapter in air power history is merely a prelude to the crusade air power advocates launched in popular culture after the war. Relying on obvious manifestations of widespread public support and sympathetic editors, publishers, directors, and producers—in short, those who controlled popular culture—air power's proponents dramatically increased their efforts to spread their message after World War II, and for a long period met with a highly receptive audience. For example, throughout the late forties and much of the fifties hardly a month went by without at least one blatantly pro–air power article appearing in such general interest magazines as *Saturday Evening Post, Reader's Digest,* or *Life.*

Judging by the wealth and content of material appearing in popular culture, the message presented by air power's champions enjoyed for a time the mantle of "conventional wisdom." That is, the mainstream of the American public was confronted with a preponderance of material that presented the revolutionary air power message with little debate. Thus for the average American, such a barrage would seem to imply that "the best minds" must agree that air power represented progressive military strategy, and any forward-thinking person would see the wisdom and inherent superiority of air power. While many raised arguments against air power's message, those arguments could hardly compete for the public's attention because of the magnitude of exposure the air power message enjoyed at the height of its impact. For example, Marshall Andrews, writing in 1950, complained repeatedly that the public was only hearing one side of the air power debate because newspaper and popular magazine editors would not accept articles attacking air power's capabilities. He further stated that anyone who questioned those capabilities was ridiculed and reviled as antimodern.[6]

Air power advocates owed the preponderance of their message to the channels through which their message was carried, and this in turn reflects the popularity of their message. While air power's champions certainly worked through "official" publications such as *Air Force* magazine and *Air University Quarterly Review,* as well as numerous aviation magazines, such venues had a limited audience that by its self-selected nature make it less reflective of the larger public. These magazines were, in effect, "preaching to the converted." Far more revealing, and therefore the focus of this study, was the message aimed at the general public as a whole. Thus by popular culture I mean media aimed at the largest audience possible. In writing books, novels, plays, and general interest magazines articles, in making feature films for theaters across the country or shows for network television and radio, air power advocates aimed their message not at government decision makers or military strategists but at the general public, the "person on the street." Furthermore, while such venues sought to be "informative," they were not news services, so they were not bound by the same investigative and objectivity standards as were newspapers, news magazines, or film documentaries. Thus air power advocates could and did work in images as well as facts, and their images were rarely balanced by opposing viewpoints.

But what makes the general interest media crucial to understanding the image of air power presented to the American public is the target audience and the reason people turned to these media. Feature films, novels, and general interest magazines sought to appeal to the widest possible audience, the mainstream middle class, and people turned to such media primarily for diversion. By creating appealing diversion, air power advocates drew a large audience that then became captive receptors for the images air power advocates sought to implant. The most bizarre examples of the dichotomy between diversion and air power images came in general interest magazines where stark depictions of nuclear annihilation were sandwiched between fashion articles and the latest installment of Tugboat Annie.

Focusing on how air power advocates presented their message through popular culture gives several revealing insights. First and foremost, it tells us what air power advocates wanted the general public to believe. Secondly, it reflects the degree to which shapers of public opinion—editors, producers, directors, and others—thought air power needed to be stressed in popular culture or would be popular with paying customers. This approach also gives, to some degree, an indication of how the public responded to the air power crusade, although one should remember that seeing a movie pitching the strategic bombing message does not mean the viewer accepted the message or became committed to it. Likewise, subscribers to magazines that regularly ran articles advocating air power themes might not even read the articles, and if they did they might not accept the argument. Still, the appearance of such themes in media that depended on paying customers is some reflection of the public mood. Finally, tracing the evolution of themes appearing in such venues indicates how popular culture, and to some extension, public mood, reacted to the air power advocates' campaign. As we shall see, larger world events and changing public mood affected how air power was portrayed in popular culture.

Who were these air power advocates? The term would seem to imply a hardcore group of activists who pushed for a singular goal or a set agenda. While this certainly describes some, the material appearing in popular culture indicates this is clearly not the case for all. Air power advocates varied in their commitment to the cause and in the goals they sought. This caveat might best be illustrated by way of an analogy. In our current popular culture the computer has its own group of advocates and enjoys something of the same "conventional wisdom" air power enjoyed in an earlier period. The gamut of advocacy runs from the hardcore computer "zealots" who seem to claim that computers will cure all the world's ills to those who see computers as an integral part of everyday life in the future and who urge "computer literacy" on everyone as a means of preparing for the future they envision. There are those who shrink back from computers, who point to dangers ahead if we "go too far" with computers, or who doubt many of the claims made on behalf of the computer. Still, computer advocates have succeeded in convincing a wide segment of the general public that computers can bring great benefits, that computers are a necessary part of modern life, and that progressive, forward-thinking individuals should indeed become "computer literate." In much the same way, air power advocates ran the gamut from hardcore zealots who made extravagant claims, such as Alexander de Seversky, to those who saw it as an important part of America's future, such as the editors of *Collier's*.

In examining advocacy groups there is often a tendency to "round up the usual suspects," to focus on individuals who might have a vested interest in the issue and then assume the vested interest motivated their advocacy. Such an approach distorts any analysis of air power advocates and their popular culture crusade. Granted, some were leading figures in the air force, and in fact there appears to be no air force leader who advocated less air power or a restriction of its mission, but their advocacy stemmed from more than bureaucratic ambition. Certainly anyone in the air force who doubted the need for a bigger air force or who questioned air power's capabilities would not get to a position of power and influence in the postwar air force, but the messages air force leaders consistently put forward in the popular culture campaign indicate that they earnestly believed the air power gospel they helped propagate and that this belief was part of their motivation in trying to make the U.S. public believe it as well. By the same token, one should not exaggerate the role of air force members in the popular culture crusade. Granted, air force figures such as Curtis LeMay played important roles in "selling" air power, but they were far out-numbered by civilian figures, many of whom never had any official connection with the air force. Some, like Alexander de Seversky and William Bradford Huie, were even an embarrassment to the air force at times and proved counterproductive to air power goals. Similarly some air power advocates were aircraft industry leaders with a vested financial interest in a bigger air force. Far more important, though, were the many more advocates who had no vested interest in advancing the air power cause. Writers, novelists, journalists, newspaper and magazine editors and publishers, playwrights, screenwriters, movie, television, and radio directors and producers, all played critical roles in spreading the air power gospel, for they decided what the public read, heard, and watched, and they did it for no apparent motive other than that they each, for a variety of reasons, believed in the cause of air power.

The diversity among air power advocates is also seen in what they believed about air power. As with the computer analogy, convictions ran the gamut from extreme to pragmatic, but all believed air power was a force that would shape America's and the world's future. Some made extravagant claims for air power, such as the belief that armies and navies were obsolete except as support units for the air force. Others felt it was America's best frontline defense in a dangerous world. Some saw air power as an amorphous concept that might best be described as the ability to do in the air whatever one wanted or had to do: bombing, seizing air superiority, supporting ground troops, or exploiting air mobility. Others, though, saw strategic bombing as the primary embodiment of air power. Most agreed that air power was more than just military planes. Anything the nation and society did on a daily basis that furthered the cause of aviation contributed to air power. Along these lines, postwar air power advocates continued the call for "airmindedness," a theme which had begun in the interwar period.[7] "Airmindedness" was a term widely used from the twenties through the fifties to indicate a state of mind that recognized the importance of aviation and sought its advancement. In much the same way people talk about the need to become "computer literate" today, air power advocates spoke of the need to make all Americans knowledgeable about aviation, air power, and the importance of the two. On the whole, though, one cannot speak of the "typical" air power advocate's view any more than one can speak of the "typical" air power advocate.

This diversity is further complicated by the fact that attitudes toward air power changed over the period in question, both among air power advocates and within popular culture. Over the course of twenty years following World War II a symbiotic relationship developed between air power advocates and the U.S. public that went through various stages. During the early years when the United States enjoyed a nuclear monopoly and the Cold War took shape, and as air power advocates focused on maintaining the wartime popular support for air power and building a large peacetime air force, the popular culture campaign stressed themes reminiscent of the interwar period, particularly the revolutionary nature of air power: air power had revolutionized human affairs as well as warfare, it had created a grave threat to the Unites States that only a strong air force could meet, and strategic bombing would paralyze any enemy's military at its industrial source.

The Soviet's explosion of an atomic bomb in 1949 and the outbreak of the Korean War in 1950 brought changes to how air power was depicted in popular culture through the mid-1950s. In responding to Soviet nuclear capability, air power advocates found themselves hostage to earlier success in depicting the lethal power of strategic bombing and had to face public realization that Soviet strategic bombers possessed the same deadly capabilities. Some air power advocates debated the value of greater air defenses for North America, but most efforts sought to portray the air force's Strategic Air Command as the best possible shield deterring a nuclear attack on the Unites States through the promise of overwhelming retaliation. At the same time, though, the Korean War forced a shift from the earlier exclusive emphasis on strategic bombing to one depicting a broader conception of air power. The end result was a set of conflicting and often contradictory images of air power encompassing overwhelming strategic forces that could somehow stop incoming enemy bombers at their source without launching a preemptive strike, along with powerful tactical and air defense forces able to meet any contingency but which could not stop a concerted nuclear attack on the United States. This development set the stage for the elevation of SAC as an icon in popular culture through the late fifties representing America's nuclear forces as the only thing standing between the United States and nuclear devastation.

By the mid-1950s, though, doubts emerged in the popular culture depiction of air power. Advocates still portrayed the air force as the best possible defense in a hostile world, but other voices questioned the wisdom of massive retaliation as national policy. More important is a subtle but perceptible shift in public mood reflected in popular culture. Joseph Corn has called the fifties the twilight years of America's romance with aviation, and the same seems to be true with its acceptance of air power as a force possessing unlimited potential.[8] Taking its place by the end of the decade was an image in popular culture that more and more depicted air power as a malevolent threat. Increasingly air power's image as the best deterrent to war had to compete with images of the Mad Bomber, best reflected in *Dr. Strangelove*'s Generals Jack D. Ripper and Buck Turgidson, both of whom threatened to plunge the world into a nuclear holocaust.

The importance of the air power crusade and the later anti–air power message in popular culture is not just what each individual advocate or critic said or believed; rather, the importance is in the images formed in American culture. There once was a time when many people, military and civilian, shapers of popular culture and average citizens, saw air power not only as the shape of the future but also as the promise of a better tomorrow. This image contributed to American society turning to air power for a sense of security through much of the fifties and to making air power the centerpiece of U.S. defense policy. The fact that at the same time air power was defined and epitomized by LeMay's Strategic Air Command and the threat of nuclear devastation is a stark indicator that images can shape popular passions in mysterious ways. Only later did the public come to see that, far from offering utopian deliverance, air power actually threatened to be the harbinger of tragedy on an epic scale, and that image was similarly shaped through popular culture. How these images were crafted is the subject of this study.

CHAPTER 2

In the Beginning
A Prologue

It really is not surprising that humans imagined great capabilities for the warplane. Since the dawn of time they had imagined they could obtain great advantage by attacking their enemies from the air. Mythology and folklore around the world is filled with images of flying creatures—both divine and mortal—and their ability to defy gravity is just one reflection of their tremendous power over earthbound creatures. In more modern times sophisticated thinkers merely added an intellectual veneer to this age-old dream. Leonardo da Vinci's famous musings of flying machines were motivated by his patriotic devotion to help fend off the invading French army and his belief that the ability to strike from the sky would present the ultimate weapon: "In truth, whoever has control of such irresistible forces will be lord over all nations, and no human skill will be able to resist his destructive power. . . . no lock, no fortress, however impregnable, will avail to save anyone against the will of such a necromancer. He will cause himself to be carried through the air from East to West and through all the uttermost parts of the universe."[1] Similarly, while in France in 1783 after the harrowing experience of the American Revolution, Benjamin Franklin witnessed the Montgolfier brothers' first hot air balloon ascension and wrote to a friend on what a great military advantage balloons would give a weak nation against stronger military powers: balloons manned by soldiers could attack without warning anywhere in the enemy's homeland, no army could be strong enough everywhere to stop a force of five thousand such balloons, and this fleet "could not cost more than Five ships of the Line."[2]

Such speculation continued right up to the eve of the Wright Brothers' first flight; in fact, it accelerated as the turn of the twentieth century approached. Some saw utopian potential in the prospect of some future warbird, as can be seen in Simon Newcomb's 1900 novel *His Wisdom the Defender.* Set in 1941, a U.S. college professor discovers an antigravity substance that he uses to power his fleet of airships. He mounts upon these ships a wondrous weapon of his own invention, and his airships have no trouble disarming the entire world, for as Newcomb writes, "no defence of person or property against an army flying the air where it chose, and pouncing down at any moment, was possible." The hero forces all nations to submit to the authority of his private corporation staffed by U.S. college students who direct all human affairs. The hero, rising above nationalism, assumes the twin titles of "His Wisdom" and "The Defender of the Peace," abolishes war, and oversees a golden age of peace and prosperity brought about by the reign of reason.[3]

By far the most frequent prophecies of this period, though, portrayed air power as a "blessed destroyer," a miraculous force discovered just in time to save the nation from some overwhelming invasion or other external threat. For example, in 1898 S. W. Odell's *The Last War; Or, the Triumph of the English Tongue,* depicts air power as one of the primary means by which Anglo-American progressivism defeats forever the forces of evil and reactionism led by Russia.[4] Products of rampant nationalism and the romanticism of war in Western civilization before World War I, air war prophecies of this sort were part of the larger cottage industry of future-war literature that I. F. Clarke identifies, and it helped shape the image of air power in popular culture as a wondrous weapon that would be the salvation of nations.[5]

The actual appearance of a working airplane in 1903 did not dampen fanciful speculation about air power; rather, the concrete reality seems to have heightened cultural expectations as the public became fascinated with aviation in general. The physical manifestation of long-standing myths and dreams, though, did awaken in some observers the fear that all-powerful warplanes might turn out to be a plague that would sweep all before it and usher in a more sinister future. The best example of this vision is the writings of H. G. Wells. Best known for such science-fiction works as *The War of the Worlds* and *The Time Machine,* Wells was also a prolific social commentator, and he perceived what the airplane's ultimate potential meant for the human race: every man, woman, and child, even society itself, would not only become targets but the focus of air power's destruction. In *The War in the Air,* published in 1908, all the nations of the world are secretly building vast aerial armadas when Germany sparks a global conflict by bombing New York City with a fleet of zeppelins. As nations around the world bomb each other, governments and civilizations collapse, and societies are reduced to small pockets living in isolation and primitive conditions. Similarly, in *The World Set Free,* published in 1913, Wells depicts the world brought to the brink of ruin by bombers carrying nuclear bombs, but in this case the threat inspires the people of the world to come together under one government that outlaws war, which ironically enforces that ban with air power—the very threat it sought to eliminate. This irony is not surprising, for as we shall see, in the real world people would turn to air power to save itself from air power. Throughout the two works Wells's message is clear: air power posed a graver threat than did the Martians in *The War of the Worlds,* for now the seeds of human destruction lay in the hands of nations and people, not some other-worldly alien, and salvation would not come through some serendipitous microbial counterattack but only through human foresight.[6]

The outbreak of World War I took aerial warfare out of the realm of fancy and, like the invention of the airplane, gave popular imagination concrete images on which to focus. It also sparked a new era in the depiction of air power in popular culture. Many who had previously speculated about air warfare were merely attempting to predict the future, not necessarily urge the adoption of any particular approach to aerial combat, let alone advocate overwhelming air power. At the same time, the few voices who had warned of danger from warplanes were seemingly belied by more powerful images stemming from the Great War: traditional warfare seemed senseless and threatening, but air warfare seemed heroic, especially since the fighter ace had given it a very popular and romantic human face. Moreover, a new medium—movies—which had been in its infancy before the war, emerged from the conflict capable of presenting cultural images far more powerfully than older forms, especially when it came to the thrill and adventure of aerial combat. Old themes still lingered—Utopianists still pointed to a shining new dawn ushered in by the warplane, others still saw it as a new "secret weapon" that would save their nation from some imagined threat, and some still warned of the potential threat of warplanes to society—but the real change in air power's cultural image came from three new cultural phenomena: the air power advocate, the fighter ace, and cinema.[7]

The interwar period saw a surge in the volume of air war images presented in popular culture, and the three new facets help explain why those images were so effective in positively shaping the public's perception of air power. One key aspect of this phenomenon was that air power advocates—those who specifically sought to advance the importance of air power or shape a specific air power agenda—began a concerted campaign to present images intended to convert the public to their new-found faith in the warplane. The most visible and vocal of these in the United States was William "Billy" Mitchell, an army Air Corps officer and a key air commander in World War I. Mitchell pioneered a new path to propagating his air power vision to the public through books and popular magazine articles, by speaking to the press, and by staging public demonstrations meant to back his assertions. There were two aspects of the image Mitchell put before the public, though, that differed dramatically from pre–World War I depictions of aerial warfare. First, while Mitchell's accounts of what air power would one day be able to do contained a great deal of speculation, they were not works of mythology or science fiction. Second, Mitchell, like several other figures around the world, attempted to develop and advance a comprehensive theoretical framework of how air power should be used and what it could accomplish if used according to theory. He not only sought to enlist the U.S. public as supporters of air power, he wanted them to support air power used according to his vision.[8]

Mitchell was not the only air power advocate active in America's popular culture during this period; a number of others—some who would later be key American air power leaders—were helping the effort. Henry "Hap" Arnold, for example, who was one of Mitchell's close associates and leader of the U.S. Army Air Forces (AAF) in World War II, wrote a series of air adventure novels aimed at teenage boys. He also co-authored with Ira Eaker, another future air general, books extolling air power to adult audiences in the years before World War II. These American figures added their voices to those of air power advocates around the world—particularly in Britain, France, and Italy—and collectively they sought to win their case in the public forum by spreading their messages through the various media of popular culture.

There were other voices advancing the image of air power in the interwar period besides the air power advocate. During the war the public had become enthralled with the fighter ace, and afterwards a steady stream of autobiographical and biographical works fueled that interest. In almost every category, World War I killed the old nineteenth-century romantic image of war, but not air warfare. In the face of protracted, dehumanizing stalemate, the image of "knights of the air" had served as a public tonic providing something, if in reality very little, for the masses to cheer about. This same dichotomy is found in the literary depiction of that war. It is significantly revealing that in much of the West, particularly Britain, France, and the United States, most written works dealing with the war were decidedly negative and portrayed its ugly, brutal side as best exemplified by Erich Maria Remarque's *All Quiet on the Western Front* and Robert Graves's *Goodbye to All That*. When it came to the air war, though, the dominant themes emphasized the excitement and chivalry of the World War I air combat. The exploits of such heroes as Eddie Rickenbacker, Georges Guynemer, and Billy Bishop were greeted by avid audiences and presented air warfare as heroic and glorious, while Cecil Lewis's *Sagittarius Rising* and the writings of Antoine de Saint-Exupéry even made flying and air combat seem existential.[9]

Special mention should be reserved, however, for the most powerful figure in the public's image of aviation, Charles Lindbergh. While he was not a war ace, the public outpouring in response to his transatlantic flight far surpassed anything seen in the ace phenomenon, and clearly he was seen in much the same light. Moreover, he was a captain in the Air Corps reserve at the time, which helped translate his notoriety to the air power cause. Lindbergh was more than just popular, and he clearly meant more to people than just the temporary attraction of a media figure. The immediate and persistent honors, official and unofficial awards, thousands of poems, paintings, and sculptures—even sermons—coming from around the world and lasting throughout his life attest to the meaning one man's flight had brought to peoples' lives, and his espousal of air power's cause throughout his life added his reputation to that effort.[10]

Nothing could beat the power of cinema, however, and much about aerial warfare made it a natural for this new medium: action, speed, danger, heroics, even gripping pathos. A steady stream of movies like *Wings, Hell's Angels,* and *Dawn Patrol* met with great success and critical acclaim—*Wings* won the first-ever "Best Picture" Academy Award. These films also illustrate the early connection between Hollywood and the aviation and air power communities. The movie *Wings* was the brainchild of John Monk Saunders, who had flown for the U. S. Army during the war, and its relatively unknown director, William Wellman, was chosen because he had flown with the Lafayette Escadrille. One of the movie's two stars, Richard Arlan, had flown for the Canadian Royal Flying Corps, while the other, Charles Rogers, was a civilian pilot who became a navy test pilot during World War II.[11] The driving force behind *Hell's Angels* was an unknown heir to a small industrial fortune, Howard Hughes, who had two real loves in his early days: moviemaking and

1. *Wings* was so effective at extolling air power it inspired Beirne Lay to become an Air Corps pilot and later a highly influential air power advocate.

flying. This film combined the two, for his goal in making the movie was to "glorify and perpetuate the exploits of the Allied and German airmen of the World War."[12] Hughes gathered around him a staff that included several aviation experts and buffs. Director Luther Reed was also the *New York Herald*'s first aviation editor, and advisor Ted Parsons had been an ace in the Lafayette Escadrille.[13] In the case of *Dawn Patrol,* the initial story came from a short piece written by John Monk Saunders of *Wings* fame, and the film's director and guiding spirit was Howard Hawks, who became one of Hollywood's leading aviation filmmakers and who had flown with the U.S. Air Service in the war.[14]

The impact these films had on "selling" air power can be seen quite literally in one example: Beirne Lay, as a student at Yale, saw *Wings* and was immediately filled with a burning desire to become an army Air Corps pilot. He fulfilled that dream and wrote about the entire experience in *I Wanted Wings,* which appropriately enough was soon turned into a movie. After World War II, Lay—himself a product of the glamorization of air power in popular culture—became one of the most effective and prolific of the postwar air power advocates and used film as one of his main media.

The new themes—air power advocates, heroic aces, and cinema—

continued as a new war loomed on the horizon; in fact, the stark threat confronting the democratic West seemed to up the ante when it came to finding the most effective defense. To many, striking at Germany and Japan through the air seemed the only hope, so Americans were reminded through nearly every popular medium that U.S. air power needed their support. Even Walt Disney got in on the act with a feature-length animated rendition of air power advocate Alexander de Seversky's book *Victory through Air Power.* The power of animation and the popularity of Disney carried de Seversky's air power message into theaters all across the country and for the first time combined cinema with overt advocacy. When war came, patriotism added impetus to the air power cause as throughout the war Hollywood and the publishing world kept up a steady stream of movies, books, and popular magazine articles touting

2. In *I Wanted Wings* Beirne Lay tells how he was inspired to become an Army Air Corps pilot and what it took to achieve that goal.

the enlightened and sophisticated nature of U.S. air power and celebrating its many contributions to the war effort.

By the end of World War II, thanks largely to images placed in popular culture, millions of Americans had come to see air power as a major component of Allied victory and as the wave of the future in military affairs. This set the stage for the postwar selling of air power through popular culture. Advocates sought to capitalize on their wartime success by nurturing public support for air power in and of itself. There was widespread support for an independent air force, but that victory needed to be consolidated by congressional action. Then the newly independent air force would need lots of support to ensure its standing vis-à-vis the other, older, services. And this effort would become especially crucial as new threats and new technology came onto the scene. Perhaps the most striking feature of this postwar popularization of air power was its sheer scope and scale. Having realized how they had gained such solid support, air power advocates also sought to capitalize on a successful formula. In short, the effort to shape America's support for air power through popular culture mushroomed in the immediate aftermath of World War II. But it was not enough for the public to support air power in general—air power advocates also sought to educate Americans on the proper uses of air power.

SHAPING THE IMAGE: AIR POWER ADVOCATES
AND THEIR MESSAGE BEFORE WORLD WAR II

American air power was born of a dream—those who saw revolutionary potential for air power saw themselves as visionaries, prophets who had grasped the ultimate shape of things to come. Air power advocates had, like others, reveled in the general fascination with aviation in popular imagination, and in that state they had "dreamed dreams and seen visions." They were often arrogant and ridiculed those who opposed their views because they believed they had "glimpsed the truth" and that their vision was as inexorable as the tide. Simply stated, the prophets of air power believed the airplane had revolutionized warfare. But advocating air power's revolutionary potential was only the beginning. Equally important to many was the shape and details of the revolution—that is, how air power must be used if it was to achieve its revolutionary potential.

Air power advocates often held conflicting views, for there was no set agenda or doctrine. To most advocates air power was more than a concept, but there was no universal plan for realizing their dream. They often considered armies and navies obsolete, not only because they were too vulnerable to air power, but also because they were incapable of decisive action. Heavily influenced by World War I and its trench warfare experience where massive armies battered at each other for four years without conclusive results, and where huge battleship navies mostly sat idly in port or on blockade duty, air power, its proponents claimed, could overleap all defenses and strike at the defenseless heart of the enemy nation. Such a blow, according to air power theorists, would be impossible to stop and would quickly paralyze the enemy society, thus delivering the world from the horrors of another prolonged war by bringing quick, relatively painless victory.

Before the Second World War, suggestions of striking directly at the enemy nation—its people and infrastructure—was a radical departure from standard military thinking. Traditional strategies in land warfare emphasized defeating enemy armies and capturing territory but did not specifically target society. Moreover, airmen stressed an offensive approach that flew in the face of orthodox interpretations of World War I: trench stalemate had proven the supremacy of defensive firepower. Finally, this approach to air power was contrary to both U.S. Army air war doctrine, which focused on air observation and support of ground troops in combat, and the public's image of the romantic fighter ace. Rather than aiding the ground battle with close air support or dueling for glory with enemy "knights of the air," air power advocates' theories envisioned air warfare as bombing the enemy's heartland. The ensuing popular culture campaign focused as much on selling the public and the military on strategic bombing as it did on the revolutionary potential of air power.[15]

The air power debate took place in Europe as well as the United States, and several European theorists had considerable impact on American air power theorists. The first to develop such theories were two Italians, Gianni Caproni and Giulio Douhet. Caproni, an aircraft designer and manufacturer, had an immediate impact during the war, as several of his writings advocated concerted bombing efforts against enemy targets and reached the highest levels among Allied decision makers. One measure of his impact on U.S. policy during the war is that John J. Pershing, commander of the American Expeditionary Forces, sent Caproni a personal note after the war thanking him for his help. Douhet's influence, although difficult to measure, had a more lasting impact. A controversial air power theorist during the war, Douhet was court-martialed and imprisoned in 1917 for criticizing Italian air policy. After the war, he spelled out his theories in a two-part work, *The Command of the Air,* published in 1921 and 1927. The first volume constituted the first public expression of a systematic plan for a war-winning bombing campaign and claimed that a fleet of bombers, striking the enemy's cities with high explosives, incendiary bombs, and poison gas would drive the enemy to either social collapse or surrender in a matter days.[16]

Two other early bombing advocates came from Britain. Commander of Britain's Royal Air Force from its creation in 1918 to 1929, Hugh Trenchard influenced American thought more through personal contact. While Trenchard focused on bombing industrial and transportation targets, he also emphasized the psychological effect such bombing would have on civilian populations. The other British theorist was B. H. Liddell Hart. An army captain during World War I, Liddell Hart became one of the leading strategic thinkers during the interwar period. He is best known for his theories on tank warfare, but he made one foray into the realm of air power with his slender volume, *Paris: Or the Future of War.* In this work Liddell Hart argued that traditional forces were as powerless to stop air power as Achilles had been at stopping Paris, and that just like that protagonist from the *Iliad,* air power could paralyze an enemy nation with one swift blow. While Liddell Hart echoes Douhet in some respects, he made a more immediate impact by reaching a wider audience.[17]

While these four figures influenced America's early thoughts on air power, the most important proponent was Billy Mitchell, who served as assistant chief of the air service from 1919 to 1925. Mitchell had little contact with aviation until 1916 when he became deputy head of the army's tiny aviation section. He soon learned to fly in his spare time and took on the cause of advancing military aviation. In March 1917, on the eve of America's declaration of war, the army sent him to France as an aeronautical observer. While it is difficult to determine who had the greatest impact on Mitchell's thinking, or when his theories first crystallized, he clearly was impressed by Caproni, Douhet, and Trenchard, and he first started forming his ideas during these early months as an observer. Mitchell was convinced the airplane had supplanted all other forms of warfare, and that the only way his vision of air power would ever come to fruition would be through changing public attitudes. With that end in mind, in 1924 he began writing articles and books aimed at as wide an audience as possible. Mitchell felt bombing gave air power revolutionary potential and that modern war against an industrial nation made its entire population a key element in the war effort.[18]

Recognizing that the public was not ready to accept such offensive plans, Mitchell did not at first write publicly about strategic bombing but nevertheless urged the army to accept it and prepare for it.[19] In a series of tests conducted off the Virginia coast between June 2 and July 21, 1921, Mitchell shocked the navy, and a host of other observers, when a group of army aircraft under his direction sank several surrendered German warships, most notably the reputedly unsinkable battleship *Ostfriesland*. Frustrated that the army and navy did not immediately come around to his way of thinking, Mitchell three years later detailed the bombing tests and outlined his grand vision of air power in a series of articles in *The Saturday Evening Post*. Mitchell's conclusion on the sinking of the *Ostfriesland* was emphatic: navies are obsolete, because aircraft can sink any ship with ease and air power can perform the navy's mission better.[20] Mitchell went even further and stated that in the air age "the destinies of all people will be controlled through the air." In the future airplanes would bomb cities with high explosives and tear gas, industries would collapse, and the nation that struck first with its air fleet would win a complete victory: "An attack from an air force . . . may cause the complete evacuation and cessation of industry. . . . This would deprive armies, air forces, and navies, even, of their means of maintenance." The following year, at the height of his notoriety, Mitchell spelled out these ideas in fuller detail: "To gain a lasting victory in war, the hostile nation's power to make war must be destroyed—this means the manufactories [*sic*], the means of communication, the food products, even the farms, the fuel and oil and the places where people live and carry on their daily lives. . . . Aircraft operating in the heart of an enemy's country will accomplish this object in an incredibly short space of time."[21]

The infamous climax to Mitchell's career demonstrates the influence of his theories on the air power debate. In 1925 Mitchell was courtmartialed for slanderous comments made about his superiors. On September 5, in response to two recent air crashes, Mitchell released a press statement railing against what he called "the incompetency, criminal negligence, and almost treasonable administration of the National Defense by the Navy and War Departments." One measure of Mitchell's stature in the public air power debate was that Pres. Calvin Coolidge personally pressed charges against Mitchell. With Mitchell being the most public air power advocate, many at the time felt the court-martial was really a trial of his theories and of air power itself. In a legal sense, this notion is clearly false. More important, though, Mitchell's critics realized they could not prosecute even such a blatant act of insubordination without dealing with Mitchell's arguments. Despite the clearly defined legal issue facing it, the court-martial elected to hear a lengthy debate on the pros and cons of Mitchell's theories. While the court-martial remained officially a trial of Mitchell's actions, the courtroom debate of his ideas tacitly acknowledged the unofficial question in many minds: did army and navy resistance to new ideas on air power justify Mitchell's comments? Whether Mitchell's theories were right or wrong, though, he was clearly guilty of the charges leveled against him, and on December 17 the court convicted him of insubordination.[22]

The court-martial sentenced Mitchell to five years suspension without pay, which Coolidge amended to five years suspension at half-pay. Mitchell resigned from the army in protest. His campaign to change public attitudes toward air power, though, brought some of the results he desired. First, and foremost, it focused public attention on his arguments in a way congressional hearings could never do and to a greater extent than did his magazine articles. Secondly, it helped bring institutional changes, albeit minor, to the army's air forces. Third, the trial gave air power advocates a martyr. The perception that Mitchell had been crucified for his air power theories crystallized those ideas for many air power advocates and added a personal sense of poignancy to their belief that they were part of a revolutionary movement. Parallels with past figures who had suffered for their faith or for a cause were inescapable and powerful.[23]

Mitchell's resignation freed him from the constraints of public office. Afterward, he spelled out his ideas in even more graphic language. For example, in an article published by *Collier's* in 1928 Mitchell stated that the essence of modern war was bombers and missiles carrying toxic gas, cities rendered uninhabitable, and nations thus reduced to impotence. Moreover, he issued a stern warning that the United States was unprepared to fight in this arena.[24] As Mitchell's depiction of air power became more graphic and shocking, though, his public following fell away. The public had found his early ideas acceptable, for they were primarily defensive. His later expressions, however, were too offensive for a nation firmly committed to isolationism and antimilitarism. His 1930 book *Skyways* sold poorly, and he found it increasingly hard to get articles accepted for publication throughout the remainder of his life.[25] Clearly Mitchell's offensive-minded strategies had outpaced U.S. sentiments, but as a new war loomed larger by the end of the decade and into the next, more and more Americans came to not only espouse many of his ideas but to reflect his enthusiasm for those ideas as well.

At the time of Mitchell's trial, many other army fliers shared his views, and he became a powerful symbol to the early air power movement. While recognizing that Mitchell was clearly guilty of insubordination, Hap Arnold nevertheless testified on his behalf and later stated that most Air Corps pilots saw the court-martial as a trial of air power. Arnold continued circulating Mitchell's theories in the following months and only escaped a court-martial of his own in 1926 by the direct intervention of the chief of the Air Service, Mason Patrick. After his resignation, though, Mitchell fell out of the mainstream of evolving air power theory in the United States, which later developed in directions he had hardly anticipated. In the final analysis, Mitchell's significance lies not in his ideas but in what he represented to the faithful followers of the air power gospel at a time when they needed a heroic role model who embodied their perceived revolution: visionary prophet, fearless crusader, selfless martyr. Mitchell became the image reassuring air power advocates that they too should persevere in the face of all obstacles, doubters, and critics. This dogged perseverance, though, also blinded air power advocates to flaws and limitations in their theories. Two examples illustrate the enduring legacy of Mitchell's image: on the eve of World War II the Air Corps dubbed its B-25 aircraft the Mitchell bomber, and in 1955, in a much more favorable political and cultural climate, latter-day air power advocates redeemed Mitchell and his theories in a cinematic paean, *The Court-Martial of Billy Mitchell*.[26]

The air power debates continued into the 1930s as images of air warfare among military and civilian air power advocates crystallized and increasingly made air power synonymous with bombing. What's more, despite the image of the fighter ace popular in movies, during the interwar period most people theorizing about air warfare came to see the bomber as the basic air weapon—all other types were variants from the standard. This conception is comparable to the army view that the infantry is the fundamental basis of land warfare and the long-held naval view that the standard warship was the battleship. One point overlooked by scholars studying the rise of U.S. strategic bombing is that many of the leading figures in developing, advocating, and implementing America's bombing doctrine, men such as Arnold, Spaatz, Eaker, and Hansell, had spent either much or most of their World War I and interwar careers as "fighter jocks." At a time when they could have benefited by perpetuating the myth of the fighter ace, and when most within the Air Corps considered fighter pilots superior to all other pilots, these men were key actors elevating bombing to the central position in Air Corps thinking.

As it emerged during the thirties, the Air Corps's bombing theory came to focus on daylight precision bombing. The theory took shape at the Air Corps Tactical School (ACTS) in Montgomery, Alabama, which had evolved into a hotbed of air power theory. As one historian observed, it "proved to be the only common location of experienced Air Corps officers who had enough time for creative thinking."[27] Officially, it was just a training school. Unofficially, though, the ACTS served as an influential "think tank" and catalyst that built grassroots support for its emerging strategic bombing theories throughout the army flying community. All faculty members certainly read Mitchell's works, but some point to other figures, such as Douhet, who also influenced their thinking.[28] Daylight precision bombing expressed great faith in air power's ability both to paralyze any nation's ability to wage war and to minimize civilian casualties. Assuming that any industrialized society, especially one mobilized for war, would have certain key industries upon which several other industries depended, the ACTS theorists believed that destroying a select number of key targets would have a magnified effect on the enemy's entire economy that would paralyze their ability to wage war. Finding and destroying these key targets placed an emphasis on accuracy, which would also minimize bombs falling on civilian areas around the target. Significantly, this emphasis on industrial analysis and bombing accuracy was a marked departure from Douhet's theories and Mitchell's post–court martial writings. Emphasizing bombing accuracy also played into cultural images of U.S. technical superiority and frontier marksmanship. Both images would help "sell" strategic bombing to the American public when the time came to employ the strategy in war. From the ACTS the doctrine of daylight precision bombing radiated out to the whole Air Corps. The school preached this new gospel to every student who went through its program until, by the start of World War II, nearly every Air Corps officer had attended the ACTS program and heard the message.[29]

As U.S. air power entered its biggest test in World War II, there is no way to directly gauge the effectiveness of the campaign to popularize it through popular culture, but there are strong indirect indications that the effort had succeeded dramatically. One such indication can be found in data gathered by Gallup polls on the question of increasing the armed forces in the years leading up to the war. The polls generally indicate a majority opinion that all forces should be increased, but the majority favoring an increased air force was consistently and markedly higher. In 1935 48 percent of those polled favored higher army appropriations as opposed to 11 percent favoring smaller appropriations and 41 percent feeling they should remain the same. For the navy the figures are 54 percent, 11 percent, and 35 percent respectively, but for air force appropriations the figures are 74 percent, 7 percent, and 19 percent respectively. This support was bipartisan and held generally the same percentages across all geographic regions. In January 1938, on the question of whether the United States should build larger forces, 69 percent favored a larger army, 74 percent favored a larger navy, but 80 percent favored a larger air force. By November 1938, shortly after the Munich Conference, the figures had increased across the board to 82 percent, 86 percent, and 90 percent respectively. Asked the same question in late September 1939, after the start of the war in Europe, the figures were 86 percent for a larger army, 88 percent navy, and 91 percent air force.[30] The question does not appear to have been asked again before the United States entered the war, perhaps because the United States had already begun increasing its military forces across the board.

Support for air power, though, had been held in check throughout the interwar period by isolationism and antimilitarism in many influential circles. Once those were swept away by the passions evoked by Pearl Harbor, the latent support surfaced, and air power seemed to many the perfect weapon. Moral qualms could easily be mollified by faith in the technological wonder that allowed the United States to bomb efficiently and humanely—both wonderful progressive images—not brutally and clumsily as enemy nations had done. The technological superiority image was reinforced by the messianic image. The airplane would deliver American soldiers from the repetition of the World War I slaughter that many expected. When daylight precision bombing became official doctrine in late 1941 and the Air Corps began selling its "pickle barrel bombing," and after the United States entered the war buoyed by images of Pearl Harbor, the public embraced strategic bombing with an enthusiasm surpassing even Air Corps leaders. This support continued even after it became clear that American bombing was neither as accurate nor as humane as predicted.[31]

World War II saw America's latent support for air power transformed into overt support. Across the country people joined in the goal to fill the skies with warplanes, and one of the most popular images of the war was one of bombs raining down on Hitler and Tojo.[32] One of the most striking and pervasive manifestations of the enthusiasm for air power in popular culture can be seen in magazine advertisements throughout the war. Pick virtually any issue of *Saturday Evening Post, Life, Collier's,* or any other general interest weekly and one will note a favorite visual image for tying into war themes: the airplane. Warplanes or air power subjects were used to pitch everything from cars to refrigerators to radios to tires. Even ads depicting ground or naval forces frequently showed airplanes in the sky overhead.[33] Another eloquent testimonial to the public's expressed faith in air power was the response to Gallup poll questions on the issue of air force independence. In July 1941 42 percent favored independence, 33 percent opposed it, and 25 percent were undecided. By August 1942, 44 percent of respondents claimed to be familiar with the issue and of those, 57 percent favored independence while 27 percent opposed it, and 16 percent had no opinion. By July 1943, apparently the last time the question was posed, of those familiar with the question 59 percent favored independence, and 41 percent opposed it.[34]

Air power advocates' efforts to shape and exploit this support during the war is a well-known phenomenon that has received considerable analysis, but several topics bear brief examination in the context of this study.[35] As late as 1941 AAF leaders Arnold and Eaker were telling the public that AAF strategy relied on industrial bombing at night, and they describe in great detail how they would achieve pinpoint accuracy despite bombing in darkness.[36] In the summer of 1941, though, when Roosevelt asked the military for force requirements if the United States went to war, the AAF presented a far different picture. To project and justify AAF requirements, the newly formed Air War Plans Division (AWPD) at AAF headquarters, staffed by former ACTS instructors, developed a comprehensive plan built around their concept of daylight precision bombing. AWPD-1, as the plan was known, took only nine days to develop, and when approved, with little dissent, it effectively made the ACTS bombing concept official U.S. doctrine.[37]

Thus when the war began and air power suddenly enjoyed overt public support, the AAF began publicizing as its main strategy a doctrine perfectly suited to the image of bombing the public was most prepared to embrace: technologically sophisticated, efficient to the point of appearing scientific, and humane in its emphasis on precision. One early example of the effort to win popular support for its bombing methods was the 1943 movie *Air Force,* a feature film seen by millions of movie-goers and which received generally favorable reviews. The film was directed by Howard Hawks, a World War I pilot and director of *The Dawn Patrol,* and AAF leaders played a central role in shaping the movie from start to finish. Arnold had consulted with Jack Warner, of Warner Brothers Studios, about the film at its inception and remained personally involved at various stages, and AAF technical advisor Capt. Samuel Triffy helped mold the central concept and write the script.[38]

The film not only depicts the exploits of a B-17 crew in the opening days of the war, it elevates the image of U.S. technical superiority and bombing accuracy to absurd levels. In one scene, according to the script, the crew drops only three bombs but sinks one cruiser and two transports. At the same time the gunners shoot down three out of six Japanese fighters before they are themselves forced to crash-land. In the movie version the bombing was cut out to heighten the dramatic effect of the final battle scene, but the gunners shoot down seven out of nine planes. While the public did not see this first display of bombing prowess, it illustrates the image Hollywood and AAF leaders wished to convey to the public. Later, in the climactic battle scene the crew joins a larger force attacking a Japanese fleet and drops three salvos of bombs sinking one tanker, one transport, one destroyer, and an aircraft carrier while shooting down three more Japanese fighters. In the film version the other aircraft decimate the enemy fleet, and nearly every bomb dropped scores a direct hit. The film's final scene, set later in the war, depicts the crew as part of the prewar "hardy band" who established the tradition of heroism, technological superiority, and operational excellence being followed by the AAF's million-man air force.[39] The message to the public in 1943 was clear: that early crew's performance became the standard upheld by all AAF crews around the world. This was the image the AAF wished to convey to the American public, but theirs was not the only voice preaching air power through the medium of popular culture.

Another major effort to popularize air power during the war was the campaign waged by Alexander P. de Seversky, who reiterated much of the technological excellence and operational efficiency messages, but who also raised dichotomous images quite out of keeping with those stressed by the AAF. Born in Russia, de Seversky grew up around airplanes and became an ace and a war hero flying for the Tsarist navy during World War I. After the Bolshevik revolution he emigrated to the United States, where during the interwar years his skill as an aeronautical engineer and aircraft designer led him to found the Seversky Aircraft Corporation in 1931, but de Seversky's poor managerial skills led to his ouster in 1939, and the firm became Republic Aviation.[40] De Seversky's greatest interest, though, was in popularizing air power. In 1921 he met Billy Mitchell and soon became one of his disciples. By the outbreak of World War II de Seversky had become a prolific author of numerous articles and radio broadcasts aimed at winning Americans of all ages to the cause of air power.[41] Early in 1942 de Seversky recapitulated the ideas he had spelled out in such magazines as the *American Mercury, Reader's Digest, Look,* and *Atlantic Monthly* in a book entitled *Victory Through Air Power.* Using the events of World War II up to that date, de Seversky argued that air power had become the decisive element of modern warfare both on land and sea. More importantly, though, he applied the industrial bombing ideas of Mitchell and ACTS theorists to the wartime situation and argued that only through air power could Germany and Japan be defeated without costly, prolonged, and bloody war. Yet another air power advocate was promising America that air power and strategic bombing could deliver it from the horrors of World War I–style trench warfare.[42] But de Seversky's message also contained a disturbing, and as events turned out, foreboding element.

In a chapter entitled "Possession or Elimination," de Seversky observed that air power was merely the latest step in the long march of military evolution that made warfare more capable of destruction. He concluded that while air power in theory gave the wielder great latitude to choose between the two extremes of possession or elimination, that is, "whether the purpose is to destroy the enemy or to capture him, whether the prey must be killed or trapped alive," in reality other factors often forced the choice regardless of the wielder's desires. For example, de Seversky states, "The deeper the civilization and the national pride of a people, the more likely it is to be subjected to the method of extermination, since such a people cannot be reconciled to living the life of the vanquished." De Seversky describes this process of elimination as "the elimination of the country as a world factor," where its people are "reduced to impotence beyond easy recovery, through the annihilation of the industrial foundations of their life," and he observes that "the very ease with which a machine-age country can be blasted into chaos from on high is an invitation to the war of annihilation." After considering all the factors he felt were pertinent to the strategic situation of war with Germany and Japan, de Seversky concludes that in both theaters, "American strategy must be geared for the war of elimination—which is as good as saying war predicated on superior air power."[43] In short, de Seversky advocated using air power in a war of annihilation against Germany and Japan to sink both countries into long-term chaos and impotence.

De Seversky's message came across most powerfully, however, when Walt Disney decided to give de Seversky a wider audience by turning the book into a feature-length movie. A self-described aviation enthusiast, Disney claimed to have concluded earlier that air power held the key to victory in World War II and felt educating Americans about air power through the film was an important civic duty.[44] The film set de Seversky's ideas into Disney's characteristically impressive and effective images, but those images conveyed the dichotomous nature of de Seversky's view of bombing in ways both subtle and overt. In numerous instances throughout the film, bombers are shown high overhead raining bombs down indiscriminately on enemy cities below, but when the illustrator gives the audience a close-up view of the scene on the ground, only factories are destroyed, reinforcing America's faith that their bombing is almost miraculously accurate.[45]

Less subtle is the macro view of the effect of such bombing. The film goes into depth in describing the Allies' military dilemma brought on by Germany and Japan possessing interior lines of supply connecting distant outposts to the industrial cornucopia of the empires' heartlands. When focusing on the German situation, the lines of communication are depicted as a spoked wheel carrying a steady stream of military hardware to its many battlefronts. Surface forces could not stop this flow, but bombers striking at the industrial heartland choked off the supply. The image was graphically rendered for the audience by showing fewer and fewer weapons coming out of the pipelines, thus allowing the ground forces to smash through the wheel's rim. This fairly innocuous depiction emphasized the military nature of the bombers' targets.

3. In *Victory through Air Power*, Disney illustrated the need for strategic bombing against Germany by depicting German industry as a spoked wheel.

When the scene switched to Japan, however, the imagery is of an octopus with outstretched tentacles grasping far-flung territory throughout Asia and the Pacific. No military hardware is shown. U.S. air power is symbolized by a bald eagle tearing and ripping at the octopus's head until it is torn to shreds and the tentacles shrivel in lifelessness.

Beyond the racist element of depicting a European adversary as an innocuous wheel while an Asian adversary appears as a creature widely regarded as loathsome and even evil in nature, there is a military dichotomy as well. The geometric imagery is very similar between the two depictions, and the description of similar tactics leading to similar results could easily lead the viewer to conflate the two images as one. In both cases, bypassing outposts to strike at the life-sustaining center leads to easy American victory. The trouble is that the methods are depicted as antiseptically efficient in one case and ruthlessly destructive in the other. The conflating of these two views of air power was all the more significant because it had such a big impact on the American public. An estimated five million Americans read *Victory Through Air Power,* and a Gallup poll claimed that between his book, articles, radio broadcasts, and the Disney movie, over twenty million Americans—or one out of every six—were familiar with de Seversky and his theories.[46] A more practical indication of de Seversky's impact is that both the AAF and the navy took steps to undercut his message fearing his theories could gain enough popular support to derail current war plans, and the navy may have been prompted to reorganize its aviation forces in part to forestall his anti-navy charges. Hoping to signal their greater airmindedness, the navy's public announcement of the plan may even have been timed to beat the premiere of Disney's film.[47]

In terms of America's actual experience conducting its bombing campaign in World War II—at times striving for and achieving remarkable accuracy against critical and vulnerable industrial targets, at other times indiscriminately firebombing entire cities—this dual imagery is remarkably accurate, but that was not the image air power advocates wished to convey to the American public. Throughout the war, then, it seems two images of American air power and the AAF's bombing campaigns coexisted side by side. During the war military and civilian leaders tried to hide or minimize the growing practice of bombing civilian targets, but this does not tell the whole story of public perceptions of American bombing, for other voices also projected images of air power that proved quite popular with the public.[48] De Seversky's popularity disseminated

4. When it came to the challenge of defeating Japan, Disney characterized the enemy as an octopus.

darker images that meshed with passions generated within the American public by the war to create a public mood advocating bombing enemy cities and civilians.[49] Anxious for revenge and desperate to shorten the war and save American lives, the public was willing to use any weapon that seemed capable of accomplishing these goals, even if it meant adopting methods that only a few years earlier would have sparked moral outrage.

Images in popular magazines not only reflected this bloodlust but to a certain extent helped shape it. A *United States News* pictograph on the eve of Pearl Harbor extolled America's ability to bomb Japanese cities, which it points out were comprised of "rice-paper and wood houses," while a wartime *Life* magazine pictograph depicted a blanket of bombers a mile wide and 117 miles long. These and other examples conveyed more of an image of brute force than precision in American air power. Furthermore, articles appeared throughout the war conveying the message that enemy cities and civilians were being bombed, and they conveyed the message in an unmistakably positive manner. For example, only one month after Gen. Curtis LeMay's devastating firebombing raid on Tokyo, *Collier's* carried a story about the development of America's incendiary bombs and how they were being put to use in Japan. The celebratory text makes clear the incendiaries are burning homes and causing large numbers of civilian casualties. The accompanying illustration shows a highway leading to a city engulfed in flames. By the road is a signpost labeled "U.S. Route 40" leading from Utah to Tokyo. Government leaders recognized the power of public sentiments for bombing, and it was one of the factors leading them to adopt civilian bombing.[50]

The United States had entered World War II with unparalleled public support for air power shaped by a long tradition of fascination with the airplane and images of its technological messianism, both of which were reinforced by promises made by air power advocates in their crusade to convert the public to the "air power gospel." Officially, American air power, centered on strategic bombing, was depicted as humane, efficient, and progressive. This was the ACTS tradition of precision bombing. Other images that predated the war and that stressed the brutal and destructive side of air power, the tradition of Douhet, reemerged during the war, and they too made a major impact on the public's perception of air power. Both images coexisted throughout the war and became potent forces shaping the popular imagination of air power. Significantly, both images promised the United States salvation through air power. The "Dr. Jekyll" image—the tradition of the ACTS—was most prominent early in the war and would remain a powerful tradition in the postwar popular culture depiction of air power, but Hiroshima and Nagasaki fixed the "Mr. Hyde" image—the tradition of Douhet—most dramatically in the public's imagination. In fact, to most Americans the atomic bomb had most clearly delivered on the messianic promise of air power in World War II.

The public's support for air power remained strong after World War II, as is dramatically illustrated by a poll conducted during the last months of the war by *The Saturday Evening Post*. When asked which of the three services they felt was most important to national defense 56.3 percent stated the air force was, while 21.8 percent said the navy, and 13.6 percent favored the army.[51] This faith in air power was built in large measure by the twin traditions of bombing that had become such potent public images and by public perception of what air power had accomplished during the war. As air power advocates strove to maintain and increase that public support in the postwar era they continued and magnified the tradition of appealing to the public through popular culture, and they continued stressing the old promises of national salvation through air power. In doing so, they relied heavily on their faith in strategic bombing as progressive and efficient—the ACTS tradition and its more appealing peacetime images—but the reality of nuclear weapons and the emerging Soviet threat in the Cold War meant the tradition of Douhet would become an inevitable part of American air power. Trying to reconcile both traditions in a peacetime popular culture crusade forced air power advocates to shape some awkward and contradictory images for the popular imagination. For awhile they were remarkably successful despite the contradictions, but ultimately those contradictions brought air power advocates frustration and, in the end, failure.

CHAPTER 3

The Air Power Revolution
Early Postwar Years

As extensive as was the outpouring of public enthusiasm greeting the advent of human flight, the sheer scope and scale of advocacy for revolutionary air power following World War II staggers the imagination. Equally amazing is that the notion of revolutionary air power enjoyed, for awhile, the status of conventional wisdom in American popular culture. Before World War II numerous individuals had come to see air power as a force that had revolutionized warfare, and through the medium of popular culture they had managed to gain a significant following among the American public. After the war, however, the number of people who accepted the notion swelled to a degree unimagined in 1941, and one detects in America's popular culture a distinct difference in the status of the claims made for air power. On a superficial level one could point to the sharply increased number of works arguing for, or extolling the capabilities of, air power. On a deeper level, though, one senses a wider acceptance of the notion that air power was more than just a synonym for military aviation, that it represented a frame of mind, a philosophy for understanding not only military aviation but its place in the wider world and in human affairs and that air power had revolutionized every aspect of life.

One reflection of this heightened status is that starting in the May 1945–April 1947 edition of *Reader's Guide to Periodical Literature* "air power" appears for the first time as a separate subject heading for listing articles.[1] Prior editions had directed readers to "See Aeronautics, Military," and the March 1959–February 1961 edition omits the heading "air power" entirely, but between 1945 and 1959, whether because of personal conviction or simply reflecting increased public usage, the editors of the *Reader's Guide,* like many air power advocates whose writing they listed, treated air power as something bigger than the sum of its parts, as a concept whose borders encompassed far more than just military aviation.

The period following World War II witnessed a virtual flood of air power advocacy works in American popular culture bombarding public imagination with the virtues of air power and the pressing need to embrace the air power revolution. This flood coursed through several channels: popular magazines, books, novels, radio, movies, television, even a Broadway play and a popular comic strip. No medium seemed inappropriate for conveying the air power message. While the message continued well into the 1960s, the torrent seems to have crested in the mid- to late fifties. The roughly twelve years following 1945 constitutes a "Golden Age" of air power advocacy in popular culture. Several factors help account for the sudden and prolonged surge in air power literature: (1) the prominent role played by air power during the war generated support for, and interest in, air power topics with the American public; (2) the threat of the Cold War and the nuclear arms race made the public susceptible to the technological messianism air power seemed to offer; and of course, (3) aviation and war topics had long been ripe fields for romanticism and high drama in many popular culture media, so combining the two in an air power piece made for a "sure winner" with the public. But no explanation is complete without taking into account the role played by air power advocates. "The faithful" had preached revolutionary air power before the war, and the events of 1938–45 had convinced them—and new converts besides—that their faith had been well placed. They saw the widespread public support the war had engendered for their cause, and they saw danger to the United States in the world around them—a danger they felt only air power could meet. All this would have been enough to prompt air power advocates to redouble their efforts after the war, but their energies were further mobilized by their fear that their critics would once again subjugate and scuttle American air power, that the public's faith did not go deep enough, that somehow the dreams of air power they had so long and fervently nurtured would once again fall short of their goal.

The air campaigns of World War II did more than anything else since the dawn of flight to bolster the air power cause and to strengthen the faith of air power advocates. First, the bombing efforts were massive undertakings, and too often size alone is enough to convince many people that something significant and effective was accomplished.[2] More important, though, the campaigns were a central part of Allied strategy for defeating both Germany and Japan.[3] The results, while hardly conclusive, were significant enough to reinforce the belief of interwar air power advocates that they had been correct in their predictions of an air power revolution. The results also impressed many other observers who were in positions to help shape public opinion. They had heard the prewar prophecies of revolution, and they came to believe that Billy Mitchell and the Boys had been right all along. Thus the air power revolution mushroomed after the war as new converts flocked to the banner, adding their voices to the old campaigners who had been preaching the air power gospel all along. Filled with revolutionary zeal, they yearned to share their newfound faith with the American public, for they were convinced the revolution had just begun and that only through mass conversion—through making the United States an "air power nation"—could air power truly achieve the potential they envisioned. This evangelistic conviction was the driving force behind the air power advocates' popular culture crusade.

The revolutionary mentality, though, went beyond the mere goal of converting the masses to support the military aspects of air power. It also spawned a revolutionary world view that sought to reshape attitudes and reinterpret past events. Air power advocates believed that air power, in its broadest sense of all activities related to aviation, called for a new way of looking at the world, both literally and figuratively. Thus in these early postwar years the popular culture campaign focused not only on advocating larger military air forces, in a larger sense it sought to "reeducate" the American people in the new "world view" that went along with the postwar conception of air power. The early years of this postwar air power crusade were frequently characterized by a simplicity, often a naiveté, in the air power advocates' claims. The Soviet Union did not emerge immediately as a widely perceived threat, and thus for several years advocates presented air power as an all-purpose answer to any threat that might arise. Moreover, technological change, specifically missiles and nuclear weapons, was in such a state of flux that no one could say with any certainty what would be the future nature of air power and warfare; this too made the air power advocates' message more general in nature.

But these early postwar years also found air power advocates free of the bureaucratic responsibilities and allegiances that would shape much of the popular culture message in later periods. The AAF was still part of the army, and thus air power advocates could make wild claims for air power without being held totally responsible for delivering on their promises. Even after the air force gained independence in 1947, air power advocates could claim that parsimonious defense budgets kept the air force from realizing its true potential. Furthermore, the Strategic Air Command, which became the focus of much of the popular culture campaign in the fifties, did not immediately emerge as an institutional force driving air power advocates' agitation. For all these reasons the claims made for air power were often highly idealistic, and at times unrealistic, in the early years following the war.

In outlining the early years of the popular culture campaign, this chapter will focus on various aspects of the air power advocates' revolutionary world view as a means of illustrating the image of air power they put before the American public. These topics include the polar concept, the new need for air force independence, redeeming Billy Mitchell's memory, the new nature of warfare, and how air power "won" World War II. By focusing on the issues stressed by air power advocates in their public works one learns not only what they said about air power and how they said it but, more important, what concepts lay behind the popular culture crusade and what air power advocates wanted the public to believe about air power.

IT'S A WHOLE NEW WORLD: THE POLAR CONCEPT

One of the most intriguing themes of the popular culture campaign was the air power advocates' notion that people needed to look at their world in a whole new way. Aviation enthusiasts had long stressed the belief that the airplane had radically redefined humanity's conception of time and space. This had been a phenomenon of other transportation revolutions, but aviation enthusiasts brought a new dimension—the third dimension—to their claims.[4] The airplane, according to its proponents, eliminated all natural and manmade boundaries, because in the air mountains, rivers, and borders are meaningless.[5] Interwar air power advocates applied much the same reasoning when they claimed the warplane had negated America's traditional oceanic isolation.[6] During World War II, though, a new idea arose that the airplane had also conquered the polar ice cap, thus bringing about a new geographical perception of the northern hemisphere. This new reality, some argued, radically changed the strategic relationship of the great powers, most of which were located in the north, and prompted new patterns of response to that relationship. Dubbed "air-age globalism," one of its key features was that some U.S. policy makers no longer viewed the United States as isolated on the fringes of great power geography by two wide oceans; increasingly they saw the nation as located in the heart of a global struggle for power and influence, and they saw World War II as a feature of that new reality.[7] After the war air power advocates largely espoused this perception and felt air power was uniquely suited to meet the new threat. They also saw that widespread public support for this notion would aid their larger cause, but to win that support meant getting the public to see the world in a new way. Thus they set out to popularize the new depiction, called the polar projection, that viewed the world with the North Pole at its center.

To understand why postwar air power advocates and others found this new image so revolutionary one needs to understand that how we depict the world helps shape our sense of geographical reality. The standard flat depiction of the earth familiar to most people at the time was the Mercator projection. This depiction suggests that the direction of travel from Chicago to Moscow is east, over New Brunswick and England. From a polar perspective, however, the shortest distance is north over the Arctic. As simple as this reorientation sounds, writers of the time treated it as a revolutionary concept. In numerous works throughout the forties authors describe this concept to their readers as if they had just unlocked one of the hidden secrets of the universe. The writers of a 1944 high school geography text, for example, devote the first three sections to the new idea and its implications. Their revolutionary attitude is best captured by the book's frontispiece, which depicts a youth enlightening an older man with a map drawn from a polar perspective, and by one of the book's review questions, which asks, "Why has the 'dreaded' Arctic come to be called the 'friendly' Arctic?"[8] William Bradford Huie, a popular writer and editor of the forties and fifties, stated in 1946 that the Mercator projection had arisen in the days when sea routes dominated international trade and travel but claimed that the needs of the air age dictated a new appreciation of the earth's surface. Postwar air power advocates saw great economic consequences for international trade and air travel arising from exploitation of this concept. For example, W. B. Courtney, a military analyst and air power advocate writing for *Collier's*, warned in a 1947 article that the United States lagged behind Britain and the Soviet Union in the development of commercial air transportation and air liners able to take advantage of opportunities presented by the polar concept and urged immediate action to avoid being locked out of the future transpolar trade routes.[9]

Air power advocates also made the polar concept part of their message that air power brought a new threat from a previously unimagined direction—a threat that only air power could meet. In a December 1945 *Collier's* article Spaatz stated that intercontinental atomic war was already a reality, because, by flying over the Arctic, a B-29 could reach any potential adversary in the northern hemisphere, "where, curiously enough, all of the great powers lie." The article includes a polar projection map of the northern hemisphere that shows the distance from Chicago to such countries as Japan, China, India, and Britain.[10] Ira Eaker expanded upon this point in a 1946 speech on the army-sponsored radio program *So Proudly We Hail:* "All the prime industrial powers of the world are located *above* the 30 degree, north latitude line. . . . Every great industrial center can be hit by a plane with the B-29's range, flying from a base near the Arctic Circle. An enemy plane could make a one-way crossing of the polar area, the shortest air route, and strike any of our key manufacturing zones."[11] Alexander de Seversky gave the concept its fullest delineation. In a 1947 article for *Look* magazine he describes the arctic region as a World War I–style no-man's land with long-range air power launched by the Soviets and Americans flying overhead. The article even included a half-page graphic illustration to reinforce the point. When de Seversky incorporated this article into his 1950 book *Air Power: Key to Survival,* he expanded the point to include its commercial implications, which he felt dictated America's economic domination of South America, but by this time many were familiar with the polar concept.[12]

The military implications of the polar concept quickly caught on in America's popular media, but its wider cultural image did not. Writers who were not necessarily connected to the air power cause soon joined the air power advocates in warning of the air threat from the north. In 1946, for example, William Veazie Pratt, a retired admiral, former chief of naval operations, and a *Newsweek* correspondent long noted for his cooperative attitude toward the army and the AAF, used the polar concept as his main argument for air force independence. In his regular *Newsweek* column Pratt stated that the arctic region would become a main theater for any future conflict, and because of its inhospitable climate, only land-based air would be able to operate effectively in that region.[13] Similarly, John Kord Lagemann, in a 1946 *Collier's* article, stated that unlike the last two thousand years where civilization centered around the Mediterranean, for the next two thousand years civilization would be centered around the Arctic Ocean. He claimed that the region above the 30th parallel contained 98 percent of the world's industry and 90 percent of the world's population. He warned, though, that this entire region was within striking range of B-29-type bombers based in the arctic region. Under these circumstances, he claimed, *"the power which controls the arctic airspace controls the world."*[14]

It is interesting to note that Spaatz's and Pratt's articles and Eaker's speech mention no specific enemy. The threat could come from any nation on the Eurasian land mass north of the 30 degree north latitude. By 1947, when de Seversky first wrote of the polar concept, tensions with the Soviets had escalated to the point that he mentions them as the West's only adversary. Finally, by February 1950 the concept of a holocaust coming from Russia toward the United States over the North Pole had become so firmly entrenched that a *Life* magazine article on the threat of aerial attack proposed a series of interlocking radar stations to protect North America.[15] By 1950, then, the concept had been reduced to a grim reality of the Cold War, but the revolutionary vision of a new world view fell by the wayside. Americans still saw the world as a Mercator projection, but it readily accepted the fact that any attack from the Soviet Union would come over the Arctic. Thus popular imagination throughout the Cold War envisioned the Arctic as a battlefield dominated by NORAD and the DEW Line, even if the larger geopolitical struggle was one of East versus West with Western Civilization centered around the North Atlantic.

Along with the physical new world view came the belief that average Americans had to become "airminded," that is, they had to develop a thorough understanding of all aspects of aviation and air power. One aspect of this called for a fundamental rethinking of America's education process. Interwar aviation enthusiasts had also urged recasting education to prepare youth for life in the Air Age, and the crux of the issue called for syllabi to include aviation and aeronautics at all levels and in all subjects.[16] The wartime geography textbook cited above is one product of this effort. After the war air power advocates picked up the refrain and claimed it was necessary for the long-term security of the nation. In 1945 an organization known as the Air Power League, which had been formed in 1944 by air power advocates to promote their cause, published a pamphlet called *The Bulletin of the Air Power League*. It included a picture of an airminded boy holding a model of an airplane, and the text states, "He is an example of the public airmindedness which must be maintained if the United States is to preserve supremacy in the air." A year later the league listed as one suggested activity of Air Power Clubs: "foster in primary and secondary schools the establishment of standardized courses in subjects related to aviation."[17] In 1949 a team of *Collier's* editors visited a University of Oklahoma kindergarten where Link trainers had been installed to "air-condition" the students. The editors pronounced themselves pleased, especially with the fact that the trainers were also surrounded by toys to combine fun with the effort to "train the kids for a grim time ahead." In 1951, after the Air Power League had become the National Air Council, it set up an education program to encourage aviation education in primary and secondary schools, an effort that gained strong air force support.[18]

The effort to encourage airmindedness extended to the general public as well. In 1945 Hap Arnold stated in the *New York Times Magazine* that "an air-minded public is the broad base of American air power." A few months later in *National Geographic Magazine* he added, "Since air power depends for its existence upon . . . the air-mindedness of the Nation, the Air Forces must promote the development of American civil air power in all of its forms, both commercial and private." Even the American Legion sought to advance air power by fostering public airmindedness in a 1947 pamphlet that stated, "We must learn quickly that Air Power has uprooted our traditional ways of life." One early indication of the widespread concern for airmindedness in connection with air power issues is a September 1945 advertisement for North American Aviation in *Collier's* magazine. The ad asks, "How do you rate in the AIR-Q test?" It then asks four questions relating to air power and tells the reader, "If you can answer at least three of the four questions on this page correctly, give yourself an 'A' in Aviation."[19]

This concern for how the American public imagined the orientation of the globe and its level of airmindedness is more than just an interesting facet of the popular culture campaign for air power; it offers a revealing insight into the mindset of air power advocates and their all-encompassing view of the place of air power in the postwar world. Moreover, it is a reflection of their conviction that air power had revolutionized more than just warfare. In their own minds this "new world view" strengthened their conviction that they had divined the true shape of modern warfare, because if they could perceive these lesser "truths" about the impact of aviation on the modern world that were unknown to "ordinary" men and women, their military prophecies must be equally perceptive. One suspects that among some members of their audience these revelations about the "new world order" had the same effect.

RECASTING AIR FORCE INDEPENDENCE:
THE UNIFICATION ISSUE

Nothing had been more divisive in the interwar period than air power advocates' claims that the Air Corps needed independence for air power to achieve its full potential.[20] For all the public agitation before the war, it may seem surprising that after World War II air force independence was not a major part of the popular culture crusade.[21] The reason for this seeming paradox is that a significant change had taken place in that the independence question was subsumed into the larger issue of military unification.[22] Air power advocates took up the cause of military unification in the name of greater overall military effectiveness but in the process served their own purposes by stressing that three coequal services of land, sea, and air forces must be part of any unified military structure.

The call for military unification began almost as soon as the war ended. Arnold set the tone in November 1945 when he called for a single department of national defense with an independent and coordinate air force, and most other air power advocates followed suit.[23] That same month Beirne Lay stated in a *Reader's Digest* article devoted entirely to the subject of military unification that despite the recent victory over the Axis, unification was needed because *"we won our war in spite of fundamentally unsound military organization at the top."* Like most air power advocates, Lay supported the army's plan for unification, which called for a single department with land, sea, and air forces under one commander, because Lay felt that the coordination system used by the joint chiefs of staff during the war had been the root of the problem during the war and would continue to prove inadequate. Lay even tried to forestall the charge that he supported unification as a ploy to gain air force independence by claiming that he did not care where air power stood in such a structure so long as national defense was unified. Given Lay's past and subsequent role in advancing the air power cause, though, plus the fact that nearly all air power advocates linked the two issues as Lay had, this claim seems less than genuine.[24]

The Air Power League threw its organization behind the cause of unification in a big way. Organized on December 18, 1944, the League's list of charter members reads like a "who's who" in America's aircraft industry, boasting over 130 names connected with various aircraft industries or businesses that could profit from advancing U.S. aviation and air power. There are, however, many and significant exceptions. The list also includes seventeen editors or publishers, including Walter D. Fuller, president of Curtis Publishing, the company that published the *Saturday Evening Post*, Henry R. Luce of *Time* and *Life* magazines, and Frank E. Gannett of Gannett Newspapers. Nine leading figures from the movie industry also appear as charter members, including Samuel Goldwyn, David O. Selznick, and Darryl F. Zanuck, along with four top administrators of such renowned research institutions as M.I.T. and the Mayo Clinic. Additionally, there are numerous figures from businesses that seem to have no connection with the flying world, such as Sears, Roebuck, Procter and Gamble, and General Mills. Furthermore, numerous private individuals, ranging from Bernard Baruch to Earl Brown, a Minnesota sheriff, became charter members. As far as the average American was concerned, the most notable member was probably movie star Clark Gable, who had served in the AAF during World War II. The League even had a Women's Committee to reach out to women all across the United States, and it was headed up by none other than pioneering aviator Jackie Cochrane, another League charter member. Military figures are conspicuously absent from the list of charter members, for the League barred active-duty personnel from joining in any capacity.[25]

The League set as its goals the standard litany of air power concerns shared in whole or in part by air power advocates: promote interest in, and the study of, air power in world affairs; educate the U.S. public in the need for a strong national air power establishment to maintain peace; and foster growth of civilian and commercial aviation. It sought to do this by making air power "the business of every American citizen," and to bring to the cause "considerable weight of popular opinion and enthusiasm."[26] One overt measure of its support for military unification can be seen in the two pamphlets it published on the subject, which gave the reader a wealth of information on why a single department of defense with a single chief of staff was good for the nation. The League's seriousness, though, can be seen best in less overt ways. First, the League was initially unique in that it sought close cooperation with the navy; an irreparable break came, however, over the unification issue when, according to League president Charles E. Wilson, the navy withdrew its endorsement of the League because the League publicly endorsed unification. Another reflection of the League's earnestness is that Jackie Cochran launched a major effort through her women's network to take the issue directly to the nation's women. Claiming that "the stake of American womanhood is plain," Cochran charged that lack of unity in the past had left the United States weak, and that such weakness must be eliminated because "if war ever comes again, there will be no 'front line.' Destruction would be visited upon our very homes in terrifying effect never before known."[27]

As with the Air Power League, air power advocates' support for unification frequently led to clashes with the navy, which opposed unification, and started a long pattern of postwar conflict between the two communities that culminated in the "Revolt of the Admirals" in 1949. Lay, for example, stated that the navy and its secretary, James Forrestal, were using delaying tactics in the public debate, hoping the public would forget about the issue.[28] William Bradford Huie was also outspoken on the issue. A prominent journalist and editor, Huie espoused air power early in World War II and in 1942 wrote *The Fight for Air Power,* detailing the air corps' interwar battles with the army and navy. After the war, in which he served as a navy officer, Huie became a leading figure in the popular culture campaign for air power, and two of the main themes he continually emphasized were the need for unification to eliminate duplication and the navy's resistance to unification. In 1946 Huie published *The Case against the Admirals,* a bitter attack filled with intemperate charges against navy leaders. He argued that even in the face of the enemy the navy placed its own best interests ahead of the nation, other services, and the lives of U.S. servicemen. Huie felt that much of the navy's force structure duplicated army and AAF missions and that the navy opposed unification to protect both this duplication and its own freedom of action. There is little doubt that advancing the air power cause lay behind these attacks because Huie also repeatedly charged that the navy sabotaged the AAF throughout the interwar, wartime, and postwar periods.[29]

The air power advocates' espousal of the unification issue was not solely for the benefit of air force independence, because many had genuinely supported the army's single chief of staff idea and saw the National Security Act of 1947 as a flawed compromise.[30] Still, the attainment of independence and a large measure of unification ended much of the advocates' statements on the subject. The fight for the twin goals created an atmosphere of animosity between the new air force and the navy, though, and passage of the act did not end all of the attacks launched by the sister services on each other.

THE REDEMPTION OF BILLY MITCHELL

Part of the drive to reshape people's views toward air power was an attempt to reinterpret past events from the air power advocates' perspective. One such attempt was the redemption of Billy Mitchell. A strenuous and controversial air power advocate, Mitchell's escalating critiques of the army's air power policies led to his being found guilty of insubordination by a court-martial in 1925. There is little doubt Mitchell was guilty of the charges against him, as Arnold himself stated in his memoirs in 1949.[31] Air power's growth in importance during the war and afterwards, though, led many to believe that Mitchell's vision had justified his actions, and air power advocates felt compelled to rehabilitate his image in the public's eye. Thus a recurring theme in the popular culture campaign was an effort to elevate Mitchell to the status of a far-sighted visionary martyred for his efforts to prepare the United States for the dangers ahead. The spoken message of this campaign emphasized how events proved the nation should have listened to Mitchell despite his traditionalist critics, but the unspoken message was clear as well: the United States should also heed postwar air power advocates' warnings about the current need for air power.

The revisionist efforts on Mitchell's behalf stretch back to at least the war years. In 1942, for example, de Seversky dedicated both the book and movie versions of *Victory Through Air Power* to Mitchell and took these opportunities to tell America that a grave injustice had occurred. In the film de Seversky called Mitchell one of history's "men of vision" who foresaw the war but was ignored and vilified. That same year and the next saw the publication of two laudatory biographies of Mitchell, one bearing the leading title *Billy Mitchell, Founder of Our Air Force and Prophet without Honor.*[32]

After the war, redemption efforts hit full stride as numerous air power advocates paid homage to Mitchell. Some of the testimonials made on his behalf were quite subtle. A sample speech distributed to all AAF units in 1946, for example, recalls the memory of fallen airmen from the war and then lists Mitchell as "foremost in our affection," for he "fought against hopeless odds . . . to have air power recognized as the mighty weapon it is." And in the play, novel, and movie versions of *Command Decision,* the hero, Brigadier General Dennis, names his firstborn son after Mitchell.[33]

Other reinterpretations of Mitchell's legacy, however, were more direct. Immediately after the war W. B. Courtney claimed Mitchell had been the pioneer of "real air-power thinking." Trenchard, he felt, had been of the same mind, but Douhet had been impractical. More important, though, Courtney claimed the Germans had been Mitchell's closest students during the interwar years and that applying his lessons made their initial victories possible. But because they did not fully trust those lessons, Courtney added, they shackled air power's true potential and were defeated by American air power. In a similar vein the Air Power League credited Mitchell with inventing the concept of vertical envelopment, that is, flying over the enemy forces to strike them in the rear. These claims that Mitchell was a pioneer air power theorist are clearly exaggerated, for as Mitchell's biographer states, "he borrowed his ideas largely from the international community of airmen which he joined during World War I."[34]

Another frequent claim was that Mitchell had foreseen World War II and its basic character, a point Huie, for example, makes repeatedly in his 1946 indictment of the navy, *The Case against the Admirals.* Huie even took to affecting Mitchell's colorful language, as in a 1949 *Reader's Digest* article when he referred to army and navy leaders who opposed air power as "the Maginot minds, the yearners for Yesterday." Arnold himself undertook a comprehensive effort to reform the public memory of Mitchell in his 1949 memoirs. Throughout his chapters on World War I and the interwar period Arnold portrays his friend and mentor as a brash but visionary patriot who sacrificed himself to gain air power for the United States. At one point Arnold states that he counseled caution but that Mitchell voiced his determination to sacrifice himself to make the army and navy listen. Arnold reports that Mitchell felt he was the only one who was in a position to make a difference, because, as Arnold quoted Mitchell, "I can afford to do it. You can't."[35]

One measure of the effectiveness of this campaign, and the widespread sympathy for Mitchell and for air power in general, is that in 1946 Congress voted a special medal to be posthumously awarded to Mitchell. This medal is frequently confused with the Congressional Medal of Honor, as, for example, when Huie states that, "Congress acknowledged the national shame and pinned the Congressional Medal of Honor upon

Mitchell's ghost." The design of the medal and its inscription, though, as well as the wording of the bill authorizing the medal, make clear it has no connection with the nation's highest military honor.[36] Still, this unique recognition of Mitchell by joint act of Congress is a reflection of the widespread sentiment after World War II that the United States was deeply indebted to Mitchell and needed to make amends for past treatment. The medal was presented to Mitchell's son, William Mitchell Jr., by Chief of Staff Carl Spaatz on March 27, 1948. Mitchell's family later tried to follow up on the official sentiments embodied in the medal by having Mitchell's court-martial conviction officially overturned. In this they were joined by the Air Force Association, and in 1956 their petition went before air force secretary James Douglas. The petition was turned down, however, in recognition of the fact that while his motives may have been laudable, his insubordinate actions could not be officially sanctioned by any military organization, even the air force.[37]

Perhaps the public culmination of the attempt to redeem Mitchell, though, was the 1955 movie *The Court-Martial of Billy Mitchell*. While the movie lies outside the time span of this chapter, its roots go back to World War II, and much of its spirit relates to the period under consideration. Little more than two weeks after Pearl Harbor was attacked, Jack Warner wrote to Arnold stating that his studio had earlier bought the rights to make a film based on Mitchell's life but that with the nation now locked in war he felt it was best not to open old interservice wounds. He asked Arnold for his "off the record" advice on the matter. Arnold wrote back on New Year's Eve wholeheartedly agreeing with Warner's reservations and stated it would be best for the nation to wait on the project. "Later," Arnold added, "when the situation is a little less acute, the picture . . . may be of real assistance from the moral standpoint." A week later Warner wrote back to inform Arnold that he would wait until some future date to make the movie.[38]

The studio waited until 1955 to make the movie, and thus it reflects elements of mid-fifties Cold War concerns, but its primary emphasis was a belated contribution to the effort to recast public memory of Billy Mitchell with Gary Cooper playing the leading role. From start to finish the film depicts the army and navy as obstinately indifferent to the capabilities of air power and Mitchell as the heroic leader of airmen in both services who see what air power can do but who are needlessly dying in their effort to keep American air power alive.[39] Mitchell's sinking of the *Ostfriesland,* for example, is depicted as a prolonged effort by the army and navy to "rig" the test to make it impossible for Mitchell to succeed. Thus he is forced to violate orders to make the test an honest assessment of air power's capabilities. Mitchell's famous press statement prompting his court-martial is cast in a similar light. With the army ignoring his repeated efforts to correct dangerous problems through official channels, and with the navy ignoring similar efforts among its airmen, Mitchell is portrayed as a heroic and selfless patriot who issues his press statement knowing it will cost him his career. Ignoring the newspapermen's efforts to get him to tone down his inflammatory charges, he replies to one reporter's question of whether this statement could get him court-martialed by stating "that is exactly what I want." The film further sanitizes Mitchell's reputation by depicting him as eschewing the public appeal his defense team, headed by Congressman Frank Reid, feels is necessary to winning the case. Mitchell, according to the movie, merely wanted to win support for air power, not discredit the army. In reality, Mitchell arranged for *Liberty* magazine to publish articles around the time of the trial to maximize his publicity.[40]

In presenting the trial itself, the film used an approach found in other works of air power advocacy, that of portraying supporters of air power as sensible and reasonable while portraying its critics as dull-witted, malicious, or biased by service loyalties. Throughout the first half of the trial, for example, the general who heads the court refuses to allow Mitchell to bring evidence that his remarks were justified because such evidence would damage the army's reputation. When Mitchell's lawyers finally maneuver the court into allowing this evidence the prosecuting attorney is reduced to a caricature of a pathetic, flustered, and indecisive man overwhelmed by the damage the evidence seems to do to his case. The prosecution's fortunes are only saved by the last-minute arrival of the army's "best legal mind" who wins by what appears as legal hair-splitting and by mocking Mitchell's predictions of the future of air power. Significantly, every one of the predictions that the prosecutor holds up for ridicule—super-sonic flight, trans-oceanic flight, and airborne operations to name just a few—had all become commonplace by 1955, thus enhancing Mitchell's reputation as a visionary before the film's audience. The highpoint of this fictional scene is the ridicule heaped upon Mitchell's prediction that the Japanese will open a war in the Pacific with a carrier-borne air attack on Pearl Harbor.

The redemption of Billy Mitchell was more than just an effort to canonize a man many air power advocates counted as a friend and mentor. Many did believe he deserved honor and the nation's gratitude and saw this movement as doing justice to one who had been wronged. Also, the new air force and its supporters needed their pantheon of saints and martyrs, and Billy Mitchell fit the bill perfectly. But as air power advocates sought the nation's support for the air power revolution in their own time, they buttressed their predictions with allusions to past prophecies they claimed had come true. Redeeming Billy Mitchell's reputation aided that effort, for if people were convinced to honor past air power prophets they might be more inclined to honor current ones as well.

THE NEW NATURE OF WAR:
THE HEART OF THE AIR POWER REVOLUTION

The notion of the warplane revolutionizing warfare is an old one. Da Vinci, Franklin, and Wells had all speculated on the tremendous advantage they imagined an aerial army would have over traditional forces. Once the airplane was invented this supposed revolution became the centerpiece of pre–World War II air power advocates. Small wonder, therefore, that after the war air power advocates returned to this notion themselves. Postwar claims for revolutionary air power took on many of the old themes, such as airplanes over-leaping traditional defenses to strike directly at the enemy's heart, but they also incorporated new themes, particularly themes driven by new technological developments that had emerged late in the war. Not all air power advocates argued the same themes, and at times they contradicted one another, but the air power revolution was a central part of the postwar popular culture campaign. Curiously, however, it was largely confined to the early postwar period.

The core of the postwar notion of an air power revolution centered on strategic bombing. Most air power advocates emerged from the war with their faith in strategic bombing as strong as or stronger than it had been before the war. As we shall see, this faith extended to an attempt to prove that strategic bombing had won the war, but it also shaped air power advocates' conviction that the main effort of any future war would involve a massive bombing campaign aimed at the enemy's industrial base. Spaatz gave this conviction its fullest expression in a 1946 *Foreign Affairs* article. Spaatz called strategic bombing "the most powerful instrument of war thus far known," because it was "the first war instrument of history capable of stopping the heart mechanism of a great industrialized enemy. It paralyzes his military power at the core. . . . it has a capacity . . . to carry a tremendous striking force . . . over the traditional line of war (along which the surface forces are locked in battle on land and sea) in order to destroy war industries and arsenals and cities . . . in fact, the heart and the arteries of war economy—so that the enemy's will to resist is broken through nullification of his means." While carefully avoiding the claim that strategic bombing won World War II, Spaatz nonetheless claimed that strategic bombing's unique capabilities meant the next war would likely be determined by air power before surface forces were able to engage the enemy in combat.[41]

Spaatz's *Foreign Affairs* article is especially noteworthy because it is one of the few postwar articles that ignored nuclear weapons and focused exclusively on conventional bombing. Most other works, including most by Spaatz, placed the atomic bomb squarely into predictions of strategic bombing's revolutionary capabilities. This is ironic because America's supply of atomic bombs remained so low for so long that for many years any strategic bombing campaign would have, by necessity, relied heavily on conventional bombing.[42] This was not the picture air power advocates projected to the public, though, for in their eagerness to portray air power as revolutionary, they routinely linked their cause to other technological wonders seen by the public as revolutionary and modern. Early public reaction to the atomic bomb showed a strange mixture of emotions ranging from fear and anxiety to awe and admiration. Despite misgivings, though, nuclear weapons for national defense enjoyed strong public support.[43] Air power advocates quickly seized on the range of public emotions toward the bomb to portray air power as at once the shocking face of future warfare and the only means of protecting the United States from grave danger.

Almost as soon as the war ended air power advocates began making predictions about what the next war would look like, and they consistently claimed that atomic weapons would be an inevitable part of future conflict. Early predictions of the inevitability of nuclear war, though, often emphasized the threat this posed to the United States, despite the fact that until 1949 the United States had a monopoly on the atomic bomb. In November 1945, for example, Arnold wrote in the *New York Times Magazine* that any future war would start with a devastating sneak attack involving atomic weapons and that the first day of battle would decide the course of the war. Arnold also introduced another aspect of the air power advocates' claim that the United States could not ignore this new style of warfare. Warning against relying on old comforting notions of isolationism and wide oceans to protect the United States from foreign conflicts, Arnold stated that America would never again have the luxury of a long period to prepare for war as it had in the two world wars. Instead, the United States would be the first target of any future aggressor and would be bombed without warning to prevent it from mobilizing its latent industrial strength. Spaatz stressed the same point a month later and added, "unless we stand in split-second readiness we will lose a future war." In a 1947 radio address Spaatz was even more specific. Atomic bombs would wipe out U.S. industry: "Chicago and Detroit could be as devastated as Hiroshima."[44]

Missiles, according to air power advocates, made the threat to the United States even more urgent. The appearance of German V-2 rockets in World War II presented the world with an image that horrified and fascinated the American public, an image that came to be called push-button warfare. The missile was such a startling innovation at the end of the war that in a September 1945 *Collier's* article W. B. Courtney predicted that "in the not too distant future the familiar airplane will be to air power as the Roman chariot is to modern land power." In his November 1945 article Arnold said that push-button war was a reality and that guided missiles would soon be able to achieve "perfect strikes" at great speed thousands of miles away. A month later Francis Vivian Drake, a frequent pro–air power commentator writing for *Reader's Digest,* claimed atomic bombs were already much more powerful than the ones dropped on Japan, and mounting these new bombs on missiles posed a grave threat to the United States. Such weapons were impossible to stop, Drake observed, noting that *"no V-2 was ever intercepted."*[45]

Air power advocates stressed the image of a nuclear threat to the United States as a means of presenting air power as the only defense against a threat that was itself based upon attack through the air. Such an approach relied heavily on the tradition of technological messianism long inherent in the popular fascination with aviation, because air power advocates were setting up an air power bogeyman and then offering air power as the nation's only hope of salvation. In this effort they became early proponents of nuclear deterrence. After painting the specter of nuclear-tipped missiles devastating U.S. cities, Arnold, in his November 1945 article, stated that the only defense against such an attack was a strong strategic air force-in-being poised to retaliate against any nation launching such an attack.[46] It is significant to note that this early enunciation of air power's deterrent role was made before any other nation had acquired nuclear weapons and before the Soviet Union emerged as the West's main adversary. In laying out this argument, Arnold presented a theme that would remain a standard feature of the popular culture crusade throughout its duration, and most air power advocates adhered closely to his original line. The Air Power League in September 1946 stated that armies and navies were in many circumstances ineffective as a deterrent but that air power was "the best preventive of aggression that exists." It then drove the point home visually on its back cover by depicting a mushroom cloud with the caption, "Peace through Air Power—Or This." The concept of air power as nuclear deterrence was at the heart of the "Air Power is Peace Power" slogan popular with air power advocates during the late forties. First introduced by Spaatz in a radio address in 1947, the theme was so common it became a virtual symbol—it even adorned the American Legion's air power pamphlets well into the fifties. The concept of nuclear deterrence was perhaps most forcefully stated among air power advocates by William Bradford Huie in a 1949 *Reader's Digest* article that he stated was meant as a warning to the Soviets. After detailing U.S. nuclear capability Huie boasted, "we can do to Russia, if Russia attacks us, what Rome did to Carthage."[47]

The postwar linking of strategic bombing with atomic weapons by air power advocates was part of an old tradition of promising quick and easy victory through air power, in this case through atomic bombing. Claiming Americans had accepted air power without understanding its revolutionary potential or the new nature of modern warfare, Spaatz, in a 1948 *Life* article, explicitly linked bombing and nuclear weapons to the notion of quick victory through air power in an effort to further the public's education and to bolster its faith. In one of his first articles written after his retirement, Spaatz reiterated the old notion that air power allowed a nation to bypass traditional defenses and strike directly at the enemy's heart. Writing in the midst of escalating tensions with the Soviets, Spaatz claimed that the Soviet Union's power rested on "a relatively few decisive target areas" and "that the precision bombing of a few hundred square miles of industrial area in a score of Russian cities would fatally cripple Russian industrial power." Spaatz even added the element of mathematical precision with his inaugural column in *Newsweek* in September 1948. Based on the TNT equivalent of the Hiroshima bomb, Spaatz calculated that ninety nuclear-loaded B-29s equaled 79,200 conventionally loaded B-17s, and since B-17s and B-24s had proven so effective against Germany in World War II, even though there had never been more than five thousand bombers at any one time, ninety B-29s with their nuclear loads should have little trouble defeating any aggressor. Huie also claimed nuclear air power could deliver quick victory. Speculating in 1946 on how a future war would be fought, he stated that two successive waves of missiles and bombers would leave the third wave of airborne occupation troops little to do in the way of mopping up. He even predicted the war would be over so quickly the navy's submarines would not have enough time to begin effective anti-shipping operations.[48]

Assurances of air power bringing swift victory encouraged an already pronounced trend for the public to view atomic bombs as wonder weapons, and thus fantastic predictions proliferated. In 1948 *U.S. News and World Report* cited the writings of air power advocates in mapping out a "Blueprint for a 30-Day War" during which the United States would bring a nation like the Soviet Union to its knees with a swift and furious "air blitz." Just as the public could be reassured with images of easy victory, though, the heightened expectation of air power's new lethality could backfire as well. In November 1945 *Life* magazine cited Arnold's writings as the inspiration for its story "The Thirty-Six Hour War," in which a sudden atomic missile attack from an unnamed enemy ravages the United States. So powerful was the image of near-instantaneous devastation from nuclear attack that another author, Russell V. Ritchey, envisioned a scenario where the Soviets had pre-positioned thirty-six atomic bombs around key U.S. cities and then demands immediate surrender. The story ends with the president presenting the ultimatum to his cabinet and asking the question that served as the story's title, "What Would *You* Do?"[49]

Some air power advocates would later back away from predictions of quick and easy victory, and they would later have to contend with heightened public fears when the Soviets developed their own atomic bomb—fears that air power advocates had themselves helped to cultivate. But air power advocates found it harder to erase public images of nuclear victory or defeat than it had been to create them. The predictions of quick victory, though, point to a fallacy that had long lurked beneath the surface of notions of an air power revolution. Running at least as far back as Douhet's *Command of the Air,* air power advocates had been promising that air power could quickly defeat any nation, and they had enjoyed considerable success in awakening public expectations for such capability. The title, "The Thirty-Six Hour War," of the 1945 story is more than coincidentally reminiscent of Stuart Chase's 1929 article "The Two-Hour War."[50] Both articles are products of the exaggerated claims made for air power in their day. Such promises seemed not only plausible to many, they also seemed to have the ring of necessity, inevitability, even desirability. But such claims were invariably based on hypothetical situations and a caricatured foe who took no defensive action and who compliantly sunk into chaos with no messy details to complicate post-war scenarios. When applied to specific situations such as World War II Germany or the Cold War Soviet Union, frictions of war not only upset the too-neat scenarios upon which the predictions had been based, they also left air power advocates looking foolish. Too often such failures left air power advocates searching for someone to blame for failure so as to protect the reputation of the air power cause.

One exception to those who saw nuclear weapons as part of an air power revolution was Alexander de Seversky. In a 1946 *Reader's Digest* article he argued that the worldwide reaction to the Hiroshima and Nagasaki bombings had grossly exaggerated the effectiveness of atomic bombs. The article brought down a storm of condemnation on de Seversky, and one might have wondered why he was swimming against the tide of public attitudes and even his fellow air power advocates who clearly shared, and helped perpetuate, the popular view of atomic devastation. The mystery became clear when his book *Air Power: Key to Survival* was published in 1950. Essentially de Seversky objected to the notion of quick and easy victory through atomic bombing. He believed air power itself constituted a revolution in warfare and that air power could, by itself, win the great war against the Soviets that he envisioned. In his mind, though, atomic bombs were just one of many tools air power would use to win that war. The war he envisioned would begin with a lengthy aerial battle of attrition over the Soviet Union where America's air force, if it listened to him and planned ahead, would seize air superiority. Seizing air superiority, for de Seversky, constituted air power's true revolutionary capability, because once it was obtained the nation could be subdued by nuclear bombing. He believed, though, that the subjugation effort would take a prolonged bombing campaign involving thousands of atomic bombs. He imagined Americans would achieve this by targeting Soviet industry, which would both paralyze the nation's defenses and convince the Soviet subjects of the impotence of the Communist regime and the benevolence of the Americans because they had not targeted the Russian population. The Russian people would then rise up, throw off their Communist taskmasters, and make peace with the United States.[51]

De Seversky's conception of the air power revolution is not only remarkable because of its fallacious notion that thousands of nuclear weapons could be exploded over enemy territory without its population feeling that it had been targeted, it also returns us to the old dichotomous traditions of Douhet and the ACTS running throughout the wartime and postwar popular culture crusade. To further their revolutionary cause, air power advocates had wedded air power to what was widely seen as a revolutionary weapon in its own right, the atomic bomb. Numerous air power advocates had stressed that air power was the only or the best means of delivering nuclear weapons, and they created in popular imagination an image that linked the two inseparably. To many in the public, nuclear weapons meant air power, and air power meant nuclear weapons, and both meant revolutionary destructive capability on a scale Douhet had never dreamed of. At the same time, though, air power advocates perpetuated the mythology of the effectiveness of precision industrial bombing. Even de Seversky stressed the precision industrial bombing image. His thousands of atomic bombs would bring relatively quick victory by bombing vital Russian industries with such accuracy that the Russian people would not feel they had been targeted: "As precision in picking out and erasing selected strategic targets improves, the toll of life will be reduced. Mass destruction will cease to be mistaken for a strategy." De Seversky even backed his point by detailing at length why civilian casualties were counterproductive.[52]

The irony of the postwar image of precision nuclear bombing, besides the fact that atomic destruction was measured in square miles, is that SAC's bombing did not measure up to public rhetoric. Overall accuracy for 1949 went from 3,700 feet to 2,300, and the winner of that year's bombing and navigation competition for B-36s won with an average score of 1,053 feet.[53] This incongruity did not matter, though, for the popular culture campaign dealt largely in images, and the image of precision and the crippling effect of knocking out enemy industry was interwoven into images of the atomic bomb's revolutionary destructive capability. One wonders if the general public, upon reflection, truly believed de Seversky's claim that atomic bombs could take out factories without killing the cities and civilians surrounding them, but on the popular imagination level the emphasis on precision and industrial targeting helped "sell" postwar U.S. strategic bombing by continuing the image that it was efficient, progressive, and scientific. The images of "pickle barrel" bombing could, in effect, mitigate the images of Hiroshima. One of the chief means of emphasizing the tradition of precision industrial bombing was the effort to establish continuity between wartime precision bombing and postwar nuclear bombing. But to truly establish precision industrial bombing as the epitome of revolutionary air power, air power advocates had to reinterpret the World War II strategic bombing campaign to prove that it had won the war just as interwar prophets had said it would.

REWRITING WORLD WAR II: AIR POWER WINS THE WAR

Interwar air power advocates had made great predictions about what air power could accomplish in war, and with massive strategic air campaigns constituting a major part of Allied strategy in World War II, postwar air power advocates naturally pointed to wartime air campaigns to prove that earlier predictions had been correct. Going a step further, though, air power advocates actually claimed that strategic bombing, and thus air power, had won the war, or at least had taken the greatest share of fight out of the enemy. This campaign ran the gamut from speeches and articles to books and movies. The wartime bombing campaign, though, was projected in a carefully contrived manner. First, it invariably emphasized the bombing campaign against Germany. This was because of a second characteristic, one that stressed the inherent wisdom of industrial bombing and the precision of U.S. bombing efforts. There were occasional references to the conventional bombing campaign against Japan, but these pale in comparison to the number of references to precision bombing against Germany. Even the atomic bombings got less notice from most air power advocates in the popular culture campaign. There were occasional veiled references that bombing had ended the war without an invasion of the Japanese home islands, but even the efforts to establish atomic weapons as part of the air power revolution rarely mention Hiroshima and Nagasaki. Instead, air power advocates presented World War II strategic bombing as a heroic struggle against both the enemy in Germany and critics at home, and their depiction was solidly within the tradition of the ACTS. World War II bombing had been efficient, progressive, scientific, and ultimately the deciding factor in victory.

Claims that bombing had won the war were controversial in official military circles, and thus AAF personnel at times moderated their statements. In the more official venue of *Foreign Affairs,* for example, Spaatz stated that strategic bombing had been decisive in the overall effort to defeat Germany but that it could not have won the war alone because time did not permit such an approach. After he had retired, though, and in the more popular arena of his *Newsweek* column, Spaatz was less diplomatic. In September 1948 he alluded to the "rubble-heaped industrial plants of Europe" as testimony to strategic bombing's effectiveness, and in March 1949 he stated that by defeating the Luftwaffe, bombing had made the invasion of Europe possible. It is interesting to note how Spaatz implies that destruction equals effectiveness, and in listing seizure of air superiority as one of strategic bombing's contributions, Spaatz neglects that that had not been the main contribution predicted for bombing both before and after the war. The Air Force Day 1946 publicity package sent out by the Public Affairs Office was also careful how it stated its claims for wartime bombing. While a sample speech states that strategic bombing was "a decisive factor in winning the war," it also added that air power cooperated with the army in ground battles and that it "worked with the Navy in patrolling the sea lanes."[54]

Other air power advocates were less equivocal. In one of the rare references to both theaters, Arnold, in a 1946 radio address, stated emphatically that the war had been won by getting "bombs on the Messerschmitt plant at Regensburg or the Zero plant outside Tokyo." W. B. Courtney expanded the point and stated flatly, "Air power caused the war in Europe. Air power won the war in Europe." He went on to explain that air power had given the Germans the confidence to launch their war of conquest but that their misuse of air power had cost them the war. Furthermore, he stated that had the Allies devoted more resources to the bombing effort, air power could have won the war sooner and with less cost. In its first publication in August 1945 the Air Power League quoted German Field Marshal Gerd von Rundstedt that "Allied air power was the decisive factor in Germany's defeat. It eliminated fuel, destroyed railways, shut off supplies of raw materials from outside Germany, smashed war production centers." And in a roundabout fashion de Seversky argued that strategic bombing did not win the war because the army and the navy would not let the AAF fight the war the way it wanted to, which also happened to be the way he had recommended. Still, he claimed, despite being relegated to a supporting role for the ground forces, strategic bombing was decisive in Europe.[55]

Such claims were tenuous on the surface because Germany had not surrendered until most of its territory had been occupied and Hitler was dead, and the navy had a valid argument that it contributed the decisive forces in defeating Japan. Air power advocates tried to prove their case through less obvious evidence, and one of the favorite tactics was to quote from the U.S. Strategic Bombing Survey (USSBS). Conducted in both Europe and Japan after the war, the USSBS was an effort to assess the effectiveness of strategic bombing on the Axis war effort. Teams of civilian and military leaders and specialists pored over records, conducted interviews, and examined target areas, then published their findings and conclusions in dozens of volumes and reports. All told, there were enough facts, figures, and statements to support just about any claim.[56] Spaatz, for example, in his March 7, 1949, *Newsweek* column, quoted the overall assessment of the USSBS: "The German experience suggests that even a first-class military power—rugged and resilient as Germany was—can not live long under full-scale and free exploitation of air weapons over the heart of its territory." Two could play at this game, though, and the navy's partisans used the USSBS to show that bombing had been a costly waste of lives and resources. James G. Stahlman, for example, prepared a pamphlet attacking air force policies, particularly its attachment to strategic bombing, and circulated it among his "several hundred" friends in the newspaper business. Stahlman, editor of the *Nashville Banner* and a former navy reservist, quoted extensively from the USSBS to show that strategic bombing had had little effect on German war production, that tactical bombing was more effective than strategic bombing, and that bombers were vulnerable without escorting fighters. That both sides could use the USSBS to their own advantage is shown by two articles published by *Reader's Digest* in a "point—counter-point" feature. Arguing for the navy, Fletcher Pratt quoted the survey to show that German war production in 1944 actually increased at the same time the bombing campaign was reaching its peak. Francis Vivian Drake countered that Pratt was misreading the USSBS, and he marshaled his own quotes to show that in 1944 strategic bombing cut output of aviation gasoline by 90 percent, nitrogen by 90 percent, and steel by 80 percent.[57]

The most effective means of extolling the contribution of strategic bombing, though, came through two works of fiction that were turned into popular movies. *Twelve O'clock High* and *Command Decision* together perhaps did more to establish the image of strategic bombing as a critical part of America's war effort in the public consciousness than all the articles, books, and speeches by all the other air power advocates combined. In the process they were crucial to projecting the tradition of the ACTS and the image of bombing as efficient, modern, and progressive into the postwar air power popular culture campaign.

Twelve O'clock High was more understated in presenting its case than *Command Decision,* but it put that argument into a gripping human story. The book was written by Beirne Lay and Sy Bartlett, two of the most influential air power advocates of the postwar period. Lay had been a student at Yale when he saw the movie *Wings* and was immediately filled with a passion to fly. He joined the Air Corps and earned his wings, then wrote about the experience in the 1937 bestseller *I Wanted Wings*. During the war he was a B-24 bomber pilot and bomb group commander, was shot down over France in 1944, and spent the rest of the war evading capture—an experience he wrote about in another memoir, *I've Had it*. Sy Bartlett, a journalist and screenwriter, was also fascinated with flying; during the war he served as a high-level staff officer in the Eighth Air Force, the AAF unit most closely associated with the strategic bombing campaign over Germany. During the war he became friends with Lay. These two were so committed to telling the air power story that before the war was over they were already discussing the need to educate the public on the great crusade of which they had been a part. After the war Bartlett badgered Lay into starting what became the novel *Twelve O'clock High!,* and a large part of the pitch Bartlett used was their mutual sense of responsibility to inform the public about the fight to make strategic bombing work. That collaboration began a long series of efforts to sell air power to the public for between them they would play key roles in bringing forth the three films collectively known as the "SAC Trilogy": *Strategic Air Command, Bombers B-52,* and *A Gathering of Eagles.*

Lay and Bartlett were quite explicit in claiming the importance of bombing to the war effort. In the novel's opening scene, set after the war, the former adjutant of the 918th Bomb Group visits the old base in England where the group had been stationed. As he stands on the overgrown runway a flood of memories washes over him, and the authors state that his tears, the first since his childhood, were not born of nostalgia, but "of the clear realization, emerging through the perspective of time, that here on this one station America might have lost the war. That this one rotten apple, decaying at a critically early juncture, almost spoiled the barrel. Americans remembered only victories. Did they know how perilously close the sequence of events at Archbury had come to destroying in its cradle the future giant of air power which, according to its victim, was the decisive factor in Germany's plunge to defeat?" The problem, and hence the plot, involves a B-17 bomb group that, under the command of an overindulgent father figure, sinks into the pit of high losses, self-pity, and plunging morale. Why one group with a morale problem threatens to lose the war for the United States, according to the authors, is that the 918th's impending collapse comes early in the war, in the fall of 1942, when many military leaders in the United States and Britain are critical of AAF theories on strategic bombing, theories that represent the ACTS tradition. Just when the AAF is under great pressure to get results quickly, when critics will use any excuse to end the effort to prove the daylight precision bombing theory, one of the few groups operating in England seems about to fold.[58]

The movie does not go into such specific detail, but it does imply the same point and with the powerful visual imagery that made it the tenth most popular movie of 1950. The movie also attached the aura of a major star like Gregory Peck to the message. The film's production team included four figures sympathetic to the air power cause. Lay and Bartlett wrote the screenplay; Darryl F. Zanuck, who had made *Winged Victory* during the war and was a charter member of the Air Power League, was the producer; and the director, Henry King, was a noted pilot and an AAF veteran of World War II. The movie was dedicated to the men who made daylight precision bombing possible and states in that dedication, "They stood alone, against the enemy and against doubts from home and abroad." In a critical scene that tells the audience why it should care, why this group is not just any U.S. fighting unit, General Pritchard, who commands the four AAF bombing groups in England, tells General Savage, played by Gregory Peck, "There's only one hope of shortening this war: daylight precision bombing. If we fold, daylight bombing is done with; and I don't know, maybe it means the whole show. We could lose the war if we don't knock out German industry."[59]

Both the book and the film highlight the effort to paralyze German industry by bombing ball-bearing factories, and in this they showcased the core of America's strategic bombing doctrine. In each version the

5. General Pritchard (Millard Mitchell, *right*) tells General Savage (Gregory Peck, *left*) that if he fails, strategic bombing will fail, and with it, any hope of defeating Germany.

justification for launching the dangerous mission is that by knocking out this one critical set of targets strategic bombing will have a magnified effect that will cripple the entire German war effort. The motif of the ball-bearing effort was based on the 1943 Schweinfurt-Regensburg raid, and it is no surprise that the authors would highlight this particular mission. Aside from its notoriety as one of the bloodiest bombing raids of the war, Lay had gone along on the raid as an observer and had written a report for Curtis LeMay, the mission leader, that was published "almost verbatim" by the *Saturday Evening Post*.[60] In both the novel and the movie the 918th successfully bombs the target and the message is clear: Savage rebuilt the group into an efficient weapon and saved strategic bombing, though in the movie it comes at a cost to Savage of a nervous breakdown. The meaning of daylight precision bombing's salvation is also clear. Because of men like Savage, strategic bombing prevailed over its critics and doubters, and this secret weapon went on to win the war.

The salvation of daylight precision bombing and its importance to the war effort, as depicted in this movie, along with its success at the box office, made *Twelve O'clock High* one of the most effective tools in enshrining the mythology surrounding America's strategic bombing doctrine in the nation's popular imagination. Not only was daylight precision bombing portrayed as a secret weapon based on Yankee ingenuity, it also pictured the Eighth Air Force as a heroic underdog winning against the odds. To the extent that postwar Americans understood the finer points of the bombing doctrine's specific tenets, their understanding was quite likely shaped or crystallized by the book and especially the movie. The image *Twelve O'clock High* put before the public, though, was one of bombing solidly within the tradition of the ACTS. The tone throughout both the novel and the movie is one that extols strategic bombing as efficient, progressive—almost scientific. It is a surgical instrument operating on only the nerve centers, leaving the vaunted German war machine unable to function. Bombing accuracy is touted throughout, to the point that, in perhaps one of the best-known scenes, and at subsequent points thereafter, any bombardier whose accuracy is not up to the group's standards is publicly humiliated by being relegated to "The Leper Colony," a crew made up of misfits.

Needless to say, the air force was as anxious to help with *Twelve O'clock High* as Zanuck was desperate to have air force assistance. In asking for aid, Zanuck wrote directly to Air Force Chief of Staff Hoyt Vandenberg, and Vandenberg got personally involved in helping production, by giving, for example, his wartime friend, director Henry King, wide latitude in his use of air force facilities. The air force even gave Zanuck and Twentieth Century-Fox a commendation for producing the movie, citing its "impressive portrayal of Eighth Air Force activities during the early stages of World War II."[61] Air force involvement, though, did little in shaping the plot or the script. The air force did object to minor plot elements, such as frequent drinking, ramming a B-17 with a tractor so it could be listed as destroyed and then used for spare parts, and a few technical errors, all of which were omitted from the film. Throughout its involvement, though, the air force did not attempt to influence the film's depiction of strategic bombing's contribution to the overall war effort. In fact, the principle reaction of all air force people who commented on the book and the script was simply an overall impression that the story was remarkably accurate. When requesting copies of the film for educational use inside the air force, Maj. H. O. Parsons, deputy adjutant general of Air Training Command, stated simply that "It portrays forcefully the responsibilities of the combat unit commander as well as those of the individual crew member and the necessity of self-discipline to the welfare of the group."[62] Thus the film's depiction of the role of strategic bombing is, like the book, solely the product of Sy Bartlett and Beirne Lay.

The other major work dealing with strategic bombing was *Command Decision* by William Wister Haines. Haines had been a successful writer before World War II, and during the war he served in intelligence in the AAF, rising to the rank of lieutenant colonel. After the war he first wrote *Command Decision* as a play in 1946. The play was so successful it moved to Broadway where it became a hit, and Haines quickly brought out a novel version in 1947 that was serialized in the *Atlantic Monthly* and condensed in *Reader's Digest*. In 1948 Metro-Goldwyn-Mayer turned the play into a movie that brought in over three million dollars and stood at eighteen on the list of the year's most popular movies. The movie's screenplay was coauthored by William R. Laidlaw, an air force reserve colonel and veteran of the Eighth Air Force, and George Froeschel. Their script followed the play closely. Like *Twelve O'clock High,* the play, novel, and film versions of *Command Decision* do not specifically state that strategic bombing won the war single-handedly. Instead, *Command Decision* claims overtly that air power could have won the war for Germany and subtly that strategic bombing destroyed Germany's real fighting strength and virtually guaranteed allied victory.[63]

Set in England in October 1943, about the time of the second Schweinfurt raid, the plot involves a fictional effort to knock out German production of the world's first combat jet aircraft. The plot clearly derives loosely from the Schweinfurt raids, for in both cases planners seek war-altering results through precision industrial bombing. The plot is also anachronistic, for it hinges on the premise that in late 1943 Germany was poised to deploy its jet (called the Focke-Schmidt 1 in the play and the Lantze-Wolf 1 in the movie) in large enough numbers to seize air superiority and turn the tide of war despite the fact that Germany did not actually introduce its Messerschmitt-262 until 1945.[64] Attacking the three factories producing the jet fighter deep in German territory will entail heavy losses, and this sets up a three-way conflict among U.S. war leaders that is the heart of the plot in all three versions of *Command Decision*. On one side are the critics of air power and strategic bombing; pitted against them is "Brig. Gen. Casey Dennis," played in the movie by Clark Gable, who believes that without strategic bombing the United States will lose the war. The third element of conflict is Dennis's superior, "Major General Kane," who worries more about publicity and the institutional fortunes of the AAF and who realizes critics will use heavy casualties as an excuse to kill strategic bombing and cut back the AAF. Haines uses this three-way conflict to narrow the focus down to the exact nature of the air power revolution.

As with *Twelve O'clock High,* the action takes place at a critical time in the evolution of the strategic bombing campaign. In this case, just as a bombing campaign is set to decide the fate of the war the Joint Chiefs are about to hold a meeting to reallocate resources for the entire war effort. For Kane this upcoming reallocation is critical, because chief among the AAF's critics is the navy, and as Haines states through one of his characters, admirals make up half of the Joint Chiefs and they do not believe strategic bombing can work.[65] When Kane learns that Dennis has started the long-planned operation, bearing the leading code-name Operation Stitch, for "a stitch in time," on the eve of the reallocation meeting, he orders Dennis to suspend the operation until after the meeting. Dennis argues this will allow a rare stretch of good weather crucial to the operation's success to go unexploited, and with winter coming on they will probably not get such a stretch of good weather again until after the German jets have turned the tide of battle.

This dilemma sets the stage for a confrontation between the two main characters that not only allows Haines to illustrate his notion of air power's true nature, it also gives him an opportunity to highlight the long struggle for American air power. Kane recounts his experiences in the interwar Air Corps when early pioneers flew obsolete aircraft, died carrying the air mail, and did everything they could to build public support. Now that they are on the verge of building a true air force, including a strategic bombing force that can win the war, Dennis is throwing the whole thing in jeopardy by incurring shocking losses. At one point he asks Dennis, "Do you realize how much the Navy wants our planes, for sub-patrol—and to protect the repairing of those battleships that air power couldn't hurt? Do you know how much the Army wants our pilots for company commanders? Don't you know the British want us to switch to night area bombardment? . . . Don't you realize the fight it's taken . . . to get us any planes at all? . . . And with time and planes and support we can [demolish] every factory in Europe. But the decision is at stake now."[66] Dennis counters that the promise of a future air force will mean nothing if Germany seizes aerial supremacy. Strategic bombing was the only means to prevent that from happening, but it had to be used immediately regardless of costs. In either case air power will decide the course of the war according to Haines. German tactical air power can deny allied victory, but U.S. strategic bombing will guarantee it. At one point Dennis tells Kane, "Sir, wars are lost by waiting. The Allies waited at Munich. The French and British waited behind the Maginot Line. . . . But if we wait . . . we'll be waiting for the Germans to put a roof on the continent . . . to confront our armies on D-Day at the Channel with an air force that's already whipped us. I'm not trying to tell you that Operation Stitch will win the war. But no battle, anywhere in this war, has been won without aerial supremacy. Operation Stitch is the price of that."[67] *Command Decision* even fits the strategic bombing campaign's high casualty rate into the context of the air power revolution. Whereas *Twelve O'clock High* treats casualties as a price of combat that can be reduced through good leadership, morale, and tactics, *Command Decision* treats the high casualty rate as a relatively small price to pay to avoid even higher casualties on the ground. In a scene near the end of both the play and the movie, General Dennis's replacement asks the advice of his intelligence officer, an old World War I artillery "retread." The major tells the general that if the German jet factories are not destroyed the major's son in the infantry, and all the other infantry troops, will have to go up against the jets when they invade Europe. When the general asks what the major would do if his son was in one of their B-17s, the major replies that he hopes he would still send the mission against the jet factories. The impression conveyed to the audience is that air power dictates the level of lethality in ground combat. Either the bombers suffer a relatively smaller number of casualties in the air or the ground forces will suffer greater casualties at the hands of superior German air power.[68]

One key element of Haines' depiction of strategic bombing is how Dennis succeeds in winning over the critics and doubters who appear in the story. Nearly everyone who is converted appears as a sensible individual throughout the work, and the rare individuals who do not come around to Dennis's arguments appear from start to finish as boorish louts. Kane, for example, appears as an unsympathetic schemer whose best days are long since past. He knows Dennis is right but surrenders to his own fears and fires Dennis for insisting on continuing the operation.[69] In the midst of the prolonged confrontation a congressional committee appears, and one of its members, Representative Malcolm, is portrayed as a caricature of the loud-mouthed, offensive politician. He objects to the high casualties of the first two missions of Stitch and flatly rejects all

6. Reporter Brockhurst (Charles Bickford, *standing, center*) hears the case for strategic bombing and is converted, as air power advocates assumed any reasonable person would be if they knew "the facts."

explanations. He holds Dennis responsible for the casualties and badgers and abuses him to the point where, in the novel, Dennis knocks him unconscious. The other congressmen appear much more reasonable and willing to listen to Dennis's explanations. Dennis eventually wins them over, and in the novel they force Malcolm to apologize to Dennis.[70] The two most sympathetic characters, though, are Brockhurst, a war correspondent, and Sergeant Evans, Dennis's orderly. Initially Brockhurst considered Dennis a tyrannical butcher, and he intended to expose him as such in the press. He is one of the first to see the wisdom of Dennis's efforts and spends most of the story marveling at the stupidity of Dennis's critics.[71] At first Evans, the ever-cynical NCO, considers Dennis just another general, but he too is converted and in the end gives up a comfortable stateside assignment to follow Dennis to his next command in the Pacific.[72]

The impression this depiction of strategic bombing's critics presents to the audience is two-fold. First, there is the unmistakable linkage between sensibility and ultimately coming around to Dennis's position. The implication is clear: any intelligent, reasonable, progressive-thinking individual would grasp the inherent good sense of strategic bombing and support postwar air power based on bombing. Those who cannot "see the light" are inescapably seen as unintelligent, pigheaded, or unenlightened. One should also note the partisan angle here as well; the characters who remain opposed all have ulterior motives—especially the army and navy critics back in Washington—that blind them to the greater good, while those who end up siding with Dennis do so because they are more concerned for the good of the nation.

The air force liked what Haines said about the bombing campaign and was thus eager to help with the movie, but it did not like the way he said it, so it kept its aid informal and unofficial. At the air force's request it received no acknowledgment for its help in the films credits. As with *Twelve O'clock High,* though, the Air Force did not try to influence the film's depiction of strategic bombing's contribution to the war effort. Because of the nature of the play, most of the action takes place indoors, and there are few flying sequences in the film, thus Air Force assistance was primarily limited to providing film footage and wardrobe.[73]

The air force objected to the play's controversial aspects, particularly the depiction of relationships between air force officers and members of Congress. Some had not liked Haines's work from the start. LeMay, for example, told Sy Bartlett he welcomed *Twelve O'clock High* because he "need[ed] something to take the taste of *Command Decision* out of [his] mouth." In early stages of communications with the studio, Maj. Gen. F. L. Parks, chief of Army Public Information, alluded to "obvious controversial elements" but stated, "I feel that a screenplay can be derived from it which will retain the dramatic values and still be approved for . . . cooperation." Less than a year later, after reading the film's first script, Maj. Gen. Emmett O'Donnell Jr., director of the air force's Office of Information, expressed approval that the writers had removed Dennis's assault on Congressman Malcolm but still found fault with Kane's assertion that interwar airmen had won favor with members of Congress by buying them liquor. The line was removed from the final script. The air force did give public aid with the movie's premiere by providing props, personnel, and the Air Force Band. And the Air Force Association presented MGM with a citation of honor for the film at its Washington, D.C., premiere. The film still remained controversial in air force eyes: when Air Training Command requested copies for training purposes Maj. H. O. Parsons noted that, while the movie portrayed many important and worthwhile subjects, students would have to be briefed before seeing it that "unfavorable characterizations of certain persons . . . which may be true in some cases are not indorsed [sic] by the USAF as being truly representative of normal conditions."[74]

The postwar air power revolution was a continuation and, in a sense, a culmination of the interwar air power revolution. Air power advocates felt they had gained insight into a whole new era where all the old ways were outmoded. Their assertions about the new way to look at the planet and the need for new educational approaches to equip young people for life in the new era enhanced their stature as theorists calling for a new approach to warfare. Given that they saw the full extent of the air power revolution, surely people would realize they must also have a unique insight into the future of war. This at least was what air power advocates thought about themselves and what they hoped others would think. The images of the new nature of warfare did appear to many as revolutionary and those images were appealing. Promises of quick, easy, and cheap victory had a powerful attraction for people with memories of two world wars. Between the revolutionary and appealing imagery air power advocates succeeded dramatically in winning the American public over to their way of thinking. A 1949 Gallup poll showed that 74 percent of those surveyed felt the air force would play the greatest role in winning a future world war. When asked again in October 1953, after the Korean War had ended, that percentage jumped to 81 percent. Two years later, when the popular culture campaign was starting to wane and the question was asked for the last time, the percentage fell to 71 percent. This faith also translated into support for a larger air force. In 1952, in the midst of the Korean War, 54 percent of Americans surveyed said the air force should be built up further as opposed to 11 percent for the army and 8 percent for the navy. Four years later, when asked what additional defense money should be spent on, 59 percent called for more strategic air power weapons while only 14 percent called for more ground forces, and 11 percent favored more aircraft carriers.[75]

But their images were also too simplistic and combined contradictory traditions. All future wars, even before the Soviet Union emerged as the main adversary, appeared as generic conflicts that could be quickly resolved with the same prescription: strategic atomic bombing. There were no complicating prewar contexts that might suggest nuclear devastation was not the answer. The war would be almost instantaneously fought and won with the adversary unable to counter, react to, or negate the effects of U.S. bombing. And finally the postwar situation never intruded on images of a future war to suggest that the wholesale atomic bombing of one's adversary might have unanticipated side-effects such as anger and resentment among the defeated population or international opprobrium for the United States. Moreover, the traditions of Douhet and the ACTS, utter devastation versus surgical, scientific precision and efficiency, were conflated into one. The atomic bomber would obliterate all before it but would also paralyze the enemy's defenses and leave innocent civilians thankful they had been spared. All of this while delivering the American people from fear and high casualties as well as easing the tax burden.

The images air power advocates placed before the American public through the popular culture campaign may have differed from images that emerged from debate in other venues, such as newspapers, Congress, or the Pentagon, but they were powerful images that shaped how average Americans viewed air power at a deep and visceral level. As such, the images of the air power revolution are important to understanding the overall place of air power in the United States as the Cold War took shape. These popular culture images would change over the next decade and a half as a result of events throughout the period, but it is important to appreciate the contours and textures of the images created by the air power advocates as the halcyon days of the early part of the popular culture crusade came to an end.

CHAPTER 4

The Revolution under Fire, 1949–53

The air power advocates' claims that air power had revolutionized warfare did not go unchallenged. Not only did critics publicly dispute their conception of air power and national defense, but other events arose that raised serious questions about the air power advocates' priorities and theories. The challenges during this period included the Revolt of the Admirals, the Soviet detonation of an atomic bomb, and the outbreak of the Korean War. Each in its own way threatened not only the air power advocates' devotion to strategic bombing but also the image of air power its adherents sought to popularize in the public's imagination. In meeting each of these trials air power advocates not only kept strategic bombing solidly in the center of their image, they also managed to fold air defense and tactical air power into their vision and make that vision even more attractive to the public. By the end of the period strategic bombing would be so firmly entrenched in the image of air power that it would become the dominant feature of the popular culture campaign throughout much of the fifties.

This period also saw changes in the shape and character of the popular culture campaign. First, it became institutionalized in that the main air power institution, the air force, became responsible to some degree for claims and statements made by air power advocates. For example, the events leading to the Revolt of the Admirals were in part precipitated and aggravated by the writings of noted air power advocates, but the U.S. Air Force got dragged into the fray. This was a reciprocal relationship, however, because the fate of the air power revolution became tied to the actions of the air force. Even if the air force was wrong, as for example in neglecting tactical air power before Korea, air power's defenders followed one of two courses. They either denied the problem or fixed blamed on someone or something else, but they never blamed the air force publicly, for that would weaken the air power cause. Second, while it may seem hard to believe when looking at some things air power advocates wrote during this period, compared to the rhetoric of earlier periods their claims became more realistic and responsible. There was no more talk of a handful of planes bringing victory in a matter of days. Sometimes they also brought bad news; General Vandenberg, while head of the air force, for example, made some rather pessimistic statements on air defense. Also, with the air force responsible for living up to promises made for air power, its partisans had to live with reality to some degree. No amount of verbal smokescreen could hide the blatantly obvious.

Third, the ranks of air power advocates would lose one face and gain several others. After playing a significant role in the days leading to the Revolt of the Admirals, William Bradford Huie would, for all practical purposes, disappear from the public air power scene. Taking his place would be Harold H. Martin and Wesley Price, both writing for the *Saturday Evening Post,* and Fletcher Knebel, a writer for *Look.* Together they would contribute a significant number of articles highly supportive of air power. The cause was also aided by what appears to be an increase in patriotic spirit among the popular magazines, most likely brought on by the heightened Cold War tension and the Korean War. Magazines like *Saturday Evening Post, Life,* and *Look* had been willing to publish air power articles before, but in this period the frequency increased noticeably, and highly complimentary pieces came from unnamed editors or from writers not usually associated with the air power cause. These magazines gave supportive treatment to other branches of the military, but their articles on air power usually adhered so closely to the air power "party line" that they amply supplemented the writings of known air power advocates. In this regard it is important to keep in mind that many leading figures controlling most of these magazines had maintained at some time or another ties with air power advocacy groups. Together with the air power advocates, they would help the air power revolution meet the challenges of this period and establish the air power image more firmly within popular culture.

THE REVOLT OF THE ADMIRALS
AND THE POPULAR CULTURE CRUSADE

The first challenge to the air power revolution was an affair commonly known as the Revolt of the Admirals. In 1949 the navy launched a two-pronged attack on the heart of the air power cause, an attack that questioned the effectiveness of air force strategic bombing and the wisdom of relying on it as the cornerstone of national defense.[1] The "revolt" clearly resulted from a combination of interservice competition for inadequate defense budgets, the navy's quest for a nuclear role, and legitimate concerns about America's reliance on strategic bombing. When the full scope of the popular culture campaign is considered, though, another element emerges that undoubtedly contributed to the navy's assault on the most fundamental tenet of the air power revolution. Ever since the end of the war air power advocates had kept up a steady drumbeat before the general public assailing the navy at every turn. Attacks were occasionally launched against the army as well, but they were rare. The anti-navy campaign, on the other hand, questioned not only fundamental aspects of the navy's mission but quite often the navy's very existence.

The early phase of the anti-navy campaign involved more than just the navy's obstruction of unification efforts. In 1946, for example, the Air Power League stated that air power had reduced the army and navy to "merely time-bound auxiliaries." That same year de Seversky fired a broadside at the navy with an article appearing in William Bradford Huie's *American Mercury* magazine bearing the inflammatory title "Navies Are Finished." Alluding to World War II, de Seversky stated that the navy refused to acknowledge that "six years of a global war in which air power proved, in every instance, to be the decisive factor might cancel out 150 years of tradition." Even the navy's seizure of island bases in the Pacific for the bombing assaults on Japan, according to de Seversky, were heroic but needlessly brought on by the navy itself by its interwar opposition to the development of long-range bombers. Relegating the navy to mere transportation support, de Seversky stated that "there simply is no fighting that navies can do which aviation cannot do more effectively and more quickly without their help." Four months later, Huie supplemented his indictment of the navy in *The Case against the Admirals* with another attack launched in *American Mercury*. Detailing navy resistance to new weapons during World War II, Huie claimed the navy was unfit to act as the nation's primary defense in an era of rapidly changing technology and defense options.[2] Obviously these were assaults on more than the navy's roles and missions or its stand on unification.

The attacks continued after the 1947 National Defense Act resolved the unification issue by creating the Department of Defense. In 1948 Huie resumed his very public assault on the navy, first with a July article in *American Mercury* charging that the navy was undermining the new unification system, wasting taxpayer money on useless projects, and trying to build a bigger air force than the U.S. Air Force. In September, again in *American Mercury*, he claimed the Marine Corps was an outdated relic that needlessly duplicated the army, and in December in *Reader's Digest* he made a similar charge about the navy's air arm duplicating the air force and attempting to seize the strategic bombing mission. Up to the end of 1948 the anti-navy campaign had been dominated by the twin firebrands of de Seversky and Huie. Other air power advocates had either voiced only veiled criticisms or couched charges in more temperate language. Spaatz, for example, stated in July that the "older services" did not understand the airmen's revolutionary zeal, and thus they put their faith in "'balanced force' based upon quantitative equality . . . rather than scientific balance in terms of a given military task." In a follow-on article he said of the navy's attempt to acquire its own strategic bombing force, "airpower has thus made its final convert. The long-standing dispute between the Navy and the airmen . . . has devolved into a jurisdictional dispute . . . over splitting up the nation's total airpower." He questioned whether the nation could afford two air forces, but in the same article voiced support for a strong army and navy.[3] With the start of 1949, however, the floodgates unleashed a torrent of attacks on the navy from air power advocates, and while few matched Huie and de Seversky for strident haranguing, most were uniquely outspoken and direct in their criticism.

Air power advocates had begun to charge in 1948 that the navy was trying to develop its own strategic bombing force, and this theme rose to a crescendo in the early months of 1949. Public attacks on the navy, along with the wrangling over the nuclear role going on inside the Pentagon, stiffened navy resolve to build the supercarrier *United States*. Spaatz inaugurated the new year and the new tone with an uncharacteristically sharp attack on naval aviation. Claiming the navy's air arm duplicated the air force, Spaatz stated that this threatened to starve both the army and the air force as well as the navy's submarine fleet. Citing World War II action in the Pacific, he claimed aircraft carriers had proven vulnerable to Japan's "second-rate air power" and would be even more vulnerable to Soviet air power or submarines. Reiterating his support for a strong army and navy, as well as strong land-based strategic air power, Spaatz stated that naval aviation's true role was helping the navy keep the sea lanes open.[4]

De Seversky weighed in on the debate with an article in *American Mercury* in which he stated that maintaining two air forces detracted from land-based strategic air power. Moreover, he claimed, it made no military sense because increased aircraft range had rendered aircraft carriers obsolete. Not surprisingly, Huie also joined in with two articles in succeeding issues of *Reader's Digest*. In March he charged that the navy was afraid of being relegated to an inferior status behind the air force and was therefore using the supercarrier, which he claimed could not handle a plane big enough to carry an atomic bomb, as a ruse to gain a land-based strategic air force of their own. The next month Huie rehashed his 1942 book *The Fight for Air Power* to argue that the army and the navy, the "Maginot minds, the yearners for Yesterday," were still trying to suppress air power against the will of the people and the march of progress.[5]

In April 1949, in the middle of this escalating public assault on the navy by air power advocates, the brand-new secretary of defense, Louis A. Johnson, a known air power supporter, cancelled the supercarrier *United States*. This move prompted the navy to launch a campaign, commonly known as the Revolt of the Admirals, to discredit the B-36 bomber and to challenge the nation's reliance on strategic bombing. Perhaps the most controversial aspect of the affair came in April when Cedric R. Worth, a civilian working in navy public relations, fabricated an anonymous document that circulated widely throughout the press and Congress. The document claimed the air force knew the B-36 was inadequate but that corrupt dealings by the bomber's manufacturer, Consolidated-Vultee, sustained its acquisition. Worth later recanted the charges but not before they prompted two sets of congressional hearings, the first in August to investigate the charges and the second in October on interservice rivalry and differing conceptions of national defense.[6] While the cancellation undoubtedly enraged the navy, the recently increased anti-navy rhetoric of the air power popular culture campaign certainly contributed to the navy's desperation.

Supporters of the navy rallied to their cause and responded in kind to the air power advocates' charges. In the midst of the controversy, for example, James Stahlman, editor of the *Nashville Banner,* printed and circulated a pamphlet arguing that strategic bombing had accomplished little during World War II to justify the heavy losses suffered by vulnerable bombers. Navy advocates pointed to numerous pro–air power articles in *Reader's Digest* in recent months and asked the editors for a chance to state their case. *Reader's Digest* did not quite grant equal time, but it did set up in the May issue a "point—counter-point" feature where Fletcher Pratt presented "The Case for the Aircraft Carrier" and

Francis Vivian Drake responded with "The Case for Land-based Air Power." The two "cases" contested in a "rigged court," for while Pratt got to state his case, Drake was given the chance to make his own case and respond to points raised by Pratt. Not only was Pratt not afforded the opportunity of rebuttal, but at no time had a naval partisan been given the opportunity to refute a pro–air power article as Drake was allowed with Pratt's article. Still, Pratt did not help his cause when he made such obvious errors as claiming that no ship was sunk in World War II when it had escorting battleships, and such inconsistent statements as claiming atomic attacks against the Soviet Union would be counterproductive yet maintaining that the Navy needed the supercarrier so it could launch nuclear attacks against targets deep inside the Russian heartland.[7]

A better effort came from Rear Adm. Daniel V. Gallery, in *Saturday Evening Post*. Gallery, alluding to the anti-navy publishing campaign, termed the air power message as one promising "quick and sure victory—at bargain rates." Attacking this notion directly and Huie by name, he got right to the heart of the fallacy buried deep in the image postwar air power advocates presented about strategic atomic bombing. First, the nuclear blitz did not fit every foreseeable conflict with which the United States could be confronted, and thus the nation needed to maintain balanced land, sea, and air forces. "While we are devastating the cities of the enemy hinterland with intercontinental bombers, his ground army may be occupying the rest of Europe. What happens then? Do we blitz Paris, Rome and Brussels?" More important, he observed, air power advocates neglected postwar realities of such a war won by atomic bombing: "We are losing sight of the fundamental fact that war is simply a means to an end. . . . Wars are fought for political objectives, and the accomplishment of the objective doesn't begin until the war is over. . . . Wholesale destruction of the populated areas of an enemy country is a poor way to promote a lasting peace." Gallery was quick to point out that he supported a strategic force of long-range bombers, and he saw a balanced and unified effort by the army, navy, and air force as the only approach to true national security. There was a strong tinge of hypocrisy, though, in Gallery's attack on strategic bombing, because the year before he had written a memorandum urging the navy to make that role its main focus and to try to seize it away from the air force. On the whole, though, the *Saturday Evening Post* article was an evenhanded and insightful counter-offensive to the attacks led by Huie.[8]

Former war correspondent Richard Tregaskis weighed in on the side of the navy in an October *Collier's* article. While stating that the United States needed B-36s and the ability to launch nuclear attacks deep into Soviet territory, Tregaskis recounted the heavy losses suffered over Germany when bombers went beyond the range of fighter cover. Without new, bigger carriers to handle modern jet fighters to escort the B-36s, and fighter-bombers to launch atomic strikes against Soviet air defenses, Tregaskis claimed the B-36 crews would be "sitting ducks." This especially because, according to Tregaskis, the B-36 was vulnerable to interception, that U.S. fighters found it easy to intercept it, and that the air force was suppressing the results of these intercept tests. He also returned to the unification issue and stated that the current arrangement meant that "the Army–Air Force axis can in effect dictate Navy strategy." As to the charge that the navy was trying to "steal" the strategic bombing role away from the air force, Tregaskis noted that navy officials had repudiated the infamous Gallery memo and that navy secretary John L. Sullivan had publicly rebuked Gallery for his comments.[9]

Air power advocates were quick to defend both the B-36 and the concept of strategic bombing as a whole. In his reply to Pratt's article, Drake called Pratt's argument a "jumble of contradictions and picturesque smokescreens," and claimed the navy was growing less realistic about future warfare. In modern war the atomic bomb was such a revolutionary weapon that it had to play a key role in any U.S. war plan, and that could only be done through strategic bombing. In defending the B-36, Drake noted that the performance differential between it and modern jet fighters was much smaller at the B-36's operating altitude of forty thousand feet, which coupled with the expectation of attacking at night, meant that "at best interception is speculative." He even reassured his readers that at that altitude America's own best fighters could not intercept the B-36. Drake also struck back by quoting the Gallery memorandum: "the time is right now for the Navy to start an aggressive campaign aimed at proving that the Navy can deliver the atom bomb more effectively than the Air Force. . . . if the Navy makes delivery of the atom bomb its major mission, the Navy can become the principal offensive branch of the national defense system." Drake charged that the only reason the navy attacked the B-36 was because it competed with navy ambitions to acquire the nuclear role and thereby dominate national defense.[10]

Spaatz, too, joined the fray. He began on May 9 with an article aimed at an old sore spot for the navy, the subject of unification. Arguing that the 1947 compromise was leading to greater service rivalry and no agreement on strategic planning, Spaatz called for reorganization similar to the original plan backed by the army and the old AAF: one chief of staff commanding all three services under one civilian secretary. In a veiled allusion to the current crisis, Spaatz claimed strategic priorities could not be set in the committee-style approach of the Joint Chiefs of Staff as it stood at that time. He felt one chief of staff, with advisors from all branches who would be removed to a separate promotion list to guard against service bias, could set strategic priorities that would then form the basis for dividing the defense budget. In his next installment, in the context of describing what he saw as a new sense of optimism in Western Europe, Spaatz attempted to minimize the impact of the navy's charge that strategic bombing could not prevent a Soviet occupation of NATO countries. Spaatz ascribed Western Europe's new spirit, in part, to its faith in the atomic bomb and U.S. air power. In a reference to the navy's charge, Spaatz stated, "Europeans feel safer because they know that American bombers give them a first line of defense. But they also realize that this line would not necessarily save them from occupation by ground forces in the early stages of another war." The reason they did not fear Soviet occupation in the early stages, according to Spaatz, was because U.S. aid was helping them rebuild their own ground forces to resist that invasion. Unmentioned in this article, though, is Spaatz's faith that strategic bombing would devastate Soviet industry, thus making it possible for the stronger, but still outnumbered, European forces to drive the Red Army out of their territory.[11]

Spaatz's most direct reply came in July with an article detailing why the United States needed the B-36. As to its vulnerability Spaatz stated, "Much nonsense has been written about whether a fighter plane can climb as high and fly as fast as a B-36. During the second world war [sic] the Lancasters and Wellingtons of the RAF were excelled by the German fighters in speed, climb, and altitude. Yet they operated successfully at night over Germany throughout the war. The B-17s in daylight, although exposed repeatedly to attacks by enemy fighters, operated successfully throughout the war." He then added, without mentioning the heavy losses suffered in these attacks, that not one AAF bombing attack was ever turned back by either German or Japanese defenses. Returning to the notion of the Red Army overrunning Europe, Spaatz stated that in such an event Soviet submarines might block the navy from approaching Europe, thus leaving air strikes launched from the continental

United States as the only means of striking back at Russia. Spaatz followed up this counterattack with another one month later addressing the navy charge that the air force's emphasis on strategic bombing was undermining tactical air forces. Despite a long trend in air force neglect of the tactical air mission, Spaatz insisted the true culprit was the effort to support two redundant air forces in the navy and the air force: "The total amount now being spent for air power by the United States is more than adequate. But it is not enough to support two air forces with duplicate establishments." This, according to Spaatz, kept the air force from acquiring forces it had long requested and left it weak in both strategic and tactical air power.[12]

As the Revolt of the Admirals wound down in October Arnold sounded a conciliatory note in a *Collier's* article. Sounding somewhat like Clemenceau, he stated that modern warfare had become too important to be formulated by service partisans in the arena of public opinion. Fixing equal blame on the army, navy, and air force, Arnold called for a "new kind of War Advisory or Planning Board" made up of high-level civilians from industry, labor, and science, as well as retired four- or five-star flag officers from all three services. Together they would sort through all claims and ideas from the three branches and weigh them "in relation to our foreign policy, war and peace objectives, international conditions and our economic situation." Arnold could afford to be magnanimous. By that point, the B-36 had survived congressional scrutiny, and the air force had been vindicated in the Congressional hearings while the navy had been chastised, Navy Secretary Sullivan had resigned, and CNO Adm. Louis Denfeld had been fired.[13]

In that part of the battle waged in the popular culture arena, air power had taken a few solid blows, but its advocates had defended their cause well enough that no serious harm had come to either the image of air power or strategic bombing. Spaatz met questions about bombings effectiveness in World War II by calling on the heroic tradition from that same war. Drake met questions of the B-36's vulnerability with facts and figures that made the air power case look very scientific. Ultimately, the charge that the navy's attack was motivated by their own desire to acquire the strategic bombing mission put the navy on the defensive and made air power seem that much more creditable. Gallery's charge that the air power advocates had forgotten that war is politics by other means, though, went unanswered. It did not have to be, because only three months later, in September, and half a world away an event took place that left the public less concerned about whether atomic bombs were suitable for every conceivable war and more worried about what atomic bombs might do in a war against the United States.

The Revolt of the Admirals took a lot out of the popular culture crusade. Whether because the public fight with the navy was a sort of baptism-by-fire leading to loss of innocence or because of the deadly serious business that followed hard on its heels, the end result was that the air power message lost its simplistic character and its naiveté. Increasingly afterward air power advocates would be the bearers of harsh realities urging Americans to "buck-up" and confront the "facts." Their message would also stress more institutional themes, that is, rather than evangelizing an ethereal notion of "air power," they proclaimed that what was good for the air force, or more often SAC, was good for the country. Symbolic of the new spirit, the air power cause lost one of its more controversial figures. After the six month blitz that helped precipitate the Revolt of the Admirals, Huie turned to other topics. Whether because of the attacks he suffered from navy advocates or because he had had a change of heart, with the exception of a mild profile of LeMay in October 1950, he never wrote another pro–air power piece again. Within two months of the LeMay article, Huie was praising Forrestal— once one of his favorite targets—as a patriotic martyr to the war against Communism.[14]

THE SOVIET BOMB AND THE IMAGE OF AIR POWER IN THE UNITED STATES

In September 1949 an American reconnaissance plane detected indications that the Soviet Union had exploded an atomic bomb. While some analysts had predicted this could occur by 1949, few in the United States, particularly the general public, were prepared for it.[15] The nation was shocked, for now the image of an aerial attack devastating the United States was more than just science fiction or air power rhetoric. In a curious twist of fate, at the very time air power advocates were striving to reassure Americans that the bomber would always get through, they faced a public desperate for reassurance that Soviet bombers could not. While it might appear at first glance that air power advocates were now caught in a trap of their own making, as events would turn out this dilemma actually worked in favor of the preferred air power role, strategic bombing. For while there would be considerable public clamor for effective air defense of North America, air power advocates would insist that no air defense, no matter how extensive, could stop a majority, let alone all, of Russia's bombers. Thus the main response to the Soviet atomic bomb among air power advocates was to stress the deterrent capability of a massive U.S. strategic bomber force. Air defense would become a vivid public image, but it is during this period that SAC and the nuclear bomber became the dominant image in popular culture synonymous with American air power.

In the early postwar years air power advocates, in their effort to convince Americans that air power was a revolutionary weapon, had attempted to shock the public with graphic depictions of modern air warfare. As both Paul Boyer and Spencer Weart illustrate, postwar scientists who opposed the use of the atomic bomb had helped create the climate of fear in their effort to shock the United States into eschewing the bomb, but in their concurrent effort to reassure Americans that air power could use the bomb to guarantee their security, the air power advocates won out over the scientists.[16] In the wake of the Soviet bomb revelation it is clear both groups had succeeded in planting nuclear fear deep within the popular imagination. Articles on bomb shelters and the likelihood or nature of a Soviet attack appeared overnight in magazines of every description. One reflection of this is that under the heading "air raid" in *Reader's Guide to Periodic Literature* prior to this event one finds no articles listed. The first edition after the Soviet bomb, however, shows not only a significant increase in articles listed under "air raid" but also two new categories, "air raid shelters" and "air raid alarms." The outpouring of articles on air raid topics continued throughout the fifties and showed no abatement until the early sixties. In fact, the first edition of *Reader's Guide* to show a significant drop is the 1961–63 edition, which spanned the time of the Cuban Missile Crisis and lists only four articles in all categories.[17]

Fears had been growing about the size of the Soviet Air Force, so when they gained atomic capability fears of imminent air attack had already been primed. Air power advocates had been contributing to that fear. In 1947 W. B. Courtney drew on images of revolutionary air power to portray the United States locked in a struggle with Russia for aerial supremacy that would decide "moral, economic and political world leadership." He portrayed himself as a modern-day Paul Revere responding to a third lantern signaling that the new threat came by air. Courtney had a grim assessment of America's standing versus Soviet air power:

"Russia is in the lead on all points of foresight, research and future war potentials." A 1947 American Legion pamphlet claimed the Soviets had 40,000 aircraft compared to the combined total of only 28,000 for the air force and navy. The pamphlet also stated that the Soviets dedicated 58 percent of their $13 billion budget to their air arm while the United States devoted only 33 percent of its $9 billion budget. The latter figure accounts for only the air force budget and does not include the substantial amount the navy spent on aviation, and the source for the figure on the number of Soviet aircraft, a W. B. Courtney article in *Collier's*, actually puts that number closer to 32,000.[18] This playing fast and loose with facts that could be easily disproved seems astounding, but at the time the Legion sought to create the image that American air power had fallen behind Soviet air power and that the gap was widening. Most people whom the pamphlet aimed to influence would react to the fear without too much thought about the veracity of the facts, much less take the time to check those facts.

A similar example of dealing in images not necessarily based on facts was the air power advocates' emphasis on the seventy-group plan. This plan had been shaped by the AAF in the closing days of World War II before any specific adversary had been identified, and in the postwar years it became a virtual shibboleth within the air power cause as the absolute minimum to protect the United States, yet the air power advocates never explained why the magic number seventy remained the same after the Soviets emerged as the main threat. Spaatz, for example, referred to the figure numerous times, including a *Newsweek* article one month before the Soviets exploded their bomb. In this article Spaatz once again bemoaned Congress's failure to provide for a seventy-group air force, authorizing instead only forty-eight groups. Not only would this action leave the air force too weak to meet its strategic and tactical missions, according to Spaatz, it would also concede to the Soviets their ambition to have the world's largest air force.[19]

The image of a threatening Soviet air force became so pervasive by the late forties that other authors began writing about it. Writing in 1948 for the *Saturday Evening Post*, Wesley Price concluded that the Soviets were "spawning giant bombers and a hornet swarm of jet interceptors," and he quoted air force secretary Stuart Symington that "Russia was building about twelve times as many planes as we were." Alluding to a potentiality soon to become reality, Price said "defense planners . . . must consider what our position would be if [Soviet bombers] should hit us after Russia acquires atomic bombs. . . . All our industrial centers would be under the gun." This image was made even more threatening when in December of that same year Frank Kluckhohn reported in *Collier's* that the Soviets were massing air bases in Eastern Siberia within sight of the Bering Sea. Making the image seem even more immediate, he observed that these bases are "not more than a 3,000-mile flight to New York and most of industrial America, a distance well within the range of moderately new bombers." After an observation flight in an air force aircraft, he claimed the runways he saw seemed long enough to handle large bombers and that the Soviets were estimated to have three hundred such bombers, capable of reaching New York. The air force had only one hundred fighters in position to oppose them.[20]

After the news of the Soviet bomb broke onto the American scene, the public felt that all the fearful images created over the last four years were suddenly real and tangible. Having been told that air power was their only hope against an air power threat, the public naturally turned to air power and expected a solution. There was more at work here, though, than just the long series of promises and exhortations coming from air power advocates. The long tradition of technological messianism that had become intertwined with the cultural fascination with aviation also played a part. Stretching back to at least the late nineteenth century, people had been conditioned to expect that salvation from any threat, even a threat from the air, would come from the airplane. With this new threat, the most obvious solution to many seemed to be the most direct—that is, to stop any Soviet bomber attack by shooting down those bombers.

Attention turned at many levels to the question of America's air defenses. Because of budget constraints and air force emphasis on strategic bombing, air defense had languished prior to this point, as can be seen in the 1948 merger of Air Defense Command and Tactical Air Command into one major command structure.[21] With the new crisis, however, members of Congress, responding to local concerns, began demanding greater efforts, and the air force initiated a series of studies to consider options. From the beginning air force leaders resisted the idea of making the air defense role their highest priority or even a priority equal to strategic bombing. They obviously could not ignore the problem and worked to increase their air defense capabilities, but with no increase in budget, those new capabilities had to come at the expense of some other capabilities, largely tactical air forces. Estimating the earliest date the

Soviets would have sufficient nuclear weapons to launch an attack as July 1, 1952, air force planners set that same date as their goal for having an operational air defense system in place. Their main efforts focused on joint ventures with Canada in building an early warning radar network and aircraft interceptor facilities across the northern fringes of North America, marshaling the scientific community to find more effective air defense methods, enlisting public support in the Ground Observer Corps to supplement radar coverage, and increasing the effectiveness of the Air National Guard in the air defense role.[22]

Another key strategy, though, involved turning public opinion to the air force's and the air power advocates' way of thinking, and here the popular culture campaign was a primary tool. Air power advocates clearly preferred strategic nuclear deterrence as the primary response to Soviet nuclear capability, but here they walked a tightrope in making their case. Sensing the public mood for air defense, they were loath to squash public faith in air power, even if it was not the preferred kind of air power, so while they voiced support for greater air defense capabilities, they subtly worked in notes of caution with their message. Spaatz's reaction in his *Newsweek* column is a good example. Immediately after the official announcement of the Soviet detonation, Spaatz called for a radar warning net and increased numbers of air defense squadrons armed with the latest jet interceptors, and he stated that the seventy-group plan might need to be revised upward. He was also quick to state, though, that the United States should continue to build up its nuclear stockpile and that the "strategic-bomber force should be increased to at least the number contemplated in the seventy-group program." His next installment extolled advances made in air defense capabilities and called for immediate efforts to build an effective radar warning system. He cautioned, however, that such a system would have limits: "While well-organized defenses might not prevent a raid, they would certainly minimize its effects. They could avert disaster."[23]

Air power advocates focused their main efforts, though, on convincing the public that strategic bombing must remain the main defense against a Soviet attack on the United States. For years air power advocates had promised the bomber would always get through. In the early postwar years they trumpeted the fact that no World War II bombing mission had ever been turned back. In the Revolt of the Admirals they used the same approach to deflect criticism of bomber vulnerability, and now they used that faith to tell the American public that the only way to stop a Soviet bomber attack was to deter it by threatening swift nuclear retaliation. One month after calling for greater air defenses, for example, Spaatz observed in his column that the "ability to launch a powerful retaliatory offensive is still our best defense against atomic attack." And in a piece written on the eve of the Korean War he stated "the atomic bomb and strategic air power are primary factors maintaining the balance of military power and thus the peace of the world."[24]

Not surprisingly, the most blunt and controversial argument came from de Seversky in his 1950 book *Air Power: Key to Survival*. De Seversky did not totally dismiss the notion of air defense, and conceded that the United States would fight for aerial supremacy over North America as well as over the Soviet Union, but he was emphatic that the best defense was a good offense. In describing the ultimate consequences of his vision he pulled no punches: "When we reduce the enemy's aerial might, we reduce his ability to deliver destruction, the atomic kind included. Should we succeed in keeping him out of our skies altogether, we will for all practical purposes have eliminated the atomic threat. True, the enemy will probably crash through to drop bombs—many or few— despite everything. But he will know that these cannot score a decision. He will be acutely aware that his own skies are wide open to our aircraft for overwhelming punishment. . . . As in any other type of bombing, the final outcome will be decided by the relative ability of belligerents to absorb punishment while carrying more of it to the enemy." This "stiff upper lip" view of air power strategy was a recurring theme throughout de Seversky's book, for he saw no way around massive casualties and derided those who offered anything but the hard facts to the America public.[25]

Perhaps the most influential statement of the faith in deterrence over air defense came from Air Force Chief of Staff Hoyt Vandenberg. In a 1951 *Saturday Evening Post* article Vandenberg made a pointed effort to disabuse the public of the notion that an air defense system could ever provide a reasonable amount of security in the event of a concerted Soviet attack. Drawing on World War II analogies, he claimed that Britain throughout the war shot down only 10 percent of the German bombers sent against their homeland despite having to guard an area only one thirtieth the area the United States must defend. He also elaborated on the difficulties inherent in aircraft interception and destruction and estimated that the best the air force could hope for was to shoot down

30 percent of an attacking bomber force. Summing up the dilemma Vandenberg stated, "There is a dangerous delusion that radar screens and complicated electronic devices will give us an airtight defense against bombing. We could tackle an engineering project that would make the Great Wall of China look like the sand trenches children dig at the seashore. We could build a steel fence five miles high around the 17,936-mile perimeter of the United States. We could place an unbroken line of radar screens on top of the fence, ring our cities with automatic antiaircraft guns. . . . We could put an umbrella of interceptor planes over the entire country—and we could not keep out a determined enemy attacking in strength." Moreover, Vandenberg added, such a system would take so much money and manpower it would render Korean forces ineffective and abandon NATO allies to Soviet occupation.[26]

The only true security, according to Vandenberg, came from strategic bombing, but the hope he offered had a shocking image implicit in its promise. Strategic bombing was the first line of defense, Vandenberg stated, because it deterred the atomic attack Americans so feared, but if that attack should come U.S. bombers would defend the United States by destroying Soviet bombers at their airfield and factory sources. How U.S. bombers were supposed to destroy Soviet bombers at their source *after* they had launched an attack Vandenberg did not say, but since the United States had eschewed a preemptive strike, the only thing he could mean was a nuclear war of attrition. Vandenberg was straightforward in stating that this would mean the United States was vulnerable to "frightful loss of life and attendant property damage," but he also said that once Americans understood it, his scenario "may not be so terrifying as it first appeared." In short, Americans were supposed to take comfort in the fact that whatever devastation they experienced in a nuclear attack dwarfed in comparison to the vengeful holocaust visited upon the Soviet Union.[27]

Many opposed the air force's lack of emphasis on air defense and continued to insist a system could be developed that worked better than the dire predictions of people like Vandenberg. One such person was Vannevar Bush, former vice president of the Massachusetts Institute of Technology and director of the Office of Scientific Research and Development during World War II. While Bush did not discount the role of strategic nuclear bombing entirely, he saw it as part of an overall balanced force. More important, he foresaw potential for effective new weapons in stopping enemy bombers. In a November 1949 *Life* article he predicted that developments in jet interceptors and guided missiles would inevitably give the defense an advantage over bombers. Little more than a year later he repeated much the same message in *Reader's Digest* and stated that advances in radar, missiles, and jet interceptors "may make it increasingly impractical to penetrate to prime targets." Bush urged that strategic bombing forces learn to defeat such systems if they were to have any hope of penetrating Soviet defenses. And in terms of a U.S. air defense system based on such innovations he stated, "We should not let anything stand in the way of bringing it to full fruition at an early date."[28]

Two of the harshest critics of the air force's air defense measures, though, were the Alsop brothers, Joseph and Stewart, who together served as long-time defense correspondents for the *New York Herald Tribune*. In 1953 they learned of the Lincoln Project, a study group formed by MIT to examine the air defense problem for the air force. Air force leaders felt the group's work confirmed their belief that there would be no affordable new or dramatic improvements in air defense in the foreseeable future, but the Alsops claimed the air force was turning a blind eye to this "official warning that the United States had become nakedly vulnerable to Soviet air attack with atomic weapons." In March Stewart Alsop broke the news of the Lincoln Project in a *Saturday Evening Post* article co-authored with noted scientist Ralph E. Lapp. The two authors gave a detailed description of numerous innovative systems, some still in development and some only theoretical, ranging from new types of radar and acoustic locating devices to guided missiles and pilotless drones. They also presented as new, ideas that were relatively old. For example, they spoke of the polar concept as if they had just discovered the secret and were sharing it with the public for the first time.[29]

More important is the fact that they were in effect playing on the old theme of technical messianism by offering a new brand of savior to deliver the nation from a new danger. In describing how several of these systems will interact they claimed "[scientists] even foresee a time when these wonderful machines will actually control the interception of enemy bombers, making the whole defense operation automatic, from the blip on the radar screen to the destruction of the invading enemy. This sounds like science fiction. But practical men are now pressing forward with the experiments in this eerie new field." The new system would not be cheap. It would cost as much as $20 billion. It would, though, destroy 85–95 percent of any incoming bomber force and protect the United States until the day when intercontinental missiles, which were also only theoretical but which the authors claimed would not be practical for many years, made the system obsolete. When the air force and the press ignored them, the Alsops charged that partisan interests in the air force and apathetic newsmen were standing in the way of the safety of the nation.[30]

A more balanced argument came from James R. Killian Jr., president of MIT, and A. G. Hill, director of MIT's Lincoln Laboratory, which had grown out of the Lincoln Project. Urging a balance between offensive strategic forces and defensive air power, the authors argued there was little use in Vandenberg's vision of victory in a nuclear war if the United States was devastated beyond the point of maintaining its way of life. The authors supported the notion of SAC as the nation's first line of defense to deter a Soviet attack but charged that SAC needlessly worried about air defense detracting from their offensive capability; in the authors' opinion the United States could support both systems adequately. Stressing their view that the air force was as committed to air defense as they were, the authors consciously limited their rhetoric by stating that a perfect defensive system was impossible to achieve, but they also observed that affordable improvements would greatly increase the percentage of enemy bombers destroyed short of their targets. The authors also dismissed the notion that such a system, as the Alsops had claimed, would stop 95 percent of incoming bombers, and while they did not quote a dollar figure, they assured the public that the $20 billion figure quoted by the Alsops was greatly exaggerated.[31]

Despite charges of neglect, the air force was committed to providing the best air defense possible with the money Congress provided, as long as it did not detract from strategic bombing capability. Still, the air force tried to discourage hope for a miracle air defense panacea. Its radio advertisements calling for volunteers for the Ground Observer Corps, for example, created images of an air defense system so weak it desperately needed thousands of civilians to help plug the gaps. One such radio spot declared, "The Reds right now have about a thousand bombers that are quite capable of destroying at least 89 American cities in one raid. . . . Won't you help protect your country, your town, your children?" At times its supporters' efforts to paint a rosy picture of air defense capabilities even left the air force worried that such optimistic presentations were counterproductive. The Air Defense Command, for example, felt a 1952 *Saturday Evening Post* article exaggerated their capabilities and might discourage Ground Observer Corps enlistment by giving the impression there was little need for further sacrifice.[32]

The inherent problem with the issue of air defense, though, was that despite whatever genuine support for it they might have, air power advocates would always see any role other than strategic bombing as detracting from the primary mission because they never felt the United States had enough air power, especially strategic air power. It was an open-ended dilemma that became a regular feature of the popular culture debate. For years air power advocates clung to the seventy-group plan when they could not get support for such a high level. With the outbreak of the Korean War, though, the air force began growing rapidly but so did its commitments, thus air power advocates began to call for even more groups. Sen. Henry Cabot Lodge, writing in the midst of the Korean War and the buildup of forces in NATO, stated in a 1951 *Saturday Evening Post* article that the recent congressional decision to build up to 95 groups was inadequate and recommended 150 groups instead. In breaking this total down into specific missions, he felt the United States needed more air defense, but then added, "of course, our most effective defense against this danger in the long view is a counter-offensive aimed at the centers of Soviet power." He called for 62 groups for strategic forces as opposed to only 38 air defense groups.[33]

Also in 1951, in a *Reader's Digest* article alluding to the new worldwide commitments, Spaatz pointed to obsolete aircraft in the air force inventory and claimed the 95-group goal amounted to only the equivalent of 50 groups, which left the air force facing 10–1 odds. In his *Newsweek* column from the same period he called for an increase to at least the World War II level of 250 groups and stressed strategic bombing as the greatest need for growth. By early 1952 he had modified his prognosis and applauded Congress for endorsing the Joint Chiefs of Staff plan calling for 143 wings but then chided Congress for delaying implementation of the plan, stating that it could lead to costly and perhaps fatal results.[34] At times air power advocates' calls for more groups even left them in conflict with the Air Force. In a June 1951 editorial, *Life* magazine sharply criticized Vandenberg for letting American air power slip behind the Soviets. Claiming to speak for the American people, the editors stated, "[Americans] not only want the best damn Air Force in the world, but they know that survival depends upon it," and concluded,

"To remain second best in the air, at this time, is to cease to exist as a nation."[35]

In their concern to maintain public support and present the best possible image of air power, air power advocates and air force supporters ended up striving to glorify both approaches for defending against Soviet nuclear attack, but invariably they did so in ways that reinforced the image that America's best defense was a good offense. An example of this is Harold H. Martin's writings for the *Saturday Evening Post*. A regular columnist, Martin wrote on a number of military topics besides air power, but during the early fifties he contributed a string of articles echoing air power advocate themes and helping their cause. In November 1950 he wrote on air defense capabilities, and while he found them to be sorely lacking, the two big culprits in his mind were the pre–Korean War budget limitations and the surprisingly early Soviet acquisition of the atomic bomb. Nevertheless, according to Martin's depiction, the air force was performing yeoman service in trying to catch up as quickly as possible: "When it became clear that we should need a strong network of defense, not in 1953 or '54, but immediately, the Air Force painfully squeezed out of its financial heart's blood $50,000,000 with which to get the permanent installations started quickly." After painting a rosy picture of improvements coming in the near future, though, Martin reminded his audience that no defensive system could be perfect and that strategic bombing was still the nation's best defense: "Therefore, those men charged with providing the tactical air defense of the United States are among the strongest supporters of the Strategic Air Command. They know the forces of that command operating against the Soviet atomic force would provide our best defense against a mortal wound in the first few days of future war."[36]

The next month Martin turned his attention to SAC. Comparing bomber crew teamwork to a baseball team executing a double-play and crewmember dedication to "novitiates studying for the priesthood," Martin presents a glowing depiction of SAC's ability to devastate the Soviet Union. He even made another contribution to the continuing legend of U.S. precision bombing by extolling SAC's emphasis on "bull's-eye accuracy," which would take out Soviet industry but spare civilians. In all, Martin was convinced SAC stood ready to defeat the Soviet Union in one massive atomic blitz, and in that he placed America's greatest hope for survival. On the prospects of a Soviet surprise nuclear attack, Martin stated that the greatest tragedy for the United States would be if such an attack caught SAC's bombers on the ground.[37]

One very unique example of air power advocates trying to balance air power's defensive capabilities while still emphasizing strategic bombing is Milton Caniff and his perennially popular comic strip *Steve Canyon*. The hero and namesake was an air force pilot, and the strip was built around his many adventures as the air force sent him to trouble spots around the world. Caniff is best described as a popularizer of air power rather than pushing specific roles, but on a number of occasions he showcased the air force's air defense capabilities. In the fall of 1954, for example, Canyon foils communist saboteurs who are delaying an early-warning radar project, and in late 1954–early 1955 he places Canyon in temporary command of an Air Defense Command interceptor squadron. Caniff uses this plot line to repeatedly emphasize the importance of ADC's Alaskan bases as the first line of defense against a Soviet bomber attack he felt could come at any time. At one point, for example, Canyon and Colonel Davey, the temporarily out of commission squadron commander, discuss how important the air defense system is to the United States. Davey observes, "If Ivan tries a quarterback sneak it's our job to stop as many of his bombers as we can, and alert our next line of defense!" Canyon, warning against complacency, states, "While we *sensible* people know [Soviet bombers] aren't there *this* minute, but that they *could* be two minutes from now!" Still, Caniff stresses that air defense could only stop a fraction of the incoming Soviet bombers. Over the long haul, Caniff repeatedly emphasized the importance of strategic bombing. The strip frequently mentions, for example, that Canyon had flown bombers during World War II and that he had flown on the famous Ploesti bombing raids. Another example is the key role a B-52 plays in a 1956 episode where Canyon decides to stay in the air force rather than accept a lucrative movie contract.[38]

The advent of the Soviet nuclear threat was a challenge to the air power advocates' emphasis on strategic bombing. The public clamor for air defense ensured the air force, not unwillingly, continued to strengthen defenses against air attack. But the air power advocates responded by mixing reassuring images of potent air defense with warnings that no defense system could avert a national disaster and that true security could only be found in strong nuclear forces to deter such an attack. Though it may have seemed contradictory, the mixed message helped keep strategic bombing at the forefront of American air power. Their strategy also went a long way toward making the Strategic Air Command the preeminent symbol of security in U.S. popular culture through much of the fifties.

IMPACT OF THE KOREAN WAR
ON THE POPULAR CULTURE CAMPAIGN

While the nation was still debating air power's response to the Soviet atomic bomb, another Cold War shock came to the American public. On June 25, 1950, North Korea invaded South Korea, touching off the Korean War. The U.S. combat experience in that war pointed out the air force's weakness in tactical air power, which began yet another challenge to the air power advocates' devotion to the preeminence of strategic bombing. Many air force defenders blamed the weakness on inadequate force levels, but critics claimed it actually stemmed from the air force's neglect of the tactical role in favor of their preferred strategic mission. Much that was said of the air power advocates' popular culture response to the air defense debate could be said of this controversy. While the air force tried to refute the charges, air power advocates set about depicting great tactical capabilities while stressing that true air power came in the form of strategic bombing.

When critics claimed the air force neglected tactical air power, they generally meant close air support. The air force *did* have a long history of turning a blind eye to providing airborne firepower to troops in forward fighting positions. The lack of enthusiasm stemmed primarily from the airmen's conviction that it was the least productive means of inflicting damage on the enemy from the air, but close air support had also gained a reputation as early as World War I as the deadliest mission of the whole air war.[39] While the air force claimed in the years leading up to Korea that it supported its commitment to provide the army's tactical air power needs, continued lack of enthusiasm is best seen in difficulties working out joint doctrine with the army and the fact that in 1948 the air force downgraded Tactical Air Command from a major command to a subordinate command within Continental Air Command. This latter move indicates another element of the close air support problem. What support for tactical air power there was in the air force generally saw it as an air superiority role, which seemed closely related to air defense—fighter pilots did not embrace close air support any more than the rest of the air force—so Air Defense Command and TAC were joined to facilitate cooperation between the two. With the air force's emphasis on strategic nuclear bombing, few air force leaders envisioned a war pitting large ground forces in prolonged combat. The difficulties in working out joint doctrine between the two services hurt close air support efforts early in Korea.[40]

On the whole the air force provided effective close air support in Korea as army leaders themselves were quick to point out. Maj. Gen. William B. Kean, 25th Infantry Division commander, stated, "The close air support rendered by Fifth Air Force again saved this division as they have many times before." Gen. Walton H. Walker, Eighth Army commander, told a group of air force evaluators, "If it had not been for the air support that we received from the Fifth Air Force we would not have been able to stay in Korea."[41] Not everyone agreed, though, that the air force was doing all it could do. The Alsop brothers acknowledged that it was doing "superbly well with what it had," but they felt the air force's emphasis on air superiority in Korea was ignoring the other half of its tactical air responsibility. Others agreed, including many army and Marine Corps officers, and enough complaints arose to prompt Congressional hearings in 1951 on air force ground support. Congress felt air leaders were hypnotized by strategic bombing and air superiority and passed legislation that same year mandating that TAC regain major command status. The air force took various steps to rectify the situation, including establishing training programs in Seoul and Japan to train air and ground commanders in air-ground coordination and pressing for more tactical aircraft.[42]

As with the air defense issue, though, air power advocates followed a popular culture "damage control" policy lest the sudden interest in tactical air power threaten the preeminence of strategic bombing. In his 1951 *Saturday Evening Post* article, Vandenberg claimed that those who sought to distinguish between strategic and tactical roles did not understand air power. Speaking of the three roles of strategic bombing, air defense, and support of surface forces, Vandenberg stated, "Although those three jobs seem pegged to different objectives, it is impossible to separate them in practice because—and this is a principle ignored too often—air power is indivisible. We don't speak of a 'strategic' or a 'tactical' Army or Navy, yet those terms constantly are applied to the Air Force." This statement introduced a complex argument that may have eluded many of his readers, but it reinforced the image of revolutionary air power, for Vandenberg went on to say that every aircraft's primary role was to "win the air battle on which final victory on land and sea is predicated." While he talked about the importance of destroying enemy aircraft in the factory or in the air, his thinking about the best way to use air power to help front line troops was best revealed when he stated, "The same bomb that knocks out one mortar on the battlefield can knock out a convoy of ten mortars fifty miles behind the front. Five hundred miles farther back that same bomb can blow up a railroad engine or a bridge, preventing the arrival of 100 mortars in the battle area."[43]

Air power advocates even connected the image of strategic bombing with that of air interdiction's magnified benefits to the ground war. Harold H. Martin, in the *Saturday Evening Post,* described a B-29 bombing raid against a North Korean rail junction feeding supplies to Communist forces. In describing the target's significance Martin quotes the group's commander during the preflight briefing: "Through it passes the main rail line from the north. It's the eastern gateway to Korea from Russia and Manchuria. The tanks that have been playing the devil with our troops in South Korea came through . . . there. The munitions from the nitrate plant at Konan to the north pass through there. There's an oil refinery there that keeps the tanks and the vehicles of the Reds on the move. . . . Between us, we'll put about 800,000 pounds of TNT on a target that's roughly 3000 feet long and 2000 feet wide. If we do our jobs right that ought to be enough." The author takes the reader through the mission in a style reminiscent of a World War II bombing mission. Rather than emphasizing bombers destroying the enemy's industrial heart, though, Martin places the mission in the context of a massive air force–navy interdiction campaign to save the U.N. position by starving the enemy of supplies.[44]

A more colorful effort, literally and figuratively, came from a *Life* photo essay complete with aerial photos of a carpet of bomb bursts and a close-up of the risqué nose-art adorning a B-29. The target for this mission was the staging area for four divisions of North Korean troops massing for an attack on U.N. positions at Taegu. Again emphasizing images of scientific efficiency, a pictograph details the grid-like pattern the bombers used to ensure every bit of the staging area was covered, but the text indicates that 850 tons of bombs were used. As in the previous example, this was not quite the "one bomb destroying 100 mortars" image Vandenberg had used, but it was stirring, and, as the author relates, when the American GIs dug in across the river saw it they "stood up in their emplacements and cheered." But to ensure no one missed the larger meaning of this image, the author added, "The 'wild blue yonder boys' of the Air Force were forsaking their strategic bombing to give help to the beleaguered ground troops."[45]

Like the longtime image of strategic bombing created by air power advocates, Vandenberg's image of air interdiction seemed inherently sensible and efficient. Why drop one bomb on one mortar when the same bomb could be used to knock out ten, or even a hundred? What Korean War air interdiction campaigns such as "Operation Strangle" would prove, though, was that Vandenberg's claims, common among most air force leaders, did not always hold true. Air interdiction racked up impressive tallies of trucks destroyed, rail lines cut, and bridges destroyed, and it frequently halted daylight movement of Communist forces and supplies, but the damage was quickly repaired and movement continued under cover of darkness. More important, Korean War experience showed that air interdiction could seriously impede efforts to mount or halt a major offensive, when the need for reinforcements and supplies was highest, but it was not effective enough to disrupt enemy firepower during periods of static warfare. Even during periods of heavy offensive action enough mortars still found their way into enemy hands to do serious damage.[46] Thus frontline troops constantly faced enemy mortars throughout the war. This limitation to air interdiction's capabilities was far too complex, though, to be widely appreciated by the general public, so the images of air power efficiency still held sway.

Air power advocates also tried to counteract criticism by showcasing air force close air support efforts. In the wake of the Inchon landing Spaatz gave air force close air support much of the credit for turning the tide of battle: "Day and night our planes bombed, strafed, observed, and harassed. The situation changed from despair and retreat to attack and annihilation." And a month later he denied army charges that the air force's favored plane for close air support, the jet-powered F-80, was too fast for the job by extolling its ability to not only defend the troops but to defend itself against enemy aircraft. Perhaps the greatest effort, though, came when the air force turned to longtime air power advocate Howard Hughes and asked him to make a movie featuring air force close air support in action.[47]

The film came out in 1952 as *One Minute to Zero.* Hughes turned to another air power advocate for one-half of the screenwriting team, William Wister Haines, author of the play, movie, and novel *Command Decision.* The movie depicts the army and air force working together closely and shows the Joint Operations Centers functioning smoothly as they receive requests for air support and expeditiously assign plentiful air assets to each mission. In one scene, for example, sixteen F-80s are dispatched to help one threatened company. Time after time throughout the movie the air force comes to the rescue of beleaguered ground troops. Army–air force cooperation is depicted as cordial, as in the friendship between the film's star Robert Mitchum, playing an army colonel, and an air force colonel played by William Talman. In one of the film's dramatic highpoints, Mitchum leads a force deep into enemy territory so it can hold up an enemy truck convoy long enough for Talman's air forces to destroy it. The plan works, but Mitchum's forces are cut off and the army cannot relieve them till morning. Talman comes to the rescue with supplies and air support but is shot down and killed in the process. The movie bears no acknowledgment of military assistance. The army refused to approve the final product because one scene, not in the original script, depicts an artillery unit shelling a group of refugees that had been infiltrated by enemy soldiers.[48]

In a similar vein the air force supported a cinematic effort to highlight U.S. tactical air power and fit the image of the fighter pilot into the image of revolutionary air power. The United Artist film *Sabre Jet,* starring Robert Stack, highlighted the F-86, the air force's frontline fighter, and used actual combat footage to add an authentic flavor. In a unique twist on later air power films, much of the plot centers on the struggles of air force wives forced to wait in Japan while their husbands flew combat missions over Korea each day. Sensing a "higher calling" of faithfully supporting their husbands so they can concentrate on their flying, the wives focus on pampering their men and trying to suppress their fears that on any mission their pilot may not return. The movie is even dedicated to all air force wives. In one critical scene Stack's wife, an ambitious combat reporter, realized that the need to support her squadron commander husband outweighed her career goals and gives up her job to embrace the domesticity she had up till that moment been rejecting.[49]

Amid the clumsy gender and family stereotyping, however, the airmen work in some revealing images. Much of the combat action involves close air support, which is depicted as very effective. One scene in particular has the group of Sabre Jet pilots working with a forward air controller on the ground. Temporarily flying F-80s because they are better at the close air support than F-86s, the pilots find every target, including one described as "along a road . . . an ammo dump; it's camouflaged—

looks like a house," and they hit each target with unerring accuracy and effectiveness. The movie also works in a major point illustrating how all forms of air power—close air support, fighters, and bombers—coordinate their efforts to save the war from being irrevocably lost. The centerpiece of this theme revolves around a "maximum effort" mission to destroy a major build-up of communist air power "south of the border." In describing the significance of this mission the film is reminiscent of *Command Decision:* the clear-sighted general trying to put the mission together must fight an obstructionist headquarters and doubters at home—in this case, their wives. Still, the stakes are too high not to run the risks, for, as the general says, if the mission fails, "the Eighth Army had better learn to swim!"

Air power advocates even turned the public concern over tactical capabilities to their own advantage. Since they never felt the air force was large enough to meet its many commitments they added tactical air power to their list of "dangerously" weak areas. Part of this effort focused on Korea. For example, some called for immediate action to reverse the inferiority of U.S. jet fighters to the MiG-15. Fletcher Knebel, writing for *Look* magazine, stated the disparity dramatically: "The fact is that the Communists can rub us out of the air there any month they want to do it" and asked, "What has happened to the American fighting plane that only eight years ago ruled the skies of the world?" Knebel laid the blame on budgetary constraints that forced the air force to design the F-86 as an all-purpose aircraft intended to perform air superiority, air interdiction, and close air support missions. This meant the much lighter MiG-15 could fly higher and faster, out-climb, and out-maneuver the F-86 in combat.[50]

Most calls for greater tactical air power, though, focused on Europe and the larger war with the Soviets many feared might come at any minute. In fact, if anyone doubted air power advocates had learned how to exploit the new public image of tactical air power, Francis Vivian Drake's 1951 *Reader's Digest* article would remove all doubt. Writing of the projected build-up of U.S. ground forces in Europe, Drake claimed they were going there with inadequate tactical air forces and asked, *"What does it take to convince the Administration that sending troops to Europe without air cover is an act of suicide?"* Pointing to Soviet air strength, he claimed they had ten thousand aircraft for supporting ground forces alone but that U.S. air strength was planned to peak out at only three thousand. Drake called on the administration to institute an aircraft building campaign to rival that of World War II so that U.S. ground troops would be protected by a tactical air force that could seize air superiority over Europe. Spaatz had stressed many of the same points three months earlier in an article, also in *Reader's Digest,* and claimed American tactical air power would face 10–1 odds in Europe. Decrying what he called the "wall-of-flesh" mentality driving America's planning for European defenses, Spaatz stated that tactical air operations had inflicted 47 percent of the casualties suffered by the Communist forces in Korea and predicted U.S. troops would face the same fate if they could not prevent the Soviets from seizing and exploiting air superiority. Like Drake, Spaatz called for a dramatically increased level of aircraft production.[51]

Even though air power advocates made public bows to the importance of tactical air power, they still cautioned that strategic bombing must remain the main focus, because it was still America's best defense. Spaatz, for example, in a 1950 *Newsweek* column, conceded that tactical air power was important to meet Cold War challenges like Korea but then stressed "[t]he B-36 and the atom bomb still constitute the military force preventing a full-scale world war and localizing the Korean conflict." And in his 1951 *Reader's Digest* article calling for tactical forces to seize air superiority in Europe, Spaatz said ground and tactical air forces should act merely as holding forces while strategic bombing won the war by bombing the Soviet homeland: "there is not the remotest chance that our ground forces can defeat the Russian Army by coming to grips with all its divisions. The Russian Army must be strangled by the bombing of the industries behind the troops." Similarly, in his *Saturday Evening Post* article Vandenberg stated that strategic bombing was the only thing deterring Soviet aggression, but if war did come with the Soviets, strategic bombing was the best means of seizing air superiority and supporting ground troops, because it destroyed planes and weapons at their source.[52]

The public effort to bolster the image of strategic bombing during this period extended to the cinema as well. In 1951 Beirne Lay, coauthor of *Twelve O'clock High,* teamed up with Paul Tibbets Jr., the pilot of the aircraft that dropped the first atomic bomb, to write the script for a movie version of the Tibbets story, *Above and Beyond.* The film did well at the box office, ranking twenty-ninth among the year's top attractions and grossing $2.5 million. The air force may have played a role in instigating the film. At the start of the project Lay told Curtis

LeMay, head of SAC, that Brig. Gen. Sory Smith, director of Air Force Public Information, told Tibbets that "the Air Force thought it timely to have his story made and would cooperate with a motion picture production." The movie tells of Tibbets's efforts to prepare and train the 509th Composite Group for the task of dropping atomic bombs on Japan. A principle subplot revolves around the extreme security surrounding the Manhattan Project and the activities of the 509th. Unable to tell his men or their families what they are training for, Tibbets is depicted as suffering under the strain of accusations from many, even his wife, that he is a martinet. While the film does not deal with the larger themes of strategic bombing doctrine or revolutionary air power, it does portray Tibbets and most of his men as heroic figures sacrificing for a greater good. This greater good is, of course, that the atomic bomb will end the war and, by extension, that in the postwar environment it will keep the peace.[53]

Taken together, the total effect of the heightened public interest in all forms of air power—strategic bombing, air defense, and tactical roles—was that air power advocates picked up the cry for more air power of all forms while keeping strategic air power as the primary focus and urging it on the public as the nation's best means of security. Wesley Price, for example, compared U.S. air power to Soviet air strength across the board in a 1952 *Saturday Evening Post* article and claimed there were glaring weaknesses in all areas that needed immediate action to reverse many years of failing to heed the air power advocates' recommendations. While the United States could not afford to neglect air defense and tactical air power, though, Price reminded his audience that the nation with the best strategic bombers held the key to aerial supremacy and thus to ultimate victory.[54] In effect the air power advocates appropriated two potential threats to the preeminence of strategic bombing in the public's eyes and not only used them to rally the public behind their quest for a larger air force, they also managed to keep popular imagination focused on strategic bombing. Thus the whole affair turned into a "win-win" situation for the air power advocates' agenda.

Much the same could be said of the whole period from the Revolt of the Admirals to the end of the Korean War. The three major threats to the air power advocates' notion of an air power revolution threatened to derail their effort to convert the public to their way of thinking about air power. The Revolt of the Admirals seemed another example of interservice bickering, but the air force appeared the winner in the whole affair. The B-36 had been vindicated of corruption charges, and the navy appeared hypocritical in trying to discredit a role it seemed to be seeking for itself. The Soviet acquisition of the atomic bomb created widespread fears for the defense of North America and threatened to divert air force efforts into the air defense mission. By showcasing air defense capabilities, though, and while continually reminding the public that the best defense was a good offense, the air power advocates retained the public's trust and continued support for strategic bombing. How many actually put their faith in Vandenberg's image of victory through destroying the Soviet homeland faster than they could destroy the United States is impossible to say. Judging by images that predominated through much of the fifties, though, it seems clear most people put their faith in keeping the Soviets at bay through the threat of retaliation. In short, the public looked to nuclear deterrence for salvation. The images raised by the Korean War were accommodated in like manner. By showing Americans that the air force could, with public support and enough aircraft, handle the tactical role while it provided air defense and nuclear deterrence, air power advocates retained control of the image of air power in the popular imagination and kept the American public solidly in the air power corner. The best indication of the air power advocates' success in defending their air power image is that shortly after the end of the Korean War a Gallup poll showed that public faith in air power as the most potent force in winning any future war jumped to an all-time high of 81 percent.[55]

Understanding the shape and contours of air power's image as it was fixed in the public imagination by the end of the Korean War is important because that image would not face another serious challenge for several years. It remained until the late fifties almost exactly what it had become in the early fifties. Yet another indication of the air power advocates' success in maintaining and expanding popular support for their vision during the period of challenge to that vision is the dominance their preferred air power role enjoyed in popular culture following the Korean War. That dominant image was strategic nuclear bombing, and it was embodied by the Strategic Air Command—SAC. So prevalent was that image that even the commander of SAC, Curtis E. LeMay, became a virtual icon, an image larger than life who represented not only his command and the air force but also the whole notion of revolutionary air power.

CHAPTER 5

The Heyday of SAC
The High Point of the Popular Culture Crusade

As the United States emerged from the Korean War the fear of monolithic, imperialistic communism was reaching a peak. Mc-Carthyites charged that communist subversion had infiltrated important segments of American society and the late war had confirmed to many that the Soviets were willing to use force to advance their goals. This "Red Scare" also heightened fears that the Soviets would like nothing better than to destroy the most powerful nation—the United States—standing between them and world domination. This fear led many to consider the prospect of a surprise nuclear attack on the United States to be a real threat. Through the popular culture campaign air power advocates had convinced many that the one factor deterring the Soviets from launching such an attack was the certainty of annihilation at the hands of U.S. strategic nuclear bombardment. After the Korean War that popular culture image shifted focus slightly. In keeping with the trend away from theoretical arguments and predictions to more institutional emphases, air power advocates less often stressed the concept of strategic bombing and instead emphasized the institutional embodiment of America's long-range strategic bombing force, the Strategic Air Command. Furthermore, rather than focusing on the need for SAC and the efficacy of strategic bombing, air power advocates sought to build public faith that SAC could deliver on the promise of strategic bombing.[1]

Air power advocates also continued to extol other applications of air power, such as air defense and tactical missions, and they sought to create an image of the air force as modern, efficient, and progressive. Articles appeared occasionally reminding the public that should a Soviet attack come America's air defense system stood ready with the most advanced systems and dedicated personnel. Other works showcased the heroism, superiority, and self-sacrifice of the fighter pilot. Some works even highlighted non-flying activities within the air force, such as research and development, and described future wonders that would keep the air force on the cutting edge of technology. There were occasional pieces bolstering the image of the air power revolution, but by and large air power advocates relied on the foundation laid in the late forties and trusted that the public still saw air power as reshaping human society.

The main emphasis, though, was on glorifying SAC, bolstering its reputation, and seeing to its every need. Numerous magazine articles focused on the command's vigilance and stressed the fact that its bombers could be launched at a moment's notice. The coverage also extended to SAC's commander, Curtis E. LeMay, making the two virtually synonymous, even to the point of anthropomorphizing LeMay's gruff and tenacious reputation into the image of SAC. One observer of the times has likened the place of SAC in America's consciousness to that of the Royal Navy in Britain or the legions in ancient Rome; to the extent that observation is accurate, that public consciousness can be largely attributed to the air power advocates' campaign to attribute America's very survival to SAC.[2] Perhaps the most notorious facet of the veneration of SAC was the series of movies made specifically to showcase the command and its needs. Collectively known as the "SAC trilogy," the movies illustrate the extent of public fascination with America's nuclear strike force.

An integral part of the SAC story in this period involves the defense policies of the Eisenhower administration. Shortly after becoming president in 1953, Dwight Eisenhower, a career army officer and commander of Allied forces in Europe during World War II, instituted a defense policy known as New Look based on the strategy of massive retaliation. Seeking economic stability and security for what he called the "long haul," Eisenhower's New Look stressed deterrence, focused on harnessing technological innovations, and relied on allied ground forces to supplement U.S. air and sea forces in the event of war. Since the United States enjoyed a considerable advantage over the Soviet Union in strategic nuclear forces, and since the prospect of matching the Soviets' ground forces promised to be difficult and costly, New Look made strategic bombing the cornerstone of America's containment strategy.[3]

That air power would become the foundation of Eisenhower's defense policy is not really surprising. Despite his long and prominent career with the army, Eisenhower had demonstrated considerable acceptance of some of the tenets of revolutionary air power. In a 1947 speech at the Air Force Association Convention in Columbus, Ohio, he spoke at length about how aviation had transformed transportation and travel and claimed the Polar Concept had reshaped international strategic relationships. More to the point, though, he stated that through vertical envelopment, what he called "aerial flanking," air power had reshaped the tactical and strategic nature of warfare, and he called the air force "our nation's best insurance against attack." Furthermore, Spaatz had stated in his *Newsweek* column that World War II had convinced Eisenhower of the need for the world's strongest air force and that since the war he had been a staunch advocate of air power in a preeminent position over the other services.[4] This does not mean Eisenhower was an air power convert, but he was sympathetic to it, and his views on fiscal conservatism meshed with what air power advocates had been saying for decades: air power could provide better defense at less cost. In fact, the thinking behind New Look followed the message at the heart of de Seversky's *Air Power: Key to Survival:* the United States could not match the Soviets in ground forces so it must rely on its technological and industrial superiority by focusing on air power.

Eisenhower's defense policies, therefore, institutionalized the faith air power advocates had been nurturing in American society for years. This official endorsement of revolutionary air power brought the air force into a dominant position within the defense establishment. That dominance is reflected in the air force receiving the lion's share of military budgets throughout much of the fifties, and in the fact that during Eisenhower's tenure an air force officer, Nathan F. Twining, rose to chairman of the Joint Chiefs of Staff, the first and only air force officer to hold that position until the mid-seventies.[5] Since the reason for air force dominance was the strategic nuclear bombing role, SAC in turn dominated the air force. This led to a period often referred to as "The Heyday of SAC," the "golden age" of strategic bombing in U.S. military history.

There was more to SAC's dominance than just official policy, though, for that dominance was also reflected in the popular culture of the period. The old cultural phenomenon of technological messianism that had led people to expect salvation from the airplane, the long years of air power advocacy nurturing those expectations by promising deliverance through bombing, and the fear of communism all came together in one time period, and Eisenhower's policies only added official sanctification. Many who believed went along willingly. Others, faced with the fears so much a part of the Cold War atmosphere of the fifties, desperately wanted to find assurances somewhere, and many were easily lulled into trusting SAC by the pervasive images. Still others who might not quite believe went along because it was national policy and they were patriotic. A graphic example of the widespread faith in SAC can be seen in a 1958 advertisement run by Kelsey-Hayes, an aircraft and missile component manufacturer. In a tribute to SAC the ad shows a smiling boy lying in bed giving the "A-okay" sign to a formation of B-58 Hustlers flying past his window. In the background is superimposed the figure of an air force enlisted man, and beneath the picture is the caption, "He awakes secure . . . thanks to 'SAC.'"[6] Because of such images displayed prominently in popular culture during the fifties and into the sixties, culturally and officially, to paraphrase Henry Stimson, air power seemed to be the one true god, LeMay was its prophet, and the Strategic Air Command the one true church.

SEMPER PARATUS: THE IMAGE OF SAC IN MAGAZINES

Magazines played a significant role in shaping SAC's image in the fifties. Numerous articles appeared in nearly every major general interest magazine, and they were nearly unanimous in the themes they stressed and the images they created. First, they were unwaveringly laudatory. There was no mistaking the editorial stand on the virtues of SAC in these articles. In fact, some of the claims made for or about SAC by such air power advocates as Francis Vivian Drake and Harold H. Martin are so exaggerated they rival some of the more extreme claims made for air power in the late forties. Second, they dwelled at length on SAC's eternal vigilance. Another standard theme was the competence, professionalism, and dedication of SAC personnel. Related to this theme were the constant reminders of the sacrifices SAC crewmembers made to be ready to fulfill their mission at a moment's notice. But the most important theme echoed old strains of technological messianism and raised expectations of salvation through air power to its highest and most overt expression. Deliverance was no longer just a vague promise based on eschatological imagery, systematic theories, or brutal predictions. Now it had a name, and that name was SAC. It even had a face, and that face was Curtis E. LeMay's. When air power advocates sought to shape SAC's image as the public's salvation in the nuclear age, general interest magazines carried the bulk of the burden. Other media, especially film, might put the message in more vivid or memorable images, but the steady flow of magazine articles ensured that the public got numerous and frequent reminders that their faith must remain in nuclear air power.

Showcasing SAC in America's general interest magazines began before the end of the Korean War. A Harold H. Martin *Saturday Evening*

Post article at the end of 1950 provided one of the first close-up examinations in the popular culture campaign. In a portent of future magazine coverage, Martin's depiction is celebratory almost to the point of being a paean. For example, the caption under a picture of a B-36 reads, "The big atom-bombers are kept in top condition by ceaseless attention to maintenance." Of the significance of SAC's forces Martin states that "this country's ability to survive a war with Russia depends upon SAC's being constantly ready to move out fast and hit hard as soon as the whistle blows." In extolling the crews, Martin stresses how much more demanding, physically and mentally, atomic bombing is than World War II bombing: "The slightest sign of stupidity, sloppiness, carelessness, indecision or confusion under stress is marked down on a check list, and a voluminous report is made which evaluates not only the proficiency of each member of the crew but the effectiveness of the whole crew." Many World War II bombing veterans, according to Martin, had to be eliminated. With public memories of wartime bombing heightened by such recent movies as *Twelve O'clock High* and *Command Decision,* this must have been powerful imagery. Martin also combined the traditions of Douhet and the ACTS by extolling both the precision of the crews' bombing and the tremendous destructive capacity at their command. The crewmembers wielded greater force than "all the power for destruction possessed by all the armies of the world, from the time of Alexander of Macedon to the present," but their "swift, sure precision" and "drill-ground precision" leads to "bull's-eye accuracy."[7]

In 1951 *Life* ran a pictorial essay on SAC, calling it "the very essence of airpower." *Life* barely mentioned the ongoing war and debates about air power roles, focusing instead on what would become standard features of SAC articles. The description of an average base emphasized security, as when a photo caption states, "SAC cooks, like all other personnel at Barksdale Field, . . . carry arms and ammunition when on duty or marching to work." The bombers were extremely complex and demanding when it came to maintenance and flying, but their range and ability to reach their targets were touted in great detail. The aircrews were highly trained and dedicated, but the sacrifices they made to remain combat-ready received considerable attention as well. Once again the twin traditions of strategic bombing melded in the article's overall image of SAC capability as it lauded both the destructiveness of the bombs SAC planes carried and the exacting precision with which the crews delivered them.[8]

The emphasis on SAC increased after the Korean War, and one of the earliest examples came from Francis Vivian Drake in *Reader's Digest* only two months after the war ended. Drake made clear the overall significance of SAC at the outset: "The free world may well stand hat in hand before our superbly trained atom-bomber crews. . . . They stand guard for all of us 24 hours a day, 365 days a year." He highlighted SAC's concern for constant readiness by detailing a headquarters security team's attempt to sneak onto a SAC base in what appears to be a stricken airliner. Drake's description of crewmembers and the demands they face presents a harrowing image: "Never has so much been demanded, both physical and intellectual, of fighting men in peacetime. . . . They are forever on a basis of war. . . . Graying hair and nervous exhaustion are common among them." The description of a training flight, said to be conducted under realistic combat conditions, is filled with a tense excitement: "'Air Force jet 123, cleared for takeoff!' The tension in the cockpit tightens like a fiddlestring. . . . 'Air Force jet 123, rolling!' 'Clear!'" Disaster seems to lurk at every turn throughout the flight, and every action is described as requiring the most exacting precision.[9]

The mood of the text is quite frankly melodramatic, but this is because Drake sees the threat as immediate and America's response to it as "reckless." Pointing to the larger Soviet air force, which he claims could maintain a continuous bombardment of the United States, Drake states that SAC funding allows only one crew per bomber, and that the crews are so exhausted after every flight that they must be grounded for four days. The solution, for Drake, is more money for SAC so it can increase its manning to two crews per aircraft. But he does not advocate a larger defense budget. Claiming SAC gets only $5.50 out of every one hundred defense dollars, he calls for increasing SAC's share by taking existing money from other forces, "that, no matter how courageous, could not head off atomic aggression."[10]

The next year *Life,* in a lengthy piece detailing the many wonders of the "Jet Age," focused much of the article on the men and planes of SAC. The tone of the article mixes images of nuclear destructive capabilities with cutting-edge technological advances being made in the air force. Modern aircraft, epitomized by the B-47 nuclear bomber, are characterized as so advanced it takes a new breed of man to fly them. Describing the B-47 as the backbone of SAC, and its crews as "[t]he foremost representatives of the jet age," the article details the B-47's mission profile and flight regimen as so stressful crews must be "psychologically decompressed to bring them gently down to a slower tempo" and so physically demanding they need a massage and steam room to "relax by sweating out their physical fatigue." Crewmembers who can withstand such pressures are so critical to the nation's defenses that, as the article quotes one senior air force officer, "When we lose one of them it's like losing the battleship *Missouri*."[11]

A unique chapter in the SAC literature came in 1955 from Arthur Godfrey. An early celebrity in the days when television's power was first being felt, Godfrey's voice reached millions of Americans through his popular radio and television programs. A high school drop-out who joined the navy in 1920 and served until 1924, Godfrey also served in the Coast Guard from 1927 until 1929, and at the outbreak of World War II he gained a reserve lieutenant commander commission and remained a long-term naval reservist. Godfrey had been using his radio and television "bully pulpit" since before the war to proselytize for the navy. In the course of his career, though, Godfrey came to know Hoyt Vandenberg, who in 1951 pressed him on his navy slant and challenged him to "put out a true story for a change." Godfrey asked, "What *is* the true story?" To which Vandenberg replied, "Go out to SAC and they'll show you." Godfrey went to SAC, heard their story, visited several bases around the world, got converted, and began spreading the word about air power in the press and on his shows. When the navy pressured him to stop he resigned his commission in 1955. The air force, bending its own medical qualification rules, gave Godfrey a reserve commission with the rank of colonel and retired him the next day.[12]

In the concluding installment of an eight-part autobiography published in *Saturday Evening Post*, Godfrey explained that his crusade for air power was the sole reason he remained active in broadcasting. Devoting almost the entire article to his cause, he explained why he thought the United States needed more air power and why the only acceptable air power was the nuclear air power of SAC. "Guided missiles, radar screens and fighter planes are no substitute for long-range bombers." Unlike most other SAC articles, this one does not purport to be a factual exposé written by a professional journalist. There are no visits to SAC bases, no descriptions of heroic SAC pilots, no flights on the most advanced bombers, just one man's opinion, and he delivers that opinion with all the certainty of a zealot. What makes this article noteworthy is the author's notoriety. As one of the most popular figures in U.S. entertainment, Godfrey's name was sure to draw millions of readers to his words. Furthermore, Godfrey details his long association with the military and aviation, as well as his close friendship with LeMay, all of which was bound to lead many readers to think he knew what he was talking about. Godfrey's reasoning was simplistic but straight forward: the Soviets were a threat and they were building a massive bomber fleet; since air defense had never turned back a World War II bomber force, the only thing that could save the United States was deterrence by having a bigger bomber fleet. Such a simplistic approach to an intractable but frightening problem was bound to appeal to many.[13]

In 1957 James Michener contributed a book-length feature, published in *Reader's Digest,* to the growing body of SAC literature. Michener had served in the navy in World War II, and in 1953 he wrote *The Bridges at Toko Ri,* a bestselling novel showcasing Korean War naval aviation. According to a biographical sketch accompanying the *Reader's Digest* article, though, he wrote this latest piece in response to the 1956 Soviet invasion of Hungary as a testament to his belief that the United States was safe from communist aggression. He wanted to tell the public about SAC, and in doing so he stresses many of the standard themes found in other SAC articles. Two events that Michener highlights, the response of a SAC base to a no-notice inspection and the annual SAC bombing and navigation competition, provide the suitable backdrop for extolling SAC capabilities. The dedicated people of Loring Air Force Base worked round the clock to bring their base through the inspection with flying colors. The description of the bombing and navigation competition stressed not only the technical sophistication of the ground and air crews but also the continuing legacy of U.S. bombing accuracy. After downplaying the legend of "pickle barrel bombing" Michener adds, "Many planes laid their bombs practically on target. And a few did actually 'hit the pickle barrel' scoring what is called a 'shack.'"[14]

While Michener's account stresses many of the standard themes he also adds a human touch. Looking at SAC "from the bottom up," Michener made enlisted members and wives the heroes of his story. His testimony to the importance of SAC to the United States, for example, comes from the mouth of a B-52 maintenance master sergeant's wife. When interviewed by Michener in the midst of a civilian evacuation of the base, she tells him, "We're at war, Mr. Michener, at war to prevent war. The rest of the nation doesn't know it, but we are." He follows a similar approach in describing the sacrifices made by the men who keep SAC running. He refers to SAC headquarters as "Ulcer Heaven" and states that most ground and flight crews are either underweight or have ulcers, piles, or back problems. He even points to an "appalling" divorce rate in SAC before 1950 as further proof of the price its personnel pay to protect the United States, and details the steps SAC took to turn the divorce rate around as proof of SAC's competence.[15]

The post-sputnik fears of Soviet missile attack brought another dimension to the SAC image. Writing for the *Saturday Evening Post* in 1958, Clay Blair reassured the public that SAC's retaliatory force would not be caught on the ground by a surprise missile barrage. In response to the Soviet missile threat, SAC instituted plans to keep one third of its force in a combat configuration ready to takeoff in less than fifteen minutes, and Blair, assessing these plans, stated, "they do the job efficiently and effectively." In fact, Blair's depiction of SAC's bombers made them appear far more capable and flexible than ICBMs. But while Blair foresaw imminent defenses against inbound Soviet missiles, he extolled the B-52's ability to defeat enemy radar and evade fighters and stated, "even in the missile age most of the bombers will get through to target and back again." In detailing future bomber advances planned by SAC, Blair fell into the pattern of excessive hyperbole. The B-70 is described as "breath-taking," "an awesome weapon system," and "comparable to developing an automobile that could cross the United States on one tank of gas." Its inertial navigation system will "automatically steer the B-70 unerringly to any point on the globe," and tests "have been chalking up amazing results."[16]

Later that same year Philip Gustafson, also writing for the *Saturday Evening Post,* detailed "SAC's new pattern of readiness to strike back from world-wide bases so widely dispersed that no attack known today could knock them all out at once." Visiting a B-47 base in Zaragoza, Spain, Gustafson provided a look at SAC forces maintaining nuclear alert at dozens of overseas bases around the world. This side of SAC, as it appeared in this article, differed little from that seen in other treatments. Their mission is just as vital to U.S. security, according to Gustafson. He quoted one flier, who stated, "My wife is always asking me why I have to sacrifice myself to save the world when all our friends lead nice normal family lives." Gustafson then provided his own answer, "I believe that most of these fellows feel there's an important job to be done for the free world. And we're all pretty lucky that they do." The crewmembers all appeared larger than life. Gustafson described one as "a deeply tanned, dark-haired gunboat of a guy. . . . one of the most competent pros in SAC, where you have to be good just to stick," "a dedicated Air Force man," "hard as nails," but still "a devoted family man." Readiness in the face of the new missile threat was also given effusive, and at times theatrical, praise: "I sleep in my underwear, with the flight suit laid out in such a way that I can step into suit and shoes in a single leap," "Everything about the area exudes an air of readiness, even the autos are cocked, not parked," and "the pack exploded out of the building. . . . We shot out on the acres of concrete apron and, veering fit to tip over, the jeep screeched to a halt . . . and everybody hit the concrete."[17]

The glorification of SAC continued into the early sixties. For example, in 1961 *Life* ran a pictorial essay focusing on how Loring Air Force Base responded to yet another inspection. The inspection gave the *Life* writers ample opportunity to present a reassuring picture of SAC's capabilities and professional excellence. Ever vigilant, SAC used these inspections, "the severest going-over the Strategic Air Command gives it units," to ensure every base is ready to do its part for security through nuclear retaliation. *Life* called the one that hit Loring "the surprise test that helps keep SAC unrelentingly ready." The inspector general appeared grim and determined in every photo, and his staff was described as "hard-eyed officers with a bagful of tricks to play." The base whips into action and earns high praise from *Life:* "Crews worked with fierce, cold efficiency to get ready for their far-ranging missions. Even the watchdogs snarled more menacingly." The legend of American bombing accuracy gets another boost in this article as well, for the inspectors found that in the bombing phase of the inspection the target "was hit on the nose every time." *Life*'s overall assessment: "SAC is more than ever on alert."[18]

The series of magazine articles throughout the fifties also extolled other aspects of SAC besides its bombers. More than just rounding out the picture to include all activities in SAC, these other articles, sharing the same laudatory tone, created a comprehensive picture that no matter what SAC did, it could do no wrong. In 1955, for example, John G. Hubbell wrote an article for *Reader's Digest* describing the survival school SAC ran for its flight crews. It taught fliers how to survive in any climate on earth should they be forced to crash-land or bail out of a stricken aircraft. Predictably, Hubbell's tenor celebrates both how comprehensively SAC is prepared for any contingency and how much SAC flight crews suffer to defend America. Another article by Hubbell in 1957 introduced the public to the new SAC air refueling tanker, the KC-135. This new all-jet swept wing aircraft was a vital addition to the SAC inventory, according to Hubbell, because it allowed bombers to refuel at their nor-mal cruise altitude and airspeed. The new capability made the range-extending operation more reliable and efficient, and, Hubbell told his audience, ensured the bombers would reach their targets deep inside the Soviet Union. Despite the fact that by this time air refueling had become routine, Hubbell managed to convey a sense of urgency as yet again the brave, dedicated professionals of SAC demonstrate that "new power has been added to the free world's biggest Sunday punch—the Strategic Air Command."[19]

The biggest addition to SAC during the fifties, though, was missiles, and despite Blair's dismissive attitude toward them, air power advocates incorporated this new capability into the image of an all-powerful SAC. Two notable figures in presenting this development were Corey Ford and James Perkins. In August 1958 the two writers collaborated on an article in *Reader's Digest* glorifying the men and mission of SAC's B-47 bases in Spain, and that same month they contributed an article in the *Saturday Evening Post* telling the story of the commander of SAC's First Missile Division, Maj. Gen. David Wade. The tone is virtually indistinguishable from SAC articles focusing on bombers. The authors say of Wade and the importance of his mission, "There's no second place in a nuclear war. . . . he doesn't propose to see this country runner-up to any power on earth." On the skill demanded of the new missileers, the authors quote Wade, "the slightest error in calculation, the least lapse in split-second timing, can spell failure," and again, "handling these complex devices executes heavier demands than any other weapons system in history." When asked where he finds such superb people, Wade responds, "Any good SAC man." All this, the authors state, will change SAC from "an all-bomber force to a modern bomber-missile force capable of reaching and destroying any enemy aggressor on the globe."[20]

Ford and Perkins returned to the subject of SAC's ICBMs in 1960 with an article in *Reader's Digest* describing the test launch of an Atlas missile. The authors described the missile with awe-inspiring hyperbole—"deadliest weapon of the free world" and "engines that de-liver 7,500,000 horsepower—enough power to light four cities the size of Los Angeles"—yet they include images of frightful destructiveness—"it looks like a prehistoric monster impatient to ravage the earth." The crews servicing and launching the missile are also depicted with a cer-tain amount of overstatement: "[they] spend long hours learning to work together with perfect precision." But the overall impression conveyed by the authors, that this awesome weapon is part of America's best hope for security, is best illustrated in their quote from the missileers' squadron commander: "We are not men of war. We're men of peace, making our contribution toward preventing another world war. But we're proud to know that if an aggressor ever forces war on this country, our Atlases are ready." With the question of the "missile gap" dominating the contemporary political debate, the authors even manage to include a subtle reminder that SAC's missile program is not getting enough funding. After the test launch, a key member of the launch team goes home to his barracks room and writes to his wife the sad news, as the authors convey to their readers, that she still cannot join him yet because "Congress hasn't appropriated funds for enough quarters on the base . . . and rents in the area have skyrocketed."[21]

A personal reflection of general-interest magazines' fixation with SAC was the concurrent attention focused on its longtime commander, Curtis E. LeMay. Born in 1906 in Columbus, Ohio, LeMay's early life was remarkably different from most air power advocates. His family was poor and moved around from town to town and state to state as his family followed what jobs his father found. LeMay entered Ohio State University in 1924 supporting his studies by working the night shift at a local steel foundry, but at the end of four years he was fifteen credits short of the requirement for graduation. He had completed the ROTC program, though, and was determined to get into the army as a pilot and through some creative efforts entered pilot training in 1928. LeMay served a succession of assignments through the thirties, completed his college degree at Ohio State in 1932, and even managed to achieve a dual rating as both pilot and navigator along the way.[22] LeMay rose rapidly in rank with the rapid expansion of the AAF starting in 1940; he entered the war as a group commander flying B-17s in England and ended the war as a major general commanding the XXI Bomber Command. After the war LeMay went on to head the Strategic Air Command from 1948 to 1957 and ended up as chief of staff of the air force from 1961 until his retirement in 1965.

During his stint as commander of SAC, LeMay became the personification of not just the command but strategic bombing as well. His personal characteristics fitted him well as a role model for the image that the air force, air power advocates, and America's leadership wished to shape for their nuclear deterrence forces. Gruff and taciturn by nature, LeMay was a forceful commander who believed strongly in strategic bombing, but Bell's palsy had also left his face mildly disfigured into what appeared to be a perpetual scowl. When LeMay took over SAC he found it to be, as Harry Borowski has described, "a hollow threat," but he quickly turned the command around.[23] He soon gained a reputation as a tough, demanding commander who drove SAC's people hard to meet his exacting standards. Many magazine articles highlighting SAC throughout the fifties focused on LeMay as the person single-handedly responsible for SAC's effectiveness and often seemed to imply that he personally invested the command with the same toughness and determination he was reported to possess.[24] The best reflections of the emphasis on LeMay, though, are the articles focused on the man himself.

In 1950 William Bradford Huie wrote his last air power piece, a profile of LeMay, for *Coronet*. Compared to Huie's articles of the previous year, this one was low-key and centered on LeMay's personality, his qualifications to lead SAC, and his commitment to its mission. Calling SAC "the cocked arm of Western civilization," Huie personalized that mission as LeMay's mission: "LeMay's job is to keep the arm ready and strong, for on his ability to strike hard hangs our principal hope for survival." Describing LeMay as "a relentless efficiency expert," Huie also claimed his reputation as "more machine than man" is unfair and that his concern for SAC's troops, as seen in his efforts to improve air force housing, inspired great loyalty. Still, Huie did not mince words when it came to LeMay's demands on his people. Speaking of LeMay's staff he quoted LeMay himself: "They know I wouldn't hesitate to order them on a one-way mission if I thought it was necessary." And in summing up the profile Huie gives LeMay the last word: "They say I'm pretty tough. Maybe I am. Right now it's a tough world we live in. This command has to operate just like we did in England or on Guam during the war."[25]

A similar profile appeared in *Life* in 1954 written by Ernest Havemann. The article received an even wider audience when it was reprinted that same year in *Reader's Digest*. Calling LeMay "relentlessly efficient," an "implacable perfectionist," and "the toughest air soldier the world has ever known," Havemann says, "LeMay and the Air Force seem to have been made for each other," and he "is ideally suited by reputation and demeanor to keep his command at the peak efficiency which world conditions and U.S. military policy demand." But it is in describing LeMay's personal impact on SAC and military history that Havemann's heroic hyperbole reaches its peak. LeMay was credited as the single agent making SAC a force Russia feared and respected. In describing LeMay's impact on SAC Havemann stated, "LeMay took SAC by the scruff of the neck, gave it one quick shake and soon had it bristling." Speaking of his development of the firebombing tactics used against Japan, Havemann called it "one of the crucial military decisions of all time, a decision that will certainly go down in history alongside such fortunate tactical choices as Washington's counterattack at Trenton." It was this reputation as much as U.S. bombers that in Havemann's opinion deterred Soviet aggression.[26]

The interest in LeMay was so great it even spawned articles detailing LeMay's private life, and the interest continued when he moved up to chief of staff of the air force in 1957. In that year, for example, LeMay joined Arthur Godfrey on an African safari that was filmed for Godfrey's television show and covered by *Life* magazine. *Life* related LeMay's off-duty activities again in 1961. His toughness was highlighted by describing his penchant for judo and photographing him in action. His perfectionism came through various other interests, such as building radios, tying his own fishing flies, and loading his own shotgun ammunition. But the article also revealed a softer side of the air force chief. He was shown training his pet dog and playing an organ, both of which were described as avid interests.[27]

General interest magazines occasionally showcased other air force leaders, such as Nathan Twining and Thomas S. Power, but the coverage was not as extensive as that given to LeMay, for it seems no other air leader sparked the public's interest as much as did LeMay.[28] He was certainly a colorful character who gave magazine writers plenty of material to work with, and judging by his encouragement of Lay and Bartlett in their movie ventures, it is clear LeMay courted public support for SAC through popular culture. It seems, though, there was something more driving the public fascination with LeMay—that it was a two-way proposition. Magazine editors and air power advocates seem to have sensed that, having put its faith in strategic nuclear bombing, the public needed a single person, a face, to associate with the image of strategic air power, one that would reassure the public that SAC could deliver on the promises of security through air power. Whether the one person at the head of SAC through most of the fifties actually fit the image of strategic bombing built up over several decades or the LeMay mystique was a media creation is hard to say. Either way, he became the embodiment of strategic bombing, and many saw SAC as a reflection of LeMay himself.

The glowing, theatrical, often celebratory air of general interest magazines in their treatment of SAC during the 1950s is perhaps the most controversial aspect of the phenomenon. Such an attitude is not surprising coming from noted air power advocates like Francis Vivian Drake, but when it was adopted by more casual advocates such as Harold Martin and John Hubbell, or by staff writers like those at *Life,* it shows how deeply the faith in air power generally, and strategic bombing particularly, had penetrated in some circles. Granted, such laudatory and melodramatic tones were products of the popular magazine genre, because they were primarily forms of entertainment and thus had to keep their material light and action-packed. Moreover, they did not bear the burden of investigative journalism or impartial judgment that magazines such as *Time* or *Newsweek* bore. Still, Hubbell's reference to nuclear war as a "Sunday Punch" trivialized a subject threatening unmitigated disaster for the entire world and contributed to the reassuring images of nuclear warfare that helped make it thinkable. And building up the leaders and followers of America's nuclear forces as larger-than-life heroes contributed to the technological messianism prompting society to look to the bomber for salvation.

A FEW GOOD MEN: THE IMAGE OF SAC IN MOVIES

The air power advocates continued their popular culture crusade through the medium of motion pictures after the Korean War, and like their efforts in general interest magazines, many of the films showcased the Strategic Air Command. Air power movies of the post–World War II era are unique in that most try to convey a message intended to shape the viewers' attitudes toward air power. While such interwar movies as *Wings* and *Hell's Angels* were consciously designed to glamorize air power, their message was limited to inspiration and did not try to plant an overt agenda.[29] This changed with the postwar air power advocates' notion of revolutionary air power, for they saw the cinema as a perfect vehicle to advance the revolution. The high point came with *Twelve O'clock High* and *Command Decision*—subsequent films would rarely achieve the power and drama of these earlier movies in conveying the air power message, but the later movies advanced an agenda nonetheless. Perhaps these later films lacked the force of the two earlier ones because they differ from them in another manner. Revolutionary air power is inherent in the message of *Twelve O'clock High* and *Com-*

mand Decision: if strategic bombing is defeated, either in the skies over Europe or in the halls of power at home, the war is lost.[30] But later films stressed revolutionary images less and less as time went on. *The Court-Martial of Billy Mitchell,* released in 1955, projected the revolutionary image of air power to a point approaching the earlier classics, but that image was woven into the main plot rather than standing alone as the main theme. The overt messages of other prominent films of this period, *Strategic Air Command, Bombers B-52,* and *A Gathering of Eagles,* focused instead on themes calculated to boost recruitment and retention and stressed revolutionary images less with each succeeding film. By the third installment of this "SAC trilogy," revolutionary images appear hardly at all. Still, all three movies conveyed one important air power image quite forcefully: they reassured the public that the dedicated people of SAC could handle the enormous job of saving the United States from the threat of nuclear war.

The principle theme of *The Court-Martial of Billy Mitchell* is the redemption of its central character, but there is also an underlying theme running throughout the film stressing the revolutionary nature of air

7. Billy Mitchell (Gary Cooper, *right*) looks on in *The Court-Martial of Billy Mitchell,* as the prosecutor (Rod Steiger, *standing*) ridicules Mitchell's prediction that the Japanese will someday bomb Pearl Harbor from aircraft carriers.

power glimpsed by Mitchell.[31] Usually this theme is a subtle but integral part of the main theme that Mitchell had been wrongly persecuted. One inescapable part of that theme is that Mitchell had foreseen the air power revolution and that if the army and navy had listened to him instead of breaking him the United States would have been much better prepared for World War II. The best example of this is when the army's prosecutor ridicules Mitchell on the witness stand for claiming that Pearl Harbor's defenses were dangerously weak and mismanaged and for predicting that the Japanese could attack Pearl Harbor with a carrier-borne attack force.[32]

It is important to note in the film's "unheeded prophet" theme the implicit image that the United States in the 1950s has seen the light, that it recognized Mitchell's vision and had put its faith in revolutionary air power. The film did reasonably well at the box office—it ended the year as twenty-eight on the list of top money makers and grossed $3 million—so millions saw its congratulatory message that all intelligent people knew Mitchell had been right all along.[33] Throughout the prosecutor's attack on Mitchell's predictions the movie audience was expected to recognize that history had "proven" Mitchell right, because every one of the predictions the prosecutor ridicules had come to pass by 1955. In the context of the fifties they were expected to pay particular heed to another prediction Mitchell made in the movie. In one scene he tries to convince a general, who later heads the panel of judges at his court-martial, of the effectiveness of bombing and tells him, "One of these days half the world will be in ruins from the air. I want this country to be in the other half." The general had not listened, but America was reassured that Mitchell's words had finally been heeded. In the movie's final scene, Mitchell walks out of his hotel after the court-martial and looks up at a formation of biplanes; suddenly the image is transformed into waves of jets streaking across the screen to the stirring strains of the Air Force Song—Mitchell's vision had finally been realized.

Another movie from 1955, *Strategic Air Command,* presents the same reassuring theme, but the image of revolutionary air power is more understated. The film began as an idea Jimmy Stewart expressed to his friend, screenwriter Beirne Lay. Both had been B-24 pilots in World War II, and both were still in the Air Force Reserve. Stewart suggested a movie about a reservist recalled to active duty during the Korean War. Lay had written a movie script about B-36s called *High Ramparts* that was never produced, so he took Stewart's idea, combined it with elements from

High Ramparts, and developed them into the story for *Strategic Air Command.*[34] Darryl F. Zanuck at Twentieth Century-Fox briefly considered the project but ultimately declined, and Paramount bought the story and assigned Samuel J. Briskin to produce the film and Anthony Mann to direct it. Lay co-authored the screenplay with Valentine Davies, who had written the screenplay for the film version of *The Bridges at Toko Ri* and who also had a brother in the air force and a son in the Air Force Reserve.[35]

The plot revolves around a famous baseball player, Dutch Holland, played by Stewart, who is recalled to active duty as a Reserve bomber pilot. With his ballplaying career just beginning to recover from his service in World War II, Holland at first resents having to interrupt it again, but he soon begins to see that SAC desperately needs reservists to remain on active duty beyond their involuntary tour of duty. His newlywed wife, on the other hand, is anxious to return to her settled civilian lifestyle. Holland finally resolves to remain on active duty because SAC's mission is so important it outweighs all personal considerations. Significantly, his wife, played by June Allyson, reconciles herself to Holland's decision because she too can see how important his new job is. The issue of reservists staying on active duty was a great concern to Lay, who told LeMay he felt SAC would be dependent upon reservists for 80 percent of its personnel for a long time and that he hoped the movie would inspire more of them to reenlist.[36]

In the process of explaining why Holland must stay in the air force the movie repeatedly stresses why SAC is so important to the nation. It is in this vein that images of revolutionary air power appear, because SAC and its strategic bombing role are depicted as the only force standing between the United States and war. When Major General Castle, 8th Air Force commander, tells Holland he is being recalled, Castle tells Holland, "Look, do you realize that we're the only thing that's keeping the peace? By staying combat ready we prevent a war?" Holland is still unconvinced and bitter until a long-service sergeant tells Holland, "Every day in SAC's a war, Colonel. Pressure's on all the time and General Hawks is breathing down your neck. We never know when the other fellow may start something, so we've got to be combat ready 24 hours a day, seven days a week." This gets Holland thinking, and the course of subsequent events convinces him he must stay in, because, as he explains to his wife, "there is a kind of war on. You've got to stay ready to fight without fighting. That's why I made this decision." With such repetitious emphasis of the same theme and the contemporary worries about nuclear war, audiences could hardly miss the point that, according to those who made the movie, the only thing standing between them and a Soviet nuclear attack was air power in the form of strategic nuclear bombing.[37]

The film also reinforces standard motifs that were part of the image of revolutionary air power. The global reach of strategic bombing is emphasized when Holland's wife finds it hard to believe he could fly from Texas to Alaska and back without stopping and when Holland's squadron flies the new B-47 nonstop from Florida to Japan. Both traditions of strategic bombing also find their way into the movie. Twice in the film the destructiveness of nuclear weapons—the Douhet tradition—are showcased. In the first instance Holland tells his wife that one B-36 with one atomic bomb could do the job of a thousand World War II bombers. Later, Hawks, a thinly disguised representation of LeMay, tells a group of B-47 crewmembers, "One B-47 and a crew of three carries the destructive power of the entire B-29 force we used against Japan." But the one bomb run scene in the movie emphasizes the continuing legacy of the ACTS tradition. Bombing from 43,000 feet, Holland's B-47 crew scores a "shack," air force parlance for a hit less than ten feet from the target. The film even includes a scene exhibiting the mystical faith often a feature of the air power advocates' message. When Holland sees the brand new B-47 for the first time the background music becomes haunting and ethereal while Holland, in awe, murmurs, "Well, she's the most beautiful thing I've ever seen in my life, General. Well, just look at her . . . look at her!"

The air force was involved both officially and unofficially in the making of *Strategic Air Command*. Lay consulted often with LeMay on the project from its earliest formative stages through postproduction problems seeking his feedback and help on numerous issues. LeMay encouraged Lay in his focus on Reserve manning problems, noting that such forces "must be in being and ready to go when the whistle blows if we are to adequately defend the country in the atomic age." LeMay also arranged for declassified SAC briefings for Mann and Davies during the early production stages and even pressed the studio to push up the film's release date.[38] The air force provided technical support for the film, which gave them the right to recommend script changes, but all their reservations were minor, and as with other air power films did not alter the basic plot or message. The main air force concern was that

8. In *Strategic Air Command* Jimmy Stewart's reaction to seeing a B-47 for the first time is almost erotic.

Generals Castle and Hawks appear to be heavy-handed and indifferent to the turmoil that air force needs created in reservists' lives, the very thing most reservists feared and resented in their active duty tours. This concern prompted revisions in the final script, most notably in the final scene where Hawks reveals his concern for reservists' hardships and repeats the message that grave national needs demand such sacrifices. The air force also requested changes in the depiction of air force members' alcohol consumption and minor in-flight procedures, all of which were accommodated in the final film.[39]

The film was a big success at the box office, and many air power advocates helped support and advertise it. The Air Force Association encouraged Lay from the outset, sponsored the film's premieres in New York City and Washington, D.C., and presented Stewart with a special medal. The American Legion also helped with the New York City premiere, and Arthur Godfrey televised it on his show and interviewed many of those attending. The film ranked as the seventh-highest moneymaker that year, and Spencer Weart points out that more people saw it than any other film on nuclear war subjects.[40]

The third major air power film of this period, *Bombers B-52*, released in 1957, also focused on one of SAC's personnel problems—retaining experienced crew chiefs. Like *Strategic Air Command,* this movie uses the issue of SAC's readiness to defend the United States as the compelling reason why people should forego greater moneymaking opportunities and an easier life as civilians. The plot revolves around a senior crew chief, Master Sgt. Chuck Brennan played by Karl Malden, who has spent twenty years in the air force, but whose daughter, Lois, urges him to retire and take a lucrative executive position in an aircraft manufacturing plant near San Francisco. Adding to the tension, Lois, played by Natalie Wood, thinks her father's position lacks respect, and then she begins dating an officer who happens to be her father's squadron commander but whom Brennan regards as an irresponsible playboy. A major subplot is that Brennan's proposed retirement comes just as his wing is slated to be the first to convert from B-47s to the brand-new B-52. Without experienced crew chiefs like Brennan, the audience is told, the mighty B-52 is worthless because it will never get off the ground.

The movie went through several name changes during its gestation, but through it all Beirne Lay, though not mentioned in the credits, played a major role. In March 1955 Jack Warner, a longtime friend of Hap Arnold and a member of the board of directors of the Air Force Association, wrote to LeMay explaining that he had hired Lay to work on the film, at that time called *Toward the Unknown.* Warner asked LeMay to help Lay and Warner Brothers "help national defense in general, and the air force in particular" by giving all the assistance he could to the film. A letter in July from Warner Brothers registering the plotline with the Department of Defense (DoD) Motion Picture Section stated that Lay was to be the film's producer. About the same time Lay wrote to LeMay that the title had been changed to *Flight Line Chief* and arranged for the project's writer, Sam Rolfe, who had written the screenplay for *The McConnell Story,* to get various tours at SAC headquarters and the NCO Academy. In November Lay again wrote to LeMay saying he was working on the first draft of the script and that the working title was now simply *Flight Line,* a title that did not seem to excite LeMay. Finally, in April 1956 Lay reported to LeMay that he had completed the second draft and was sending it to Jack Warner for final approval.[41] According to the credits for the final film, however, Rolfe wrote the story, Irving Wallace wrote the screenplay, and Lay played no role at all.

Perhaps because of Lay's ambiguous role, this film's presentation of revolutionary air power themes is far less than any air power film up to this point. The movie is clearly a work of air power advocacy, and revolutionary motifs are present but less often than in earlier films. As in *Strategic Air Command,* the air force and strategic nuclear bombing are presented as the only things keeping the peace and protecting the United States from nuclear devastation. In a tense scene where Brennan explains to his daughter the importance of what he does, he tells her, "We got to keep our ships and our crews combat ready. And when they're ready no one will dare lay a hand or a bomb on us and maybe someday that will keep you and your children alive!" The film even places the air power revolution into a historical perspective when the wing commander tells one of his B-52 crews, "For centuries it's been the job of a successful general to win wars. But in this nuclear air age it's the job of a successful general to prevent wars. Now we think that the way to prevent wars, to deter major aggression, is through superior long range nuclear air power, poised and ready to takeoff at a moment's notice." As with previous films, *Bombers B-52* also employed traditional images of strategic bombing's effectiveness, but unlike previous works it stresses only the tradition of Douhet. In a scene where crew chiefs are undergoing training for the new aircraft, an instructor tells the class, "on a single mission one [B-52], just one, can carry greater destructive force than that of all the bombs dropped by the entire Allied air forces during the whole of World War II."[42]

But revolutionary themes could be easily overpowered by human drama. The tension between Brennan and his daughter over her embarrassment with his rank and job, and that between Brennan and his squadron commander, first over the latter's reputation as a carouser, and later when he starts dating Brennan's daughter, creates dramatic scenes that compete with the main plot. The main plot, that Brennan is important to the air force and should stay in, does remain the focus throughout, and through an improbable plot twist in the film's climax all parties show their dedication, but this is hardly revolutionary. Much the same could be said for people remaining in the army, navy, or marines. In the final analysis, *Bombers B-52* extols the air force as preeminent in national defense, but the revolutionary themes as the basis for that preeminence, which had been a feature of previous films, are much more understated.

Still, the air force was anxious to lend support and gave considerable aid. Of course, the air force requested changes as a condition of its help, but as with other air power movies the objections were superficial and

9. In *Bombers B-52*, Lois (Natalie Wood, *right*) finally realizes the needs of the country and air power must come first and tells her father (Karl Malden, *left*) she wants him to stay in the air force.

did not change the basic nature of the film. Several individuals objected that there were too many aircraft accidents and in-flight incidents in the original script, including a B-52 blowing up in mid-air. In fact, Donald Baruch, head of the DoD Motion Picture Section, hinted that Boeing had got wind of the high accident rate and requested changes.[43] The final version included only two in-flight problems—a stuck landing gear and an in-flight fire—but in each case the heroic actions of crewmembers save the aircraft with little damage. Both SAC and the air force objected that the film did not seem to raise the status of NCOs much. SAC mentioned specifically the daughter's embarrassment that her father is only a "sergeant grease monkey," but this did not change the depiction of the daughter's attitude.[44] Despite these complaints both SAC and the air force were quite pleased with the overall story. While it may not have stressed revolutionary air power, it did glamorize the air force, NCOs, and the B-52, but more importantly it highlighted SAC and its nuclear role in national defense.

Like the general interest magazine campaign, the effort to venerate SAC through movies continued into the early sixties. In 1963 Universal

Studios released *A Gathering of Eagles* starring Rock Hudson. The film grew out of a conversation between LeMay and Sy Bartlett, co-author with Beirne Lay of *Twelve O'clock High*. LeMay expressed his concern to Bartlett that recent novels like Peter George's *Red Alert,* at the time being turned into *Dr. Strangelove,* would harm SAC's reputation. Bartlett "instantly" saw the need for a movie to explain to the public SAC's importance. He then wrote the story on which the screenplay was based and produced the film. Delbert Mann, who as a bomber crewmember in World War II flew thirty-five missions and who had always wanted to make a movie about bombers, directed the film.[45]

Much had changed by the early sixties, though. As the next chapter will show, air power was under attack from several directions and images of revolutionary air power seemed naive and had almost totally disappeared from popular culture. Of all the movies highlighting strategic air power, *A Gathering of Eagles* deals with revolutionary themes the least. Like the other two films of the SAC trilogy and the SAC articles of the fifties, it showcased SAC in complimentary terms, but there was little more to its message than the reassuring images of SAC vigilance in ensuring effectiveness, that its people were dedicated and made great sacrifices in performing their mission, and that SAC's positive control procedures virtually ensure that no one could accidentally or maliciously start a nuclear war. The plot involves a base armed with both B-52s and ICBMs that had just failed an operational readiness inspection, or ORI. In the wake of this failure the wing commander is fired and Colonel Caldwell, played by Hudson, is sent to whip the base into shape for a repeat inspection in the near future. In searching for weaknesses Caldwell finds several people who do not live up to SAC's demanding standards. One such case is the base commander, an old pilot who had excelled in the SAC of pre-Sputnik days but who had trouble adjusting to the new SAC of missiles and the need to launch all aircraft within fifteen minutes of warning.[46] The stress of the new high-pressure SAC had driven him to excessive drinking. Another problem is the vice wing commander, Caldwell's best friend, who refuses to make the hard decisions that SAC's mission demands of all its commanders. Caldwell, who has no problem making the hard decisions regardless of personal feelings, fires both commanders and drives the rest of the base's personnel so hard morale begins to slip.[47]

Complicating the plot and accentuating the pressure on Caldwell is his new wife, who does not understand why he needs to be so hard.

10. Colonel Caldwell's (Rock Hudson, *right*) cool handling of an in-flight emergency illustrated how strong and trustworthy the people of SAC were in contrast to depictions of mad airmen in *Dr. Strangelove* or automatons in *Fail Safe*.

Other wives come to her with complaints about what Caldwell's training and alert schedule are doing to their family lives, but Caldwell turns a deaf ear to her entreaties to relax the pressure. She befriends the base commander's wife and is thus shocked to find out her husband has fired him, and when the former base commander attempts suicide Caldwell's wife blames her husband. Thinking the high pressure is unnecessary, she feels she is seeing a side of him she never knew existed and plans to leave him. Before she leaves the re-inspection team arrives. Instantly all morale problems are forgotten as the entire base leaps into action performing heroic feats to ensure the base passes this time. As one character says while watching Caldwell struggling with a command problem, "There's a man I thought I'd never be rooting for." The sudden and universal concern to pass the inspection convinces Caldwell's wife that the pressure was real and necessary, that her husband is not unusual—that everyone shares the sense of urgency in meeting SAC's standards. In explaining to Caldwell that she now sees that she was wrong, she tells him of an airman who had just undergone an emergency appendectomy, "Do you know the first thing he asked about when he came round? His wife or his children? No, he wanted to know how his plane did in the ORI."

All of this undoubtedly conveyed a very positive image of SAC to most of its viewers when the movie first came out, but the movie assumed its audience recognized and accepted that SAC was critical to national survival. The revolutionary themes that had been part of earlier films are almost entirely lacking. There are no speeches about how SAC or air power in general is the only thing standing between the U.S. people and nuclear annihilation. There are no people agonizing over whether what they do is so important it justifies staying in the air force when loved ones urge them to pursue more lucrative civilian careers. In fact, one of the biggest hardships suffered by the family of the fired base commander is that now they are poor and their son must drop out of Stanford. The closest the film comes to conveying the threat of nuclear devastation is when, in the midst of an alert exercise that has sent the crews and their aircraft to takeoff positions at the end of the runway, Caldwell says to his vice wing commander, "The way things are this could be the real thing." His companion replies, "You never know." Command post then broadcasts an announcement that it was an exercise and the crews are visibly relieved. An audience not conditioned to see SAC's mission as America's only hope for deterring nuclear annihilation might miss much of what prompted the film's sense of urgency and why SAC had such demanding standards. Anyone unfamiliar with the tense days of the Cuban Missile Crisis might even assume that the pre-Vietnam air force must have been obsessed with looking good on inspections and that all SAC commanders must have been martinets.

In the context of the early sixties, though, the air force thought highly of the film and gave it considerable support. But giving technical assistance had recently become a problem. In the wake of controversy over the level of army support in the making of *The Longest Day,* Assistant Secretary of Defense for Public Affairs Arthur Sylvester launched a reevaluation of military assistance to commercial films. The study led to a new set of guidelines for military assistance and reluctance on Sylvester's part to authorize future assistance. Bartlett was one of the first to request support under the new rules, and though he submitted a request so closely complying to the new guidelines that Donald Baruch, head of the DoD Motion Picture Section, labeled it "the Bible," Sylvester turned Bartlett down claiming the film was just another movie to boost the air force's image. When LeMay, by now air force chief of staff, heard that support had been refused, he personally intervened and gained Sylvester's quick compliance. Despite the detailed requirements list submitted to Sylvester's office, Bartlett got considerably more support on location at Beale Air Force Base in California and at SAC headquarters. LeMay was quite pleased with the final result: he claimed that of all the air power movies this one came the closest to conveying "a true picture of what the military was all about." The public did not share LeMay's sentiments. In a reflection of the changed public mood toward air power, the movie finished out the year at only forty-eight on the list of most popular movies.[48]

Before leaving the "SAC trilogy" one common feature bears consideration. Critics have focused on the depictions of family relationships shared by several air power films of the postwar era, particularly *Above and Beyond, Strategic Air Command, Bombers B-52,* and *A Gathering of Eagles.* In all of these films female family members, usually wives, rebel against the demands the air force makes upon their husbands or fathers. Invariably, though, the female character "comes around," accepts the demands, and is reconciled with the male character and the needs of the air force. Some critics see this plot device as merely an extraneous romantic digression detracting from an otherwise good movie; others have seen it as a reflection of the sexist expectation that women are supposed to submit to male authority and the dictates of hierarchical society, especially within the context of the Cold War.[49] This latter observation is valid and important, but for the purposes of this study it is also important to note that the near ubiquity of this depiction of family strife and how it is resolved hints at yet another effort to convey the importance of air power to contemporary audiences. In every case the source of conflict is the airman's commitment to the air force stemming from his sense that its mission is vital to winning the war, in the case of *Above and Beyond,* and to keeping the peace in later movies. When family troubles arise the airman points to the higher cause—air power's importance to the nation—and in only one case, Sergeant Brennan, does the male *temporarily*—and reluctantly—agree to abandon that cause. By the end of each movie, though, the course of events has "reeducated" the female family member, and she accepts the sacrifice in the name of what air power is doing for the country. In Sergeant Brennan's case, his daughter, realizing that what her father does is important and honorable, frees him to do what he wanted to do all along—remain faithful to air power for the good of the nation. In an era when domestic bliss was elevated to unprecedented levels, the recurring theme of family strife in films that celebrated the source of that strife seems calculated to convey the message that revolutionary air power is so important to the nation that it even outweighs the family unit and the institution of marriage. There was also the unmistakable message to women: revolutionary air power was so important that they must accept the patriotic duty to sacrifice their desires in the name of supporting the airmen who served that cause.[50]

Other air force roles besides nuclear strategic bombing appeared in popular culture throughout the period, but such features were not as frequent as features on SAC, and the images created were generally crafted to supplement the heroic and capable image of the air force in general, not challenge the dominant position of SAC. One example is a 1955 *Saturday Evening Post* article written by Frank Harvey highlighting TAC's nuclear fighter-bombers. With the nuclear role dominating military planning in the Eisenhower administration TAC sought and acquired a share of the nuclear mission.[51] In detailing that nuclear role, though, Harvey portrays TAC's nuclear mission as supplementing SAC's. Calling SAC America's long-range "Sunday punch," he describes TAC's nuclear force as a "Free World Fire Department, with the mission of settling 'little wars,' like Korea, before they can grow big." As with magazine articles focusing on SAC, Harvey paints his subjects as efficient, dedicated, and larger-than-life heroes, and in the process further trivializes the subject of nuclear war. Not only is the prospect of all-out nuclear war with the Soviet Union reduced to the image of a "Sunday punch," but nuclear weapons can even deliver the United States from another frustrating "small war" like Korea by rushing around the world at jet speeds dropping atomic bombs on every trouble spot.[52]

Two movies from this period focused on other aspects of the air force, and they each received a unique form of air force endorsement. In 1955 Warner Brothers released *The McConnell Story,* a movie about Joseph McConnell, a leading ace during the Korean War who later was killed while testing new aircraft. The film highlights the air superiority role of tactical air power in the heroic tradition of the fighter ace but little more. There is no larger vision that air power was the decisive element in Korea or that tactical air power was superior to strategic air power. It was just a story about a heroic airman who died in the line of duty. Universal's 1956 film, *Battle Hymn,* told of a World War II fighter pilot, Dean Hess, who accidentally bombed a German orphanage killing 37 children. Driven by guilt, he becomes a minister but in 1950 rejoins the air force and is sent to train South Korean fighter pilots. When the test of battle comes, Hess finds he can kill again and shoots down two enemy aircraft. The real story, though, comes in Hess's efforts to found and protect an orphanage for Korean refugees. While this film also showcases tactical air power, its real message is one airman's humanitarian spirit.[53]

What makes these two films unique is that both were introduced by air force generals at the beginning of the movie. General O. P. Weyland introduced *The McConnell Story* and spoke briefly about how U.S. freedoms were secured throughout American history by countless men like McConnell. In *Battle Hymn* Gen. Earl E. Partridge, who had commanded the Fifth Air Force in Korea during the war, said that Hess's story "is an affirmation of the essential goodness of the human spirit." On one level these introductions serves as an endorsement that went beyond the usual practice of military support for motion pictures. The presence of a uniformed officer of the highest rank served as a powerful visual affirmation that the film represented the air force. On another level, though, these introductions serve as an indication of just how thoroughly popular culture had come to embrace air power. In the mid-fifties an air force general introducing a film might have been unusual but not unthinkable. Such a scene at the start of any war movie after Vietnam, on the other hand, can scarcely be imagined.

Television provided a new and increasingly powerful medium to showcase air power, and the wide range of air force roles were highlighted, but strategic bombing generally appeared as the ultimate definition of air power. In 1953 the ABC series *March of Time* broadcast an episode titled "The Air Age." While it featured aviation of all sorts since the dawn of flight, particularly Korean War fighters, much of its emphasis focuses on the contribution of strategic bombing to World War II. The show even extolled the B-36 for its size and destructive capability.[54]

In 1956 CBS launched a year-long series, *Air Power,* a weekly documentary-style show narrated by Walter Cronkite. Like the *March of Time* episode three years earlier, this series outlined aviation developments throughout the history of flight and showcased virtually all air power missions. Numerous episodes focused on the contributions of tactical forces in both World War II and Korea, and air defense received considerable attention. In fact, the premiere episode was a dramatization of a Soviet air attack against North America and depicted how the

United States and Canada would attempt to stop the incoming bombers. In this dramatization, though, air defense forces could not stop all the bombers, and the audience was told that the only hope for avoiding nuclear devastation was the threat of retaliation that would leave the Soviet Union more devastated than the United States. Several later episodes focus on strategic bombing in World War II, depicting it as a new weapon that could destroy a nation's ability to wage war. In case anybody missed the connection with postwar nuclear bombing, one episode stated that in the nuclear era one plane with one bomb could do what it took sixty thousand men to do to the Romanian oil refineries at Ploesti. Another episode, titled "The New Doctrine," compared Soviet and U.S. nuclear bombing capabilities and extolled SAC's efforts to remain ahead of the Soviets in nuclear bombing. The series concluded with a final reminder that security could only be gained through a strong bombing force to deter a Soviet attack on America.[55]

Television also gave Arthur Godfrey his greatest opportunity to put his air power advocacy before millions of Americans on a routine basis, and this was undoubtedly where he had his greatest effect. Godfrey broke into radio in 1930, but his popularity did not really begin until after World War II. Godfrey's success on radio led to his transition to television in 1948 with a televised version of *Arthur Godfrey's Talent Scouts*, which ran on CBS until 1958, and *Arthur Godfrey and His Friends*, which aired on CBS from 1949 until 1959. Both shows were enormously popular. He is the only star in television history to have two top-rated primetime shows at the same time, and his popularity, which ran strong through the mid-fifties, made him a media celebrity.[56] Godfrey also wrote articles and gave speeches and interviews, but judging by his correspondence with LeMay, he did most of his air power work on his television shows.

Godfrey championed a strong air force, and thus one of his pet concerns was recruitment and retention. He touted air force enlistment on his show for its education opportunities, and he worked to improve retention by improving air force morale. Two key efforts in this area were boosting military pay and easing the loneliness of duty at isolated bases, and in both he used his television shows as a soapbox to rally support.[57] Godfrey's military pay efforts offer a revealing example of his effectiveness in garnering tremendous public support through his television shows. Having invited Senate Majority Leader Lyndon Johnson to his Virginia farm in 1958 for some "gentle persuasion," Godfrey reported

LBJ's reaction to a pending pay raise bill: "The bill will never be reported out of committee—will never reach the floor—will never come to a vote—and if it is, will be defeated!" After a week of urging his audience to write Congress on the issue, Godfrey related a call from Johnson: "Will you cut it out! [The mail] is up to the ceiling here." The bill passed shortly thereafter.[58]

Godfrey's main concern, though, was SAC, and his television show gave him frequent opportunities to help build its public support. He highlighted SAC and its concerns on the air, he filmed portions of his shows at SAC bases, and he plugged SAC movies, all the while sending out his simple reassuring message to millions of viewers that their only chance for security was through strategic nuclear deterrence. One incident illustrates dramatically both Godfrey's championing of SAC and his impact. On his April 2, 1956, episode of *Arthur Godfrey's Talent Scouts,* Godfrey held up the latest copy of *Air Force* magazine, the official publication of the Air Force Association, and described it as "very, very important." That particular issue was entirely dedicated to SAC and contained fifteen articles written by various SAC leaders, including Curtis LeMay. Godfrey told his audience, "Steal one, borrow one, buy one if you have to . . . but get a copy and read it from cover to cover. Every American must know the things that are in this magazine." This created a problem for the AFA, however, because *Air Force* is not sold to the general public—it is only sent to Association members. The AFA told Godfrey they had three hundred extra copies they would give to anyone who asked for a copy, but when Godfrey passed this along to his viewers, the AFA was inundated with requests. As James Straubel, longtime editor of *Air Force* and author of a history of the AFA, relates the sequence of events, "Hardly had he finished when our phones began ringing with calls from people who wanted their copies of *Air Force.* And then the telegrams began to arrive, until we had requests for 160,000 copies beyond our regular print order." The AFA produced a condensed version to meet this sudden windfall of public interest.[59]

The dominant role of nuclear bombing in America's official and cultural defense thinking was a curious episode in U.S. military and cultural history. Despite critics, faith in strategic air power remained strong in both official and unofficial circles through much of the fifties, but in the second half of the decade criticism escalated in both realms. In military and diplomatic areas observers noted that massive retaliation left few choices between Armageddon and acquiescence. If a "small war" flared up, the United States had too few conventional resources to meet most threats, so U.S. leaders had to choose between using nuclear weapons or accepting an unpleasant situation. Both the French disaster at Dien Bien Phu and the crisis in Laos illustrated America's restricted options.[60] The inflexible nature of massive retaliation stems from a fallacy long buried deep in the air power gospel. Just as early aviation enthusiasts had felt the airplane freed them from the constraints of gravity and physical barriers, air power advocates felt the warplane freed them from many traditional constraints of war. When theorizing about strategic bombing, for example, they rarely stopped to consider under what circumstances bombing an enemy into submission would be an appropriate strategy or, more important, when it would be inappropriate. Moreover, they did not consider what sort of postwar relationship the United States could hope to maintain with a nation that had been bombed to the point of collapse. Nuclear weapons only aggravated this fallacy.

The Kennedy administration moved U.S. defense policy away from a slavish reliance on nuclear obliteration, but official policy could not easily alter cultural attachment to images of salvation through nuclear air power.[61] The same technological messianic images that made easy victory through air power such a compelling notion for air power advocates also drew the general public like a siren song. The fallacy of strategic bombing suitable for all occasions exerted a powerful attraction to a society deathly afraid of the communist threat but confronted with the intractable complexities of the Cold War. In the second half of the fifties, though, and continuing into the early sixties, voices arose in popular culture questioning the image of air power in general and strategic bombing in particular. This popular culture counterrevolution started out tentatively but by the early sixties rose to a crescendo and created an alternate image—an alter-ego as it were—of the Mad Bomber that competed with the popular image of SAC. The counterrevolution would not totally eliminate the hold air power had gained on the public's imagination, but it would change the nature of public debate on air power issues and to a great extent end the air power popular culture crusade.

CHAPTER 6

Disturbing Visions
Air Power's Critics Strike Back

Opposition to the image of the bomb began in popular culture almost immediately after the atomic bomb blasts at Hiroshima and Nagasaki. Most notable in this regard was John Hersey's *Hiroshima,* published in 1946. The book was a bestseller, was reprinted in *The New Yorker,* and was read in half-hour installments over ABC radio. Other works also appeared that same year. Hermann Hagedorn wrote an epic poem, "The Bomb that Fell on America," and in March, Lewis Mumford's "Gentlemen, You Are Mad!" appeared in *Saturday Review.* About this same time the *Bulletin of the Atomic Scientists* emerged as a forum for antinuclear debate.[1] With the exception of Hersey, though, these and other works were obscure or reached a relatively small segment of the public, and they represent a minority view toward the atomic bomb. Furthermore, all of these works focused on the bomb itself, not the image of air power. Before World War II there had been considerable debate over the morality of bombing, and some even denounced air power as a scourge on humanity, but after the war such concerns faded away as debate focused on the atomic bomb.[2] This lack of opposition to air power continued for the most part until the mid-fifties and left air power advocates a clear field to preach their revolution.

For several years air power advocates exploited their opportunity and through popular culture preached faith in air power with considerable success. But the emergence during the early fifties of the image of strategic nuclear bombing and SAC as the ultimate expression of air power wed the air power revolution to nuclear weapons to such an extent that support for air power meant support for nuclear warfare, while opposition to nuclear warfare increasingly meant opposition to air power. In the last half of the decade growing segments of the American public began having serious doubts about nuclear weapons, and as a result they began questioning faith in air power.

In the latter half of the 1950s several factors helped spark a dramatic surge in the antinuclear movement in the United States. Both Spencer Weart and H. Bruce Franklin credit the launching of Sputnik in 1957 with the dramatic rise of antinuclear sentiments and literature, and that event undoubtedly was the main overt impetus, but there was something more, something less tangible, that helped make the cultural atmosphere ripe for dissension through the late fifties and early sixties.[3] A contributing factor to the growing fear of nuclear weapons was a vague but increasingly perceptible loss of faith in the revolutionary promise of air power. Some of this can be traced through what *did* appear in popular culture between 1956 and 1964, but it can also be detected in what *did not* appear or what was no longer present. What *did* appear beginning in the last half of the decade was a series of novels making the first tentative assaults on the images of air power, and in the early sixties the trend quickened with escalated attacks. These novels did not signal an all-out abandonment of faith in air power, a point born out by the fact that movies made from the early novels tended to dilute or downplay the anti–air power sentiments. In the early sixties, though, the films made from novels with anti–air power sentiments retained and even heightened the attacks on air power images.

This chapter will examine the shape of the anti–air power literature in popular culture, but one should also note what *did not* appear, or more precisely, what was no longer present. Something had changed in pro–air power circles and in society's response to air power. As the fifties wore on the air power popular culture campaign emphasized less and less the revolutionary image of air power. Each succeeding installment of the SAC trilogy contained less emphasis on revolutionary themes. Magazine articles bear out this trend as well. Increasingly emphasizing institutions, especially SAC, few articles extolled the brave new future of air power as had characterized much of the pro–air power material of the late forties. In 1948 *Collier's* had devoted the better part of an entire issue to the forty-fifth anniversary of the Wright Brothers' first flight, but the seemingly more significant fiftieth anniversary in 1953 drew far less coverage. In 1954 *Life* published an article harkening to the great air age ahead, and it published another in 1956, but these are conspicuous for being exceptions. Perhaps the best indication of this lack of emphasis is the fact that the 1959–61 edition of *Reader's Guide to Periodic Literature* omits the category "air power," a heading it had listed since its 1932–35 edition.[4] The 1956–57 CBS television series *Air*

Power cast its subject in a revolutionary context, but individual episodes frequently stressed that it was a revolution that carried both dangerous and beneficial portent.

Something had changed in U.S. society too. The simple faith in air power built up in the late forties and nurtured through the early fifties was slipping away. The impact of Sputnik in awakening public fears should not be minimized, but this was not the first nuclear-related shock the Soviets had inflicted on the U.S. public—the difference in public reaction in 1957 as opposed to the 1949 Soviet atomic bomb blast is revealing. As in 1949, a spate of articles appeared in general interest magazines after Sputnik reassuring Americans that air power had an answer to the new threat. Many of these articles told the public that SAC's bombers were still a relevant deterrent, but others hailed the rapid development of new missiles that the air force would use to deter a Soviet missile attack.[5] These assurances did not allay fears as had the earlier campaign, though, for it seems the public was no longer in the mood to accept blind faith in air power. Perhaps part of the answer can be found in the fact that the new threat came in a new form. In 1949, when faith in aviation—and thus air power—remained high, people could put their trust in our airplanes to beat their airplanes, for thus was the only way the Soviets could deliver their bomb. In 1957, however, the new danger came in the form of a rocket—with public fascination in aviation being eclipsed by the relatively new interest in space travel, people feared the rocket had trumped the airplane.

What was behind this declining faith in air power? That is a tough question to answer, for it hinges on intangible factors like images, moods, and attitudes often reflected in non-events such as what was no longer said or shown. Furthermore, support for air power did not disappear quickly or completely by any means. Still, public moods do change, and several factors favoring public faith in air power had changed. For one thing, much of the earlier faith in air power stemmed from the long-standing fascination with aviation in general. But by 1957 flight was becoming a commonplace phenomenon that many had grown up with or were coming to take for granted. Secondly, with new wonders such as spaceflight, television, and computers edging out the airplane as the symbol of high technology, air power no longer seemed so revolutionary. Yet another factor was the air power advocates' shift in emphasis from revolutionary themes to the air force's institutional needs. Essentially, air power's evangelists abandoned the eschatology of their faith—air power's redemptive qualities—for the mundane bureaucratic aggrandizement of the organization supposedly embodying that faith. Furthermore, when critics began launching attacks on both air power and the air force, air power advocates defended the institution as opposed to defending the faith. Thus institutionalization of air power in the air force wed the air power revolution to the fortunes of a bureaucratic organization, led the air power advocates away from their original vision, and paved the way for public disillusionment in the United States. All of this would tend to weaken the technological messianism investing air power with its seeming powers of salvation.[6]

Weart offers a theory in a related context that may give yet another explanation for why people lost faith. In discussing why many eventually fell silent on the nuclear debate he points to "cognitive dissonance," that people often choose to ignore the "dissonance" or discrepancy between their fears and their actions when the options become too complex for easy solution.[7] In the air power context this could have been a factor, for as long as the United States had a nuclear monopoly or SAC bombers and air defense seemed to offer a reasonably valid measure of protection, people could put their faith in air power to protect them from enemy air power. Missiles that could strike suddenly with little or no warning, however, made countering the Soviet threat too complex for easy faith, but the unilateral disarmament that some advocated did not offer much of an alternative either. Increasingly people chose not to choose. They could not abandon air power, but they could no longer continue the naive faith either.

For whatever reason, people began to lose faith in air power, and one reflection of this is the publication, and increasing popularity, of works in popular culture that questioned or attacked the dominant image of air power. Starting in the second half of the fifties and accelerating through the early sixties, novels and movies escalated their attacks and drew ever-larger audiences. By the end of the period depictions of air power that would have been unthinkable in the early fifties were becoming bestsellers and classics. These works not only reflect the loss of faith in air power, they undoubtedly accelerated it as well. They also changed another aspect of the popular culture air power debate. By 1963 works that unquestioningly lauded air power were becoming rare. *A Gathering of Eagles* was the last film glorifying SAC; it did poorly at the box office, and it was the last positive depiction of air power until well into the 1980s. The same was true of general interest magazines. Positive portrayals would still appear, especially in *Reader's Digest,* but the new tone is best captured by James Atwater's 1963 *Saturday Evening Post* article examining SAC's *Minuteman* missiles. While it gives SAC's side of the story thoroughly, the old cloying praise is gone and is replaced with guarded respect and healthy skepticism.[8]

Assaults on air power from the mid-fifties to the mid-sixties, then, both indicated and spurred the public's loss of faith in air power. It is ironic in a way that one of the leading causes of the demise of the air power cult would be popular culture, because popular culture had been such an effective tool in building that cult from its earliest days in the first place. In a sense air power advocates learned that "he who lives by the sword dies by the sword."

THE EARLY YEARS: A CHANGE OF TONE

At least as early as 1956 works began appearing in literature that took the first tentative steps toward questioning the cult of air power. The trend continued through the decade with the attacks becoming increasingly bold and straightforward. Some of these novels were turned into major motion pictures with "big name" stars like Robert Mitchum, Steve McQueen, and Robert Wagner, but the movie studios lagged behind the novelists in their willingness to challenge the air power gospel. In every case the film version toned down the anti–air power elements that had been major features of the novel upon which it was based. Perhaps the changes were made because studio executives still felt an attachment to the air power cause; perhaps it was simply that they believed audiences were not ready to see their air heroes depicted as borderline pathological killers. In either case, this reluctance to undermine the image of air power in film reflects the slow and incremental change in attitudes toward air power in popular culture.

One 1956 novel, Ward Taylor's *Roll Back the Sky,* is a good example of the tentative nature of early negative depictions of air power. The book is a psychological drama dealing with the bombing campaign against Japan in the last six months of World War II. Taylor was a career air force officer who flew B-29s in the Pacific theater during the war; he returned to that subject in this novel written while he was still in the air force. The plot revolves around a B-29 pilot and his crew and begins about the time of the March 9–10, 1945, firebombing raid on Tokyo. The image of air power, as conveyed through the thoughts and reaction of the pilot,

11. The novel *Roll Back the Sky* explores the psychological impact of the firebombing missions over Japan on the men who flew those missions.

his crewmembers, and the entire group of which they are members is, at best, schizophrenic.

On one level the novel seems to be just another story about men in war. The pilot, Richardson, his crew, and many others fear death and sweat out each mission. There is also the familiar love triangle when Richardson, who is married, falls in love with a Red Cross volunteer stationed near his base on Saipan. On another level, though, Taylor seems to be building toward an indictment of strategic bombing. Early in the novel when Richardson's crew flies on the Tokyo firebombing mission, their first sight of the city, already in flames, is described initially as a lovely scene: "In a chilling, menacing way it was beautiful. . . . It was not unlike a flaming sunrise . . . a delicate pink." Almost immediately, though, it turns to a horrible spectacle: "In a few seconds . . . the glow had changed enormously. It was no longer beautiful. Now it was a pulsing, angry red. At its base the color faded and became streaked with white; at its top the tone was orange, and there was a fitful flicker."[9]

After the flight some of Richardson's crewmembers start experiencing medical problems. His radar operator complains of a foot injury and begins acting strangely, one of his gunners experiences an unsettled stomach, but most serious is his bombardier, Wilson, who begins suffering from stomach problems and headaches. The author links this sudden onset of physical maladies to the crewmembers' reaction to the firebombing. In explaining his sudden ailments to Richardson, Wilson says, "looking at those fires was like looking down into the door of a furnace, and I thought about all the people burning down there and how they must hate me and want to kill me, and I couldn't blame them. . . . I was just all sick inside and I felt like I couldn't move. . . . I was afraid of them, afraid they'd kill me. I could feel them hating me and wanting to kill me. I can still feel them hating me.[10] Moreover, the whole unit experiences a psychosomatic onset of mysterious problems. Most noticeable is the group commander, who seems to be slowly decaying before their eyes until he is killed on a bombing mission.[11]

But just when it appears Taylor is building to a powerful statement, he backs off. Wilson's problem becomes a main focus through five chapters and climaxes on a firebombing mission over the target. Before the mission he told Richardson he was too sick to fly, but the pilot, sensing that Wilson was just scared, orders him into the plane. Wilson's fear mounts through the flight, and then just short of the target he abandons his bomb sight. Richardson, in an "animal-like" rage, confronts him, and without a word spoken by either, Wilson returns to his position and completes the bomb run. Afterward, Wilson explained that Richardson had forced him to confront and conquer his fear, and thereafter he performs like the perfect bombardier.[12]

After this Taylor says little more about bombing and turns instead to Richardson's feelings about war. In this vein, though, Taylor does not question the nature of air power, or even modern warfare, but war in general. Richardson had always wanted to be a soldier and had joined the AAF hoping to find glory and fulfillment in war. What he finds, however, is that war is just fear and death. There are no heroes. One could sense in this a repudiation of the glory of air power that was often a part of the air power advocates' message, but Taylor does not develop this theme. Instead Richardson repudiates the quest for glory and finds that the real meaning in life is a personal affirmation of hope. The realization bursts upon him in the midst of combat as he struggles with his own fears. He discovers that only through hope for the future will he find meaning in life, and he thus rediscovers his love for his wife. What we have, then, is a book that raises questions about air power and its effect on the human spirit but which pushes the point fitfully and never drives an anti–air power message to the point that would make it a true attack.

The other novel dealing with air power published in 1956 was James Salter's *The Hunters*. Another psychological study, the story revolves around a fighter pilot's experiences in the Korean War. Born James Horowitz, Salter had been a fighter pilot during the war, and undoubtedly the novel reflects his perceptions of that experience. The fact that he published under the pen name "Salter" suggests he may have intended it to be something of an exposé.[13] The central character, Capt. Cleve Saville, is in some respects an antihero in that he rejects the heroic image of the world in which the war has placed him, the world of fighter pilots in an F-86 group based in South Korea. Throughout the novel, though, as the reader learns about the fighter pilot world, its heroic image emerges as a pathological ideal of perverted and inverted values. By ultimately rejecting this heroic image, therefore, Saville actually turns out to be heroic. But Saville dies in the course of combat, having never achieved the highly sought status defining a hero in the fighter world, the status of ace. In Salter's depiction, all who do reach this status are grotesque caricatures of depravity, while virtuous or admirable characters fall far short, thus conveying the image that success as defined in the world of pilots can only be achieved by the most antisocial elements.[14]

By all measures short of combat, Saville should be honored in his world. He was a superb pilot in peacetime who had flown with the air force acrobatic team and had won a prestigious air-to-air fighter competition. When he arrives in Korea his group commander, who had flown with Saville before the war, is glad to have such a famous pilot in his unit and makes Saville a flight commander. Saville, though, is also depicted throughout the novel as a sensitive, thoughtful individual, as best seen when he courts a young Japanese woman while on leave in Tokyo. The same aggressive nature that made Saville a good fighter pilot also compels him toward the goal of becoming an ace, but as aerial victories elude him, he becomes at first frustrated and then introspective. In the meantime, he watches the methods used by his fellow fighter pilots who achieve success, and he is increasingly revolted. He searches for what it is within himself that makes him feel that failing to become an ace equates to personal failure. In the end, he achieves his second kill by shooting down the leading enemy ace but rejects the accolades by ascribing the victory to his wingman, who died on the mission.[15] By the time Saville dies, four missions short of the end of his tour, he is at peace with himself and the fact that he won true honor by remaining virtuous even though the fighter world sees him as a failure.

In direct contrast to Saville are the two figures in the novel who achieve the most success in the fighter pilot world but who act despicably. One is Lieutenant Pell, a new pilot straight out of training. Pell is an egotistical loner desperate for glory and willing to do anything, moral or immoral, to become an ace. Pell is placed in Saville's flight and immediately starts undermining Saville's reputation with the other flight members and the group's leadership. The other villain is Colonel Imil, the group commander. Imil was an ace in World War II and an ace again in Korea. He cares about one thing and one thing only: chalking up the best kill record for his group. In a dramatic scene that reveals both Pell's and Imil's true values, Pell abandons his element leader during combat to pursue and shoot down his fifth enemy aircraft, thus obtaining the coveted status of ace. His element leader, left unprotected by his wingman, is killed, and Saville demands that Pell be grounded. Pell lies about what happened, and Imil suddenly turns on his old friend, berates him in front of the entire unit, and says, "A man with five victories, and you want me to ground him? What's wrong with you? He ought to be a flight commander."[16]

Other characters sharpen the perversity of the dichotomous world of the fighter pilot. Major Abbott, another World War II ace who seems to have lost the winning edge, is treated like a pariah by everyone in the group and feels like his life has lost all meaning. He is transferred to a staff job in Seoul, but he cannot stay away and comes back to visit. The two element leaders in Saville's flight, Corona and Daughters, figure out what Pell is doing, but Daughters is killed by Pell's betrayal, and Corona returns home at the end of his tour wanting nothing more to do with the air force or airplanes. The other members of the flight, Lieutenants Hunter and Pettibone, young and eager, follow Pell everywhere, worship him, and ape his ways, but like stereotypical toadies they gain no achievements of their own. High-ranking group staff officers, whose only fault is that they have no kills, are berated and ridiculed in front of lower-ranking officers, while lieutenants who do have kills are shown the deference and honor usually reserved for those of much higher rank. Taken together the world of fighter pilots portrayed by Salter seems to be a place where society's standard virtues such as honor, loyalty, and teamwork count for nothing, and personal victory, even at the cost of a comrade's life, is the only virtue recognized. This was hardly an image of air power ushering in a better world.

When *The Hunters* was made into a movie in 1958, however, many of the negative elements were considerably softened. Saville's character was radically altered. Instead of a sensitive man who is disenchanted and finally killed by the perverted world he finds in Korea, he is a hard man who is softened by the compassion he learns while at war. Pell becomes a hip, cocky loner who matures into a team player willing to sacrifice himself to save his buddies. Imil is reduced to almost a bit part, but in the dramatic scene where Pell's actions cause the death of his element leader, Imil appears as a man trying to be fair in the face of conflicting accounts and who promotes Pell, after a stern verbal reprimand, because there is no one else to fill the now-vacant position. The novel's minor character, Major Abbott, is elevated to a supporting role as Lieutenant Abbott, a man whose fear of combat drives him to excessive drinking and who closes himself off from his wife and anyone who tries to befriend him. The new theme of the story is the redemption the airmen find in the mutual interdependence of air combat. When Abbott is shot down Saville crash-lands to save him. Pell, disobeying orders, returns to strafe enemy troops pursuing Saville and Abbott, and is shot down by ground fire. Together the three men, each of whom had shown antisocial character flaws up to that point, make their way from deep inside enemy territory to the safety of their own lines and on the way shed their old ways and become truly heroic figures.[17]

Ironically, when Twentieth Century-Fox sought technical support to make the movie the air force objected to the radical plot changes. The air force had suggested the novel to the studio as a story it would like to see turned into a movie, and after obtaining the rights Twentieth Century-Fox submitted a story synopsis that followed the novel to a remarkable degree.[18] The air force's initial reaction was guarded. In August 1956 Baruch cautioned the studio that "[t]he Air Force indicates that the background of the story may offer some problems in extending full cooperation." The air force seems to have been concerned about the large amount of aerial filming that might be required: a 1957 letter granting official support warned, "The studio should be advised, with great emphasis, that the granting of such cooperation does not automatically assure them of the use of the large number of aircraft and amount of equipment that they might desire."[19]

By the next year the script had undergone the radical changes outlined above, and suddenly the air force threatened to withhold cooperation. Claiming it had liked the book much better and that it had given initial approval based on a synopsis following the book, the air force complained that there were no redeeming characters in the script. They objected to Saville's lack of feelings and his pursuit of Abbott's estranged wife and to "the 'switch-blade knife' characterization of Lt. Pell." In fact the air force considered both characters to be "punks." Predictably they resented the frequent drunkenness of Abbott, and they considered Imil's brief portrayal as little more than a "bellowing clown." Finally, they dismissed the redemption element, the rescue of Abbott, and the escape from enemy territory as superficial action and adventure and felt the changes had subverted "what was fundamentally an honest fictional study of jet aces and what made them effective 'Hunters' in the Korean War." Ultimately the air force and the studio reached a compromise, because the film was made with considerable air force help and was approved for release, but the elements objectionable to the air force remained.[20]

The whole episode betrays a curious logic on the part of the air force. Granted, the characters of Saville and Abbott were degraded considerably from the novel version, but Imil is totally rehabilitated from a characterization of the worst sort of unscrupulous commander, and Pell is toned down considerably. Most important, though, is that Saville, Abbott, and Pell are all redeemed by the end of the movie, and the image of the air force is highly reassuring. To characterize as "fundamentally honest" a novel portraying successful fighters as twisted and unscrupulous, while everyone who possesses any normalcy and decency fails by the fighters' standards and either dies or goes home in disgust indicates the air force either did not understand the deeper meanings or did not find them repulsive. It objected to excessive drinking and adultery but accepted promoting those who obtained glory by getting their leaders killed.

It is significant that both *Roll Back the Sky* and *The Hunters* were written by air force pilots writing about their own experiences in war. Up to this point almost all fliers had been air power advocates, and from the earliest days of flight they had been among its greatest, and loudest, champions. Furthermore, air power advocates had nearly always maintained a solid front in proclaiming through popular culture that air power was an unqualified benefit to humanity. In 1956, however, two pilots, both having the clearest possible view of what air power could do, presented some disturbing images of air power, jaded images that suggested air power might not be the progressive enlightening force the public had been led to believe. Their images suggested that air power ate at the heart of the human spirit, and they presented these images through the same medium—popular culture—their fellow airmen had long used to propagate the image of air power's innate nobility. But Taylor and Salter did not directly attack air power as a danger to the world. That attack would not come for several more years.

PAST AND FUTURE WARS: TWO FRIGHTENING IMAGES

In 1957 and 1959 two novels appeared that further questioned the reputation of air power in the general public, and in each case the intensity of the challenge was escalated above that which had gone before. The damage was all the greater to the air power cause because both books enjoyed greater notoriety than the works of Taylor and Salter, but in each case the movie that issued from the books toned down the negative air power images. The first was Nevil Shute's *On the Beach,* and the second was John Hersey's *The War Lover.* Taken together, the novels and the movies illustrate that while some voices were willing to raise serious questions about the promises made for air power, others were still reluctant to press the point too far.

On the Beach is not, strictly speaking, an anti-air power book. More antinuclear in its message, it still presents some negative images of air power, especially if one remembers that air power advocates had made air power and strategic nuclear bombing synonymous and the fact that Shute had been a Royal Air Force pilot. More important, though, the book attacks nuclear war, and since bombers were still the only way to deliver nuclear bombs in 1957, any attack on nuclear war became an attack on air power's primary image. Between the novel and the film millions saw that negative image. The book was a bestseller, was serialized by over forty newspapers, and sold more than any other book on nuclear issues. The film was also a hit. It was the eighth most popular film of its year and grossed over $6 million. More people saw it than any other nuclear movie except *Strategic Air Command.* The popularity of the book and film posed such a clear threat to public support for America's reliance upon nuclear air power that the Eisenhower administration considered attempts to discredit the movie, and government experts attacked Shute's notion that bombs could wipe out all life on earth.[21]

The central premise of the novel is that a nuclear war involving several nations in the northern hemisphere has elevated atmospheric radioactivity so high that all animal life dies. The radioactivity is working its way south, and people in Australia monitor its spread as they await their doom. The plot revolves around how people deal with impending death. Much of the action is pedestrian as people strive to maintain normalcy while the clock ticks down, and there is the obligatory romantic interest, but this is what gives the book's antinuclear message its power. Shute reveals few glimpses of what happened in "the Short War," but it is not a reassuring view of air power.

The Short War, as the Australians call it, lasted only thirty-seven days, and during that time, according to scientific estimations, at least 4,700 nuclear weapons were detonated by all sides. The duration certainly complies with those air power advocates who predicted short wars in the nuclear air age, but the novel's outcome was hardly the happy results promised by airmen. The number of nuclear weapons and the worldwide tragedy that results also served as Shute's response to those air power advocates, such as de Seversky, who said thousands of nuclear weapons could be used against an enemy nation and still leave its society intact. The most negative image of air power, though, is the description of how the war started and how it was conducted. It began in the midst of an Arab-Israeli war when Albania dropped a bomb on Naples, Italy, and some unknown country bombed Tel Aviv. The United States and Britain intervened with demonstration flights over Cairo, and the Egyptians retaliated by launching six long-range Soviet bombers with Soviet markings against Washington, D.C., and seven against London. One got through to Washington and two to London. Most of the statesmen in both capitals were killed, which left decision-making to military leaders who launched a retaliatory strike against the Soviets, discovering only too late that it was a mistake. By then chaos reigned as critical decisions devolved to ever-lower echelons of military commands. In the midst of the Soviet-NATO nuclear war another one breaks out between China and the Soviet Union, and at one point near the end China was being run by an air force major.[22]

What the reader sees, therefore, is that air power has made nuclear war too easy to start, impossible to defend against, and because of its speed and destructive capability, impossible to control if unanticipated events occurred. In short, air power in the form of strategic nuclear bombing was too inflexible to serve as any rational form of defense or wage any rational form of warfare. If anybody missed this point, Shute drove it home explicitly. When one character suggests the problem was that nuclear weapons had become too cheap and readily available to even the smallest country, another character counters, "Another was the aeroplanes. . . . The Russians had been giving the Egyptians aeroplanes for years. So had Britain for that matter, and to Israel, and to Jordan. The big mistake was ever to have given them a long-range aeroplane."[23]

None of this background information made its way into the movie, though. When the question of *how* the war started arises the characters all say that no one knows the specific details. In response to the question of *who* started the war, though, the answer becomes philosophical and the guilt communal. Everyone started the war by relying on nuclear weapons. When an Australian scientist is asked who started the war he replies, "The war started when people accepted the idiotic principle that peace could be maintained by arranging to defend themselves with weapons they couldn't possibly use without committing suicide. Everybody had an atomic bomb and counter-bombs and counter-counter-bombs. The devices outgrew us, we couldn't control them. I know, I helped build them, God help me. Somewhere some poor bloke probably looked at a radar screen and thought he saw something, knew that if he hesitated one thousandth of a second his own country would be wiped off the map so, so he pushed the button, and, and the world went crazy."[24]

Thus the film emphasized an antinuclear message and only indirectly implicates air power in the disaster. By conveying its message in the powerful visual medium of the cinema, though, the film was quite effective. People were seen leaving theaters in tears, and others pointed to the effect the film had on shaping their views on nuclear issues.[25] Negative images of nuclear war in 1959 could not help but undermine public faith in nuclear air power even if air power was not directly incriminated in the unfolding tragedy.

A much more direct attack was launched against the image of air power in 1959, one that focused expressly on the image of strategic bombing. John Hersey, the author of *Hiroshima,* created an image with his novel *The War Lover* that might best be described as a photographic negative of the image presented in *Twelve O'clock High.* The parallels

12. In *On the Beach* a philosophical scientist (Fred Astaire, *left*) explains what he thinks really started the war: nuclear weapons were too powerful for humans to use rationally.

between the two novels are striking. The setting is the same, the B-17 bombing campaign against Germany in World War II. Both novels set the climactic scene in the same air battle, the bombing raid on *Schweinfurt*. Both even end with the hero's plane ditching in the English Channel. Each is also a psychological study of the men who fly the bombers, and each focuses on the impact of one pilot particularly. The title character of *The War Lover,* though, is not the heroic image of General Savage but instead a psychopathic B-17 pilot, Capt. Buzz Marrow, who like Savage is meant to embody air power itself. The second main character in *The War Lover,* the story's narrator, is Marrow's co-pilot, Lt. Charles Boman, a thoughtful humanist whose growing understanding of Marrow represents society's awakening awareness of air power's true nature. Literary critics see *The War Lover* as a tale of survival, of the humanist learning to survive in the face of all things that destroy life, but for the purposes of this study it is important to view the novel from the perspective of what Hersey saw as the destructive force threatening humanity.[26]

In the novel Marrow clearly, even repetitiously, emerges as a twisted psychotic obsessed with destruction, but his obsession is solely associated with airplanes. So repetitious and grotesque are Marrow's faults that clearly Hersey is trying to demystify the image of air power through this one character. As Laurence Goldstein has observed, "Hersey understands the dead-end of the aerial technician's vision" and that the novel offers "an alternative to Air Power as a dominant cultural myth." Throughout the novel Hersey depicts Marrow as the perfect flier. He flies by instinct, almost as if he and the airplane were one. But Hersey's portrayal has strong sexual overtones. When Marrow first sees the B-17 that has been assigned to his crew he says, "Some torso, huh? . . . Just seeing that thing makes me feel horny. I can't wait to get my hands on her." He later christens the ship *The Body,* but as Marrow later explains, the reference is not to a female body but to his own: "*The Body* . . . is my body. And when I fly I'm just pushing along with *The Body* sticking out in front of me. It's part of me." After their first bomb run, Marrow tells the bombardier that when he had heard the words "Bombs away!" he experienced the best feeling he ever had short of sex. Marrow's representation also conveys a perverse image of the tradition of Douhet long embedded in U.S. strategic bombing. In describing Marrow's reaction when looking at strike photos, Boman says he looks like "a man who has just taken a big slug of strong booze, when the throat burns and the first relaxing ecstasy shoots through the chest—with the difference that he seemed to be able to savor that first stab, prolong it, hold onto it." At another point Marrow says of a bomb run gone bad, "I didn't care where the f—[*sic*] we dropped those bombs as long as it was on a city. You can't win a war being squeamish. Chicken s—[*sic*] doesn't win wars. You have to kill *somebody.*"[27]

The character of Boman serves as an example to the American public as he slowly comes to realize Marrow's true nature. Through him Hersey hopes to enlighten the public about the real character of air power and how they should respond to it. At first Boman, like the popular imagination's response to aviation, idolized Marrow and put great trust in him to get the whole crew safely through their tour. Slowly, though, he comes to realize Marrow's skill and bravado are just a facade, that he is an empty shell and his love of war and thirst for destruction threaten to get them all killed. More important, Boman comes to realize Marrow threatens to squash all humanity, all that is good in Boman's spirit.[28] Helping him toward this realization are two supporting characters who are the first to figure out what Marrow really is.

The first is Lieutenant Lynch, an intellectual representing the rational response to air power. So much of the appeal of air power had been rational—it just seemed to make sense that if bombs were dropped on key enemy industries it had to have a magnified effect on their war-fighting capabilities. Lynch on several occasions indicates that, in his view, such thinking is only superficially efficient, that beneath the surface it is barbaric. On one occasion, for example, after Lynch explained to Boman the superficiality of Marrow's attitude toward war, Boman asks what brought up such an observation seemingly out of the blue, and Lynch replies: "it strikes me that in this century something awful has been let loose among the so-called civilized peoples, something primitive and barbaric. . . . If I can do my part in keeping this worst side of mankind in hand, I'll be satisfied, whatever happens to me." What happens to Lynch is that he is killed, and in describing the scene Hersey reinforces the intellectual theme by stressing repeatedly how his brains were splattered all over the cockpit.[29]

More important is Boman's British girlfriend Daphne. A sensitive, introspective woman, she first senses Marrow's spiritual emptiness and represents Hersey's response to air power's emotive appeal. Aviation had exerted a strong emotional hold on popular imagination, and in the postwar environment Cold War fears had turned that emotional attachment into a desperate faith that air power could save the United States from the Soviet threat. Through Daphne the reader learns that Marrow, and by extension air power, is just a thin veneer of strength and potency that in reality is a greater danger that perpetuates war. Part of Daphne's insight comes from the fact that she had known other fliers and that Marrow's sickness is not confined to him or to U.S. airmen. She had been engaged to an RAF bomber pilot who was so obsessed with killing and destroying that when his first tour ended he transitioned to night fighters so he could go on killing and destroying. "He was like a blood brother to [Marrow]. . . . As like as two peas in a pod."[30]

Daphne's most important insight, though, concerns what Hersey considers to be the true character and significance of men like Marrow. This comes most clearly when she describes to Boman her crucial exchange when Marrow tried to seduce her:

> I understood, then. It was from [the RAF pilot] that I understood. I said, "I know all about you."
> "What do you mean?" He halted, like a soldier challenged by a guard at night.

I said, "That feeling when the plane shudders because the bombs are falling out. . . . The feeling you have—you have that stirring down there, don't you Major?—when you start the bombing run."

Now he looked astonished. And you could see creeping into his face the first sign of caving in, the first realization that the world knew all about him. Six billion pairs of eyes staring at him. He was trembling. . . . He sat down. All the flame was out. He hung his head and squeezed his hands between his knees.

"You little bitch," he said. Then he put his hands over his face and began to shake out dry sobs.

Then speaking of men like Marrow and her RAF pilot she tells Boman, "I think we ought to worry . . . more about what's going to come of those who enjoy [war] too much. They're going to inflict their curse on the rest of us in peacetime. . . . They're going to pass it on to their children. We'll have other wars. . . . I don't know what we can do about these men, how

13. In the movie version of *The War Lover* Daphne (Shirley Anne Field, *left*), confronts bomber pilot Buzz (Steve McQueen, *right*) with her knowledge of what he truly is: a psychopathic killer.

you can educate this thing out of them, or stamp it out, or heal it out—or whether you can get rid of it at all." Boman's growing understanding of Marrow's true nature imparted to him by Lynch and Daphne changes his attitude toward flying and air power. At first he had loved flying and yearned to be, like Marrow, the perfect pilot. He even subscribed to the pilot mystique: "We had the illusion that between aviators there was a mysterious bond, that we were sharers of a secret. . . . It was much later, with Daphne's help, that I realized that . . . his dream in the sky and mine were far apart in kind." Concurrent with his awakening understanding of Marrow is his growing disillusionment with bombing. Early in the war he had "thought of the enemy as a pickle barrel," but the more he learns about the realities of bombing the more disturbed he gets. He starts having nightmares about his victims below, "a crowd of innocents with upturned Picasso faces," where he sees himself in the crowd as one of the victims and at the same time in the sky as one of the perpetrators. By his twenty-fourth mission he has come to associate the sounds of exploding bombs with the end of civilization. By the time of the great Schweinfurt raid Boman's twin crises—his new understanding of Marrow and his revulsion with bombing—have joined in his mind as one. "I had a despairing view of the world and of what men were making of it. . . . There would never be peace so long as there were men with Marrow's taint."[31]

The movie version of *The War Lover* came out in 1962, and by this time the cultural climate was more open to assaults on the image of air power, but still the studio held back somewhat. The film version was not altered as dramatically from its literary original as was *The Hunters,* but it lost much of Hersey's anti–air power tone. For example, the co-pilot, renamed Bolland in the film, does not struggle with the ethics of bombing. The image of bombing is also transformed from the tradition of Douhet found in the novel, to the tradition of ACTS, as when a strike photo reveals that one squadron bombing through broken overcast scored ten direct hits on the targeted submarine pens. Even *Twelve O'clock High* did not claim bombing was that accurate. The movie is mildly antiwar but not necessarily anti–air power, for the message is confined to one lone misfit who loves killing too much—the psychotic pilot, who in the movie is named Rickson. Daphne quickly sees that Rickson loves war like her former lover, but her lover is said to have been a paratrooper, not an RAF pilot; moreover, she does not suggest Rickson is part of a larger force perpetuating war. Everyone knows Rickson should be grounded, including Rickson's superiors, who appear competent and dedicated, but they reply with resignation that he is a great pilot who gets the job done and that wars need a few individuals who are willing to kill. In the end the crew is lucky to survive when Rickson's megalomania burns out and, rather than admit defeat, dies in a fiery crash, but the near-tragedy seems more the work of one crazed individual than a larger social pathology.[32]

By the beginning of the sixties, therefore, the novels *On the Beach* and especially *The War Lover* were reflective of a growing trend in popular culture challenging the pervasive image of air power and helping create doubts about what air power might mean for the future of the human race. The movie industry, as had been the case with *The Hunters,* had not gone as far in critiquing air power as the novels had, but these later movies did present images that might have been unheard of in the late forties or early fifties. The fact that this same mid- to late fifties period was also the period of magazine articles idolizing SAC and of movies like *Strategic Air Command* and *Bombers B-52* should serve as a reminder that not everyone agreed with the depictions of Salter and Hersey. Still, the works considered thus far in this chapter indicate that there was a segment in society questioning the air power image and finding an increasingly powerful voice in popular culture to present their doubts. This of course meant more people were exposed to an alternate image of air power than the one they had heard almost exclusively through the mid-fifties. This situation changed dramatically in the early sixties, however, as a series of books appeared that launched the most severe attacks on air power ever in postwar popular culture, and most of them were turned into movies that were as severe, if not more so, than the original novels.

A NEW VISION IN THE SKY:
EARLY SIXTIES AND AIR POWER AS THREAT

The increasing level of concern over air power from the mid-fifties on was a part of the larger growing concern over nuclear weapons. A survey taken only months after Sputnik showed that 75 percent of those surveyed felt hydrogen bombs would be used against the United States in any future world war and that such attacks would kill 70 percent of the population. Fueled by such sentiments, the antinuclear movement grew dramatically through the late fifties and peaked around 1963. Surveying titles listed in *Reader's Guide to Periodic Literature,* Spencer Weart reports that antinuclear articles rose dramatically in the late fifties and reached a peak in the early sixties. Because of the intimate connection between nuclear weapons and the dominant image of air power, the antinuclear movement became inextricably intertwined with the growing doubts about air power. The twin heightened concerns even became a factor in the 1964 presidential election, for many saw Republican candidate Barry Goldwater, a reserve air force general and staunch air power supporter, as "nuke-happy." Some pundits went so far as to twist his campaign slogan, "In Your Heart You Know He's Right," to "In Your Heart You Know He Might." It is not surprising then that the early sixties saw a significant escalation in the tenor and popularity of attacks on air power's image. The changing public attitude was not complete. The same survey that found such concern about nuclear war also found that 60 percent of those surveyed felt the United States should continue making nuclear weapons. Positive depictions such as *A Gathering of Eagles* continued, and some magazine articles still highlighted SAC's mission, but as we have seen, even these reflect a changed attitude. The new wave of anti–air power works appearing in popular culture, though, represents the highest level of anti–air power sentiment since the end of World War II and in turn helped erode public faith in air power still further.[33]

The first of the new generation of attacks came in 1961 with Joseph Heller's *Catch-22.* Using the media of farce and satire, Heller sets his Cold War concerns into the world of a B-25 bomb group in World War II Italy. If *The War Lover* is a photographic negative of *Twelve O'clock High, Catch-22* is its demented nightmare version. Heller had been a B-25 bombardier in Italy during World War II who flew sixty combat missions, but his novel is not a loony memoir of his experiences during the war. Writing during the Korean War, Heller said that he had in mind the next one, World War III, and he waited for a more favorable cultural climate before publishing his work. A complex and allegorical story, *Catch-22* has numerous levels of meaning, and as each level plumbs deeper meanings, the novel presents increasingly frightful images of air power. A bestseller, the book sold over five million copies by 1970 and was made into a disappointing movie that same year. The novel quickly became a classic in American literature, thus ensuring that Heller's images of air power would live on for generations.[34]

Even a superficial reading of *Catch-22* presents a highly damaging

14. The novel *Catch-22* depicts the air force as populated by a bunch of lunatics.

attack on air power's image. As opposed to the image of dedicated and trustworthy airmen put forward in the forties, Heller's AAF seems an insanely inverted world were the most despicable acts are perceived as normal. Group commander Colonel Cathcart has his men bomb an Italian village for no other reason than to obtain good strike photos, because he is convinced civilian targets yield the best bomb patterns. Mess officer Milo Minderbinder starts out trading government property on the black market and expands his operation until the entire AAF is integrated into his corporation, M&M Enterprises. His corporate motto, "What's good for M&M Enterprises is good for the country," is an obvious parody of former head of General Motors and Secretary of Defense Charles E. Wilson's "What's good for General Motors is good for the country" and ties air power into the image of the military-industrial complex. Mind-erbinder even makes a deal with the Luftwaffe to bomb his own airfield in exchange for buying his excess products.[35]

Other characters are no better. Some appear pathetic, as in squadron commander Major Major, who had been promoted to major from private simply because his name was Major, and who is so afraid of his responsibilities he jumps out his office window whenever anyone comes in. Others appear subject to bizarre delusions of grandeur, as with General Peckem, a Special Service Corps commander who schemes throughout the novel to bring every bomb group in the AAF under his command. Every character exhibits some form of abnormal behavior, but the harmless ones fall victim to the dangerous ones as they destroy everything standing in the way of their schemes. Indeed, the only "heroes" often appear craziest of all, but they are heroic because they escape. One pilot, Orr, ditches his plane on every mission as he practices for his escape and finally, after yet another ditching, paddles a life raft all the way to Sweden. Yossarian, the main character, fights the system throughout the novel, tries to avoid combat, and in the end, inspired by Orr's example, sets off on his own escape to Sweden.[36]

On a deeper level, though, air power appears as a malevolent evil. For one thing, as H. Bruce Franklin observes, Heller twists the oft-heard claim that bombing won World War II into an image that bombing won the war for the "enemy," the enemy being all the corrupt, conniving, and grasping people who use the air force for their own perverted ends.[37] This of course should not be taken literally but as a reflection of Heller's view, shared by other air power critics at the time, that in pushing their revolutionary image air power advocates had placed in preeminence a military mindset, strategic nuclear air power, that threatened to obliterate everything in the name of saving the United States from communism. Second, Heller dwells on the depersonalization airmen are inflicting on the world. Representative of this is the death of Snowden, a B-25 gunner killed on a bombing mission. Throughout the novel Heller reveals more and more of "Snowden's secret" as Yossarian comes to realize, along with the reader, the significance of how Snowden dies. When the details are finally revealed, Yossarian bandages the wrong wound only to find out too late that Snowden has been eviscerated by a piece of flak. The truth then dawns on him: all that is vital to humanity is pouring out of the wound inflicted by the new order just as Snowden's vital organs spill out of his wound onto the aircraft floor. "He gazed down despondently at the grim secret Snowden had spilled all over the messy floor. It was easy to read the message in his entrails. . . . The spirit gone, man is garbage. That was Snowden's secret."[38]

What salvation was there for Heller if air power was actually damnation? His picture was not reassuring. For Orr and Yossarian it was escape to a place far enough away that they were out of the airmen's reach. But this was only individual salvation, because the threat still remains. As Yossarian says when told that his running away may actually help the schemers succeed, "Let the bastards thrive, for all I care, since I can't do a thing to stop them but embarrass them by running away." For everyone else all Heller could suggest was to find the courage to persevere, like the chaplain who could not muster the courage even to believe in God but who, buoyed by Orr's example, finally resolves that he will persevere against the Colonel Cathcarts and the General Peckams.[39] Not everyone caught these higher levels of meaning, and the humor might have kept others from taking even the more obvious meanings too seriously, but *Catch-22* injected at least a note of cynicism into the popular culture image of air power, and in many people's imaginations it dealt a severe blow to the notion of air power as a redeeming force.

A more serious and dramatic attack on air power was the 1962 novel *Fail-Safe* written by two political science professors, Eugene Burdick and Harvey Wheeler. Published the same month of the Cuban Missile Crisis, the novel benefited from contemporary fears of nuclear war. It became not only a bestseller, selling over two million copies, it also was the only nuclear-related novel to make the top ten list of bestsellers for a given year. The novel remained on the *New York Times* bestsellers list for thirty-one weeks and was chosen as a Book-of-the-Month selection. In another reflection that changed attitudes toward air power were becoming more widespread, *Fail-Safe* was serialized by a magazine that had done so much to lionize SAC throughout the fifties, the *Saturday Evening Post*. The plot centered on SAC's Positive Control system, the so-called "Fail Safe" system, that relays orders for nuclear bombers to attack the Soviet Union. In the novel the system culminates in a "black box" in the bomber's cockpit. After the bombers are launched a light is supposed to illuminate, indicating to the crew that they are to strike their targets. Because of a faulty condenser in a "Fail-Safe Activating Mechanism" at SAC headquarters, an attack indication is sent to six bombers, one of which reaches and bombs Moscow. To atone for the disaster and avert a Soviet counterattack, the president, a thinly veiled representation of John F. Kennedy, orders a SAC bomber to bomb New York City.[40]

This is not a story like *On the Beach* where air power is only tangentially implicated in the disaster. For Burdick and Wheeler airmen are the disaster. They have been entrusted with machines of infinite destruction, and they have entrusted machines with determining when to unleash that destruction. More important, though, the airmen have themselves become machines, unthinking, unfeeling, incapable of understanding anything but the linear logic of nuclear warfare and its dictates. In describing the training SAC crewmembers undergo to ensure they attack or refrain from attacking as ordered, the authors state, "The tests, the indoctrinations, the training—all were designed to convert normal American boys into automatons." The most graphic image of the "automated" SAC crewmember is the commander of the group of attacking bombers, Colonel Grady: "He *was* an automated man. . . . There was only flesh and bone; there was no heart. There was intellect, but it lay inert, unmotivated by emotion." The culmination of the machine motif comes when Grady refuses to obey a direct order from the president, coming to him by radio, to abort his attack and return to base. Arguing that he is not authorized to accept orders once past his fail-safe point, Grady cannot adapt to situations outside his rigid training.[41]

The air force objected to the premise of the novel, but as with their reaction to Salter's *The Hunters,* the airmen did not seem to catch the deeper implications of the charges made about air power's inherent danger. Assuming the attack by Burdick and Wheeler was directed against SAC's system, the air force defended the system and missed entirely the message that air power itself was the danger along with the people who made up the system. A memorandum prepared by Col. A. A. Arnhym, special assistant to Gen. Thomas Power, commander of SAC, epitomizes the official air force response. Arnhym argued that the authors did not understand the system. There were no "black boxes" like the novel described, and any order to attack had to come from the president and was relayed verbally in an encoded message that then had to be checked by multiple members of every crew on every aircraft. Since the problems in the novel could not arise in SAC's system, the system *was* safe. Nowhere does Arnhym seem to recognize that the authors saw SAC's unthinking faith in the system—the very sort of faith he himself was evincing—as the real danger.[42]

Others came to the air force's defense, and while they focused on the reliability of SAC's people as well as its system, they flatly rejected any notion that America's nuclear air power could inadvertently or inappropriately bring the world to ruin. For example, in 1963 Donald Robinson wrote a reassuring article for *This Week Magazine* that *Reader's Digest* reprinted in its pages. Robinson related in great detail the various aspects of the Positive Control system, and with each facet he emphasized that no mistake was possible. He also outlined SAC's efforts to ensure no one "madman" or even several working together could possibly launch a nuclear attack. As with the SAC articles of the previous decade, Robinson showered SAC with fulsome praise, but his total dismissal of annihilation by mistake reinforced the image that airmen accepted the hair-triggered apocalypse Burdick and Wheeler attacked. Another major effort was Sy Bartlett's film, *A Gathering of Eagles*. Emanating from his conversations with LeMay that *Fail-Safe* would erode the public's faith in SAC, Bartlett showcased SAC's Positive Control system. Various scenes showing procedures in the SAC command post, activities in a wing command post, and crewmembers decoding alert messages reassured the public that SAC was in constant control of all its wings and aircraft at all times. But other images of airmen knocking themselves out for a commander they hate and ignoring the effects their mission had on their families actually reinforced the Burdick and Wheeler image of SAC automatons.[43]

In 1964 Max Youngstein turned *Fail-Safe* into a movie that followed the novel almost to the letter. Youngstein was a member of an antinuclear group known as the National Committee for a Sane Nuclear Policy, or SANE, that formed in the wake of Sputnik, and he actively pursued the film rights using his like-mindedness with the authors as a bargaining lever. Youngstein did add some features to the movie. One gripping, if implausible, scene added to the image of the SAC automaton. After Grady refuses to listen to the president's order to break off the attack, SAC headquarters puts Grady's wife on the radio, and she hysterically pleads with him to return, but even to this the unbending pilot turns a deaf ear. The other major addition comes after the president tells the premier that New York will be bombed. Reinforcing Youngstein's disarmament views, the president then lectures the premier that both countries built the system that caused the disaster and now both sides must work together to destroy that system.[44]

Not surprisingly, the air force refused to help with production, which hurt the film's visual authenticity. But since the book had raised such controversy over its less-than-authentic presentation, theatergoers could

15. Even a hysterical wife can't convince the automaton pilot to violate SAC's training in *Fail Safe*.

hardly have expected to see an accurate depiction of air force flying. And go to the theater they did: in its first three months the film grossed $1.8 million. Patrons undoubtedly went hoping for the same gripping drama found in the book, and they were not disappointed. If anything, the movie made some of the novel's most dramatic scenes even more powerful. As a result, millions more saw the disturbing images Burdick and Wheeler had presented about the nature of air power, and they saw them put forward in a very powerful way.[45]

Probably the most notorious chapter in this period's assault on the image of air power came with Stanley Kubrick's 1964 macabre masterpiece, *Dr. Strangelove*. The movie was based on an obscure novel written in 1958 by Peter George titled *Red Alert*. Kubrick, who had already made one antiwar movie with his 1957 film *Paths of Glory*, wanted to make a movie about inadvertent nuclear war, and in 1961 he discovered George's novel. Deciding that *Red Alert*'s serious and technical tone would work better as a nightmarish comedy, he enlisted George and screenwriter Terry Southern in his effort to create the script. The three also collaborated on a novelization of the film, also titled

Dr. Strangelove. The two novels, mere shadows of the film version, did not sell well. Thus in a reversal of the late-fifties trend where movies did not press their anti–air power message as far as the novels, the film version of *Dr. Strangelove* presented the strongest attack on airmen and was seen by more people. The film was the fourteenth-favorite film of 1964 and grossed over $4.4 million.[46]

Red Alert was a classic example of the modern version of the "future war" novel popular before World War I, and as such it conveys a generally positive view of air power. This is not surprising because George had been an RAF pilot.[47] In the preparedness tradition of "future war" literature, George's work saw the "missile gap" as the ultimate cause of the near-disaster of which he writes, because the general who launches the bombers to attack the Soviet Union does so to start a war before the first Soviet missiles are operational and while the United States has a temporary advantage. As opposed to the insane "Gen. Jack D. Ripper" of the film version, a quite sane General Quinten believes America's avowed policy never to launch a first strike leaves it at a disadvantage that, once the Soviets have large numbers of missiles, makes it only a matter of time before the United States is destroyed. For this reason, sensing a brief window of opportunity, he launches an attack that he hopes will be followed by an all-out U.S. nuclear attack. The positive view of air power is borne out not only by the image of bombers saving the United States from eventual destruction but also in the novel's depiction of U.S. air power as technically sophisticated and its airmen as motivated and highly proficient. The novel ends on a strong preparedness note. When the disaster is narrowly averted both the president and the Soviet ambassador agree peace will only be ensured once both sides are armed with ICBMs, because the threat of mutual annihilation will keep each side from launching an attack.[48]

Kubrick saw great potential for farce in George's novel, and in the process of reworking the story no institution or person escaped his attack, but air power clearly emerges as one of the chief culprits. The president, the Soviets, the army, and academic theorists all come in for a good roasting. Even the film's lone hero, RAF Group Capt. Lionel Mandrake, often appears to be a twit as when he ceremoniously comes to attention and orders General Ripper to give him the code that will allow him to recall the attacking bombers. Arguably, though, the characters most memorable for their lunacy are air force officers. Gen. Jack D. Ripper, clearly in the grips of advanced psycho-sexual delusions, orders his planes to attack in an effort to foil what he thinks is a communist plot to undermine the United States by polluting its people's "precious bodily fluids." Maj. "King" Kong, pilot of the only B-52 that fails to receive the recall signal, is a caricature of the uncouth but dedicated yokel who rides an atomic bomb out of the bomb bay whooping like a cowboy riding a bronco. Air force general and chairman of the Joint Chiefs of Staff "Buck" Turgidson, after learning of the Soviet "Doomsday Device," stakes out the strategy for the post-apocalyptic Cold War by declaring, "Mister President, we must not allow a mineshaft gap!"[49]

Like Burdick and Wheeler, Kubrick sees the danger of air power as more than just a failure in the system starting an unintended nuclear war. Once again the threat comes from the people who populate the air power world, but in *Dr. Strangelove* the problem is not that airmen are robots. Rather, airmen are so fanatically wedded to their faith in air power and their paranoid view of a world filled with threats only nuclear bombing can meet that they threaten to plunge the rest of humanity into

16. In an iconic scene from *Dr. Strangelove*, Major "King" Kong rides a nuclear weapon to his own—and the world's—destruction.

oblivion. Ripper's paranoia stems from his own sexual insecurities and conspiracy fixations, and his solution is to unleash the bombers. Kong so relishes the thought of nuclear warfare he personalizes it as "nuclear combat toe-to-toe with the Ruskies." Even after learning the "Dooms-day Device" will destroy all life on earth if so much as one bomber reaches its target, Turgidson cannot help reveling in the capability of the bomber to "always get through." Standing in the war room, his arms outstretched imitating a B-52 flying at low altitude, he exclaims, "If the pilot's good, see, I mean if he's really sharp, he can barrel that baby in so low, you ought to see it sometime, it's a sight! A big plane like a '52! Vroom! Its jet exhaust frying chickens in a barnyard!"

The worst part of the film's depiction of air power is that there is no escaping these mad airmen. Even the oft-touted virtue of the dedicated SAC personnel becomes a vice. When all efforts have failed to stop the bomber an onboard malfunction prevents it from releasing its weapons, and the world seems to have been granted a reprieve. The "heroic" dedication of Kong, though, solves the problem and the bomb is dropped on target. But even the looming death of all life on earth for the next hundred years does not shake airmen from their fixations. After hearing of the idea of setting up underground cities so a few thousand Americans can live on and repopulate the country Turgidson urges continued reliance on air power in the new era. Counseling the president he states, "I think we oughta look at this from the military point of view. I mean, supposing the Russkies stashed away some big bombs, see, and we didn't. When they come out in a hundred years they could take over."

As with *Fail-Safe,* the air force refused to help with the production, but that did not preclude Kubrick from making a movie that proved to be quite popular. Kubrick did request air force assistance, but the depiction of their Positive Control system precluded any cooperation. Undeterred, Kubrick used models for the flight scenes and his imagination for much of the rest. As with *Fail-Safe,* realistic depictions of air force procedures did not really matter, especially since Kubrick's medium was farce. The humorous element, though, may have backfired. The film was very popular. Two New York City theaters broke opening day attendance records, and long lines withstood freezing weather to see the film, but some observers claimed moviegoers were too busy laughing to take the movie as seriously as Kubrick had hoped. Still, its anti–air power images became fixed features in popular culture. To this day people ask

B-52 pilots if they keep a Stetson on board as Major Kong did. More important, however, *Dr. Strangelove,* along with *Fail-Safe,* marked the complete abandonment of any hesitancy in Hollywood to portray air power in a negative light.[50]

Yet another indication of changed attitudes in the early to mid-sixties is the writings of some erstwhile air power advocates. Some, like Sy Bartlett and Ira Eaker remained actively in the fight to the end. Others, though, while not necessarily becoming anti–air power, showed signs that their thinking about air power had changed along with society. One such example is William Bradford Huie. After a brief stint as a notorious air power advocate in the late forties, Huie almost completely dropped from the air power scene after the Revolt of the Admirals. He went on to other causes, most notably civil rights and military injustice. In this latter area he wrote *The Execution of Private Slovik* in 1954 and *The Hero of Iwo Jima* in 1962, but another work in 1964 indicates an evolving attitude toward air power. After World War II rumors circulated around the world that the pilot of the *Enola Gay,* Paul Tibbets, driven by remorse, had gone insane or had become an alcoholic or a criminal. Those rumors had their basis in the story of Maj. Claude Eatherly, a pilot in the 509th Composite Group, who had flown the Hiroshima weather ship that determined where the first atomic bomb would be dropped. After the war Eatherly sunk into a life of drinking and petty crime. He later claimed his role in the "crime of Hiroshima" led to his actions and that the air force was persecuting him to keep him from sharing his guilty conscience with the world. At Eatherly's request Huie wrote a book about the sordid affair.[51]

Given Huie's two most recent works on military injustice, one might have expected this story to be a denunciation of the air force. On the other hand, given Huie's past as a rabid air power advocate one might have expected it to be a whitewash of the air force. What he actually wrote was an even-handed account where he lets the facts speak for themselves. He denounces neither the air force nor Eatherly. Eatherly appears as a glory seeker who brought his troubles upon himself. Disappointed that he did not get to drop one of the atomic bombs, he later tried to glorify what role he did play. After the war he wanted to stay in the air force but was thrown out in 1947 for cheating on a training exam. He later signed on as a mercenary hired to smuggle guns into Cuba for a right-wing group plotting a coup, and then he was to bomb

Havana when the coup broke out. Caught and arrested for this crime, he spent some time in jail, after which he drifted in and out of various jobs and Veterans Administration mental health facilities where he was diagnosed with mild stress disorders. In what appeared to be both an effort to stay out of jail and another attempt to gain glory, he seized on the story of a guilt complex for his role in Hiroshima and played up to various antinuclear groups around the world.[52]

What makes *The Hiroshima Pilot* seem to be a transitional work is both its neutral stance toward the air force and works that Huie wrote later in his career beyond the period of this study. In 1975 he wrote *In the Hours of Night,* a novel based on events of the late forties. The story embodies Huie's belief late in life that after World War II the United States should have led the world toward universal disarmament under an international peacekeeping force. This is a sharp departure from the man who in 1949 warned the Soviet Union, "we can do to Russia, if Russia attacks us, what Rome did to Carthage." In forgetting that he had been one of the leading proponents of relying on a large nuclear-armed air force, Huie's disassociation from air power seems to have become complete. This new conviction remained with Huie for the rest of his life, for around the time of his death he told *Contemporary Authors* he was working on a story titled *How America Failed Mankind.* Huie called this story "the most important story of the twentieth century, for it is the story of the men who made the atomic bomb and who . . . worked desperately to prevent the bomb from becoming a national weapon."[53]

In another example, Fletcher Knebel, author of several pro–air power articles for *Look* during the fifties, gained considerable notoriety in 1962 with a novel that portrayed the air force, along with the rest of the military, in a very bad light. Earlier, in 1960, he had joined with Charles W. Bailey II in writing a journalistic history of the development and use of the atomic bomb in World War II, *No High Ground.* The account was an evenhanded treatment of the events and included a section examining the effects on the people of Hiroshima, but it also detailed some of the negative consequences of the bombing and the troubled consciences that had arisen since 1945. Its somber and uneasy ending reflected the growing divisions on the subject of nuclear weapons and air power within American society at the time of its publication.[54] Two years later Knebel and Bailey again collaborated on a book that was as big a shock to the military as *Fail-Safe* had been to the air force that same year. The book was *Seven Days in May*.

The story of an attempted military coup, *Seven Days in May* fell hard on all the services, but the leader of the plot is a charismatic air force general who is chairman of the Joint Chiefs of Staff. Gen. James Mattoon Scott, whom the authors describe as "a blend of the best of Eisenhower and MacArthur," was a fighter pilot and an ace in both World War II and Korea, and he had brilliantly commanded all air assets in a war in Iran against "the Communists" that had only recently ended unfavorably for the United States.[55] The prominent role played by Scott put the air force in the forefront for the onus in this novel, but air power in general got a black eye because of the main reason for the coup attempt. The president, Jordan Lyman, used international fallout from the war to gain an international nuclear disarmament treaty that the Pentagon had almost universally opposed. Worried the Soviets would cheat on the treaty and attack the United States once it had destroyed all its nuclear weapons, Scott orchestrates a plot involving virtually every branch of the military. Once again airmen see air power as the only solution to international tension and are willing to resort to the most extreme measures rather than relinquish their vision.

There are several redeeming military characters, chief among them being the hero of the story, Marine Col. "Jiggs" Casey who uncovers and helps foil the plot. Another military figure who remains loyal and plays a key role in bringing down the conspirators is a top air force leader General Rutkowski, commander of Air Defense Command. Also Admiral Palmer, Chief of Naval Operations, refuses to go along with the plot, but these characters cannot erase the stigma the novel placed on the entire military.

The book quickly became a bestseller, remaining on the bestseller list for 49 weeks, and was soon made into a movie. The movie version dropped the Iran War motif and made the disarmament treaty the sole reason for the plot. It also strengthened the role of Scott, played by Burt Lancaster. For example, unlike the novel, the plot is foiled only after Scott had already launched the coup. All of these changes made its anti–air power message stronger, though it retained its negative image of all the services. Columbia pursued the project and inquired about military support, and when they were turned down they appealed to the White House but to no avail. Columbia dropped the project and Paramount bought it but did not pursue Pentagon support. Instead, the director, John Frankenheimer, used subterfuge to film what few shots with military backgrounds he needed. Military help was not critical to the movie and the final product was none the worse for not having it, for the film proved quite popular at the box office.[56]

William Wister Haines, author of *Command Decision* and co-screenwriter for the film *One Minute to Zero,* did not change his views quite so much as had Huie and Knebel. In 1964 he published *Target,* a novel about World War II intelligence gathering. Haines returns to an old theme: the plot involves two intelligence analysts who go into recently liberated Strasbourg to gather information on a factory that had made parts for German aircraft. Their goal is to discover where the Germans were building the ME-262 jet fighter. Once again Haines credits allied bombing with gaining air superiority, and once again the new German jet threatens to regain air superiority and turn back the course of the war. There are occasional references to how effective U.S. bombing had been, as when the Strasbourg factory owner tells Brett, the U.S. agent, "Your bombing had almost extinguished piston plane manufacture on the eve of the Allied invasion and the Russian summer offensive." Again the factory owner states, "Your bombing last winter brought German aircraft production almost to a standstill."[57]

The novel, though, also betrays a strong undercurrent of cynicism toward precision bombing that stands in stark contrast to the depiction in *Command Decision*. In a London staff meeting, for example, the head of the target selection committee, frustrated at their inability to determine where the factories are located, comments, "don't take it too seriously. We've still got plenty of hospitals and orphanages to prang." And of Brett, Haines states, "he had read Douhet, Seversky and the propaganda of the Army Air Corps." An infantry colonel Brett encounters on his mission tells him, "Well, I'll hand it to you flyboys. . . . you'd won this war three times before I hit Africa and twice before I hit Marseille. . . . There's just one thing I would like to know: with all this victory through air power. . . . What are us dogfaces doing out here in the mud?" The most recurring theme, though, is frequent references to the heavy toll in casualties and property caused by inaccurate U.S. bombing. Throughout his journey across France Brett encounters the scars and animosity generated by "precision" bombing, especially in Strasbourg.[58]

Not all air power advocates drifted away; some clung to the "true faith," but they were invariably relegated to the margins as they sounded more out of step with society. Spaatz ended his literary career just as the new decade was starting. His last *Newsweek* column ran on Apr. 17, 1961, and he went out arguing for the B-70 bomber, a plane that was never built. The next year Ira Eaker began a column carried by the Copley News Service for eighteen years and offered to as many as 1,400 newspapers each week. Most of these newspapers, though, were small city and local papers. In 1963 Eaker claimed his column was carried by "over 31 papers weekly," thus Eaker seems more like "a voice crying in the wilderness." He continued supporting air power topics like the B-70, but he also wrote on anticommunism and pro-business topics, and with the growing antiwar and antimilitary sentiments in the wake of America's escalating involvement in Vietnam he often wrote to defend the war and the other services.[59] Eaker did get one shot at taking his air power message to the "big time." In 1963 Arthur Godfrey was a frequent guest host on the *Tonight Show,* and he and LeMay conspired to get Eaker on the show as a guest on June 6, 1963. Eaker sent ahead of his appearance a list of questions for Godfrey to ask him. The questions covered the range of topics from national defense to the state of bomber capability, so it appears he had ample opportunity to put his air power message before a large audience. Compared to the old days, though, this was a small opportunity.[60]

Clearly, the new tenor was not just a product of how air power was presented in popular culture—the audience had changed considerably as well. More and more, those who clung to the old message seemed out of touch with mainstream America. A good example of this change can be seen in Arthur Godfrey's fall from the pinnacle of his former stardom. Once one of the most popular and influential radio and television personalities, by the late fifties Godfrey's audience began to fade away. Network executives tried various recombinations of the old format but to no avail. Finally in 1958—the beginning of his last year as the host of his own television show—a CBS executive leveled with him about where they saw the source of his problem. "He had turned into a complete bore with only three topics of conversation": his farm, his airplane, and Curtis LeMay and the air force. Godfrey still had a loyal following, as his orchestrating support for a military pay raise that same year illustrates, but it was a dwindling segment of the nation.[61]

Another example of air power advocacy out of step with the United States was Nathan Twining. After retiring as chairman of the Joint Chiefs of Staff in 1960 Twining wrote "a hard look at U.S. military policy and strategy," as the subtitle of his *Neither Liberty nor Safety,* published in 1966, proclaimed. An analysis of U.S. military and diplomatic strategy throughout the Cold War, Twining's views might have been mainstream in the early fifties, but in the changed atmosphere of the mid-sixties they were extremist. Pointing to a "fear psychosis" desperate to believe the "Russian Bear had become a fun-loving, happily domesticated beast," Twining attempted to rally the American public to remain staunch in the face of nuclear dangers. Speaking in favor of strategic bombing, for example, he said opposition to it was prompted by "an instinctive moral objection to . . . the subjugation of civilian populations to the hazards of war" and then mocked such morality for preferring that the hazard be borne by young men in uniform on a far-off battlefield.[62]

Curtis LeMay also remained true to the air power gospel, but here too the one-time paragon of U.S. determination became a symbol of the reactionary fringe. Like Twining, LeMay tried to get Americans to "buck-up" and accept the sacrifices of a hard line in the fight against global communism. In his 1965 memoirs, for example, he offered his oft-quoted formula for ending the war in Vietnam: "My solution to the problem would be to tell them frankly that they've got to draw in their horns and stop their aggression, or we're going to bomb them back into the Stone Age." Such sentiments were out of step with the predominant views, however, and he drifted further into the outfield of political and military debates. No better example of this exists than the fact that the man who was once lauded as America's best hope for peace and security ended up as the running mate of an extremist third party candidate, George Wallace, in the 1968 presidential elections.[63]

By 1964, then, cultural views toward air power had gone through a dramatic evolution. The air power advocates' popular culture campaign had not come to a complete halt, but it was a mere shadow of its former self. Some advocates had changed their tone considerably, while others had drifted away to other pursuits. More important, those who remained found their message relegated to the outskirts of the new cultural debate. Where once air power advocates had promised quick, easy, and painless victory through air power, now they lectured Americans on the need to accept greater sacrifices and suffering. Their message had not really changed in its fundamental premise, though. What had changed was society's response to their message. Fears of nuclear devastation had risen to new heights since 1957, and this prompted many to reexamine their faith in air power. When they did so they found a long line of critics raising increasingly sharp attacks on the image of air power, and the old faith could not stand up under the assault. With the old faith gone and new fears of nuclear war rising, the exhortations of LeMay and Twining suddenly sounded like something out of *Catch-22*—or worse, *Dr. Strangelove*.

CHAPTER 7

Conclusion

Air power's popular culture crusade was a unique and curious chapter in U.S. military and cultural history. On one level air power was the result of an invention, the airplane. On another level, though, it was the product of widespread fascination with aviation and a faith stemming from this fascination that exhibited characteristics of religious devotion. It seems no coincidence that air power's era of domination in the U.S. military structure began during a period of enchantment with aviation and in an atmosphere of grave international danger. The wondrous new invention was going to save the nation. Likewise, the erosion of faith in salvation through air power seemed to coincide with the fading cultural fixation with the airplane as flying became commonplace, and new wonders, like space travel, captured the public's imagination. In the interim, though, air power advocates reflected and exploited the love affair with the airplane in their effort to convert the nation to the gospel of air power.

Postwar air power advocates had come a long way since the interwar era in winning widespread public support for their cause. Taking advantage of both the cultural fascination with aviation and the unprecedented public support for air power generated by World War II, they had used popular culture as a prominent part of their campaign to "make America an air power nation." Following a trail blazed by Billy Mitchell and others, they shaped their faith into a message that extolled air power's revolutionary potential and promised not only salvation from the dangers of war but also a better tomorrow through air power. Placing their message in those forms of mass media that many Americans turned to for entertainment and diversion, air power advocates made their image of air power a major part of the popular imagination's conception of security in a time of danger. Outside factors, especially the fear of communist aggression and Soviet attack, aided air power advocates in gaining support for their cause, and thus they crafted their popular culture campaign to present air power, specifically strategic nuclear bombing, as the best defense against the communist threat. When other factors, such as the Korean War and interservice rivalry, challenged the image they had hoped to instill in the public consciousness, air power advocates outmaneuvered the challenges and kept their image relatively intact. For a brief time that image, embodied by SAC, dominated the public's notion of national defense and security.

In the last half of the fifties, though, other challenges arose that weakened public faith in the air power advocates' image. New critics arose and cultural attitudes changed. Aviation was no longer the new and fascinating image it once had been, and from the mid-fifties on, writers emerged who projected a jaundiced view of air power. The change had only just begun, though, and these few early attacks were mild compared to later works. Significantly, when such works were turned into major motion pictures with big-name stars, the anti–air power message was softened considerably. Air power advocates also confused the institutional well-being of the air force with advancing their air power cause. The biggest challenge, though, was the awakening fear of nuclear devastation during the late fifties, a fear that rose sharply in the early sixties. Sputnik had shocked the nation in 1957, but so had the Soviets' explosion of an atomic bomb in 1949. Unlike the earlier crisis, however, many rejected the naive faith in air power and began to see air power itself as part of the larger problem. Recognizing the connection between public faith in air power and acceptance of nuclear warfare, critics of nuclear weapons advanced their cause through works in popular culture that sought to undermine that faith by presenting air power and airmen as grave threats. Once again, these attacks on air power built slowly. The 1957 novel *On the Beach* implicated air power only indirectly, and the 1959 film said even less. The works of the early sixties, though, *Dr. Strangelove, Fail-Safe,* and *Catch-22,* for example, took on the image of air power directly. These new attacks were unique both because they would have been unheard of ten or fifteen years earlier and because they were so popular.

Between declining fascination with aviation and recurring images of the "mad bomber," the American public rapidly lost that curious kind of faith that seemed to invest air power with almost mystical properties. The technological messianism that had led many to look to nuclear bombers for salvation from the threat of nuclear devastation was exorcized, and public imagination began to see the nuclear bomber for what it was: a brutal weapon that should be reserved for only the most brutal necessity. No longer did magazine articles proclaim in effusive prose that nuclear bombers were the answer to every military conflict. Even the 1963 film, *A Gathering of Eagles,* the last of the "SAC Trilogy," lacked most of the old images of revolutionary air power. Similarly, there was a new and more realistic attitude toward air power in popular imagination. People outside the air force community no longer spoke of "Air Power," as if it were bigger than the sum of its parts. Instead they saw it as part of a larger U.S. military structure. The general public did not turn against air power completely. In a sense they accepted it as a facet of modern warfare, and the air force enjoyed generally as much support as did the army and the navy. An indication of the new public attitude is how outrageous and out of step with the times LeMay's proposed solution to the Vietnam dilemma sounded in 1965 and how naive it sounds today.

Technological messianism was not purged from the U.S. consciousness, though, for it seems Americans still look to technology, and increasingly science, for salvation from complex problems. Such expectations need a simple-minded fascination with the technology in question, though, and as aviation became less fascinating and people learned more about the complex problems of nuclear air power, images of deliverance could no longer be maintained. More and more from the late fifties on, technological messianism moved on to other wonders, particularly space flight in the sixties and perhaps computers today. Similarly, enthusiasm for flying has not disappeared entirely. Crowds still flock to air shows where aerial demonstration teams like the air force's Thunderbirds and the navy's Blue Angels are a big hit, and every year thousands join the air force hoping for a chance to become pilots. The big difference since the early sixties is that few outside air power circles seriously believe air power can single-handedly handle any military situation that arises. Aviation still retains vestiges of its old romantic imagery in popular culture today, but generally such images have reverted to a simpler time, hence the recurring romantic motif of the biplane and the World War I ace.

Thus on the eve of America's deepening involvement in the war in Vietnam there was a significant gulf between what the air force and air power advocates believed air power could do and what the public was willing to support. Many in the air force in 1965 agreed with LeMay's strategy for winning the war. Latter-day air power advocates point to the massive bombing raids on Hanoi during the Linebacker II operation in December 1972, which hastened the signing of the peace accord in early 1973, as a vindication of modern air power. In fact, to this day there is a strong belief among many that the Linebacker II raids ended the war, and that if Johnson had unleashed the bombers in 1965 the way Nixon had in 1972, the same results would have been obtained sooner.[1] Few Americans would have supported such a policy, though. Long before 1972, air power had become a widespread symbol of the excessive and counterproductive means being used to prosecute the war. For many Americans air power in Vietnam came to symbolize bombed-out villages, widespread defoliation, and jets fruitlessly hunting lone snipers hidden in triple-canopy jungles, and the public generally found these images disturbing. Clearly the public had widely repudiated the sentiments expressed in 1955 by Frank Harvey when he extolled the image of bombers using nuclear weapons to stamp out brushfire wars in all corners of the globe.[2]

Air power's previous image as the epitome of high technology warfare actually came back to haunt air power advocates during the Vietnam War. Hard pressed to explain why the world's greatest air force could not defeat an underdeveloped country like North Vietnam after they had proclaimed for so many decades that air power could win any war, all air power advocates could do was complain that they were not allowed to conduct the air war the way they wanted, and they called for more bombing. With wide segments of the public already questioning the level of aerial destruction, claims that air power could only work against a minor power like North Vietnam if the bombing effort was escalated did not enhance the public's faith in air power. To many Americans it seemed this high technology weapon could only win by sinking to uncivilized levels of barbarism.

The use of air power in Vietnam was hardly the only controversial element of that war, and the air force was not the only government agency drawing fire from those who opposed the war effort. Still, on the eve of America's most controversial war, air power had experienced a rapid fall from grace in the eyes of the American public. Furthermore, air power advocates had not yet adjusted to the new public attitudes toward their cause or their favored methods. The gulf between the airmen and the American public would widen during the war and plunge the image of air power to its lowest point in public esteem since the 1930s. That image would slowly regain ground, but it never approached the level of public trust enjoyed in the mid-fifties. Even the dramatic results of the air campaign during the Gulf War and the sight of precision-guided munitions striking with inerrant accuracy could not awaken the old faith in the preeminence of air power. Significantly, works in popular culture since Vietnam that portray air power in a positive light, such as Tom Clancy's novels, show air power serving in a crucial but supporting role alongside the army and navy.

America's fixation with air power after World War II was a passing phenomenon, and its reoccurrence seems hard to imagine. The key ingredient in the cultural recipe leading to faith in air power—a society so fascinated with the sudden reality of human flight as to ascribe messianic properties to the airplane—was a simplistic and innocent public consciousness that will never come again. Familiarity has not bred contempt toward the airplane, but it has bred nonchalance. Americans are so far removed from that naive frame of mind today it seems hard to believe people once expected salvation from a mere machine. Reading some of the exhortations of air power advocates from the late forties or the general interest magazine articles about SAC from the mid-fifties generates feelings of amusement today, and even some measure of embarrassment. Still, to understand the rise of air power after World War II to a level of dominance in America's military structure, one must understand the cultural attachment to air power, how air power advocates reflected, fostered, and shaped that attachment, and how they used it to build an air power empire based on strategic nuclear bombing.

In a larger sense, though, the postwar air power phenomenon also illustrates the importance of images in shaping any society's attitudes toward the military and toward warfare in general. Torn between conflicting emotions, fearing war but fearing attack, suspicious of militarism but venerating its heroes, every society has complex images of war and its own military structure that shape its attitudes toward military policy. Even the most authoritarian government cannot ignore these public attitudes completely. Recognizing this, every branch of America's military structure has long conducted its own campaign to influence public opinion and shape its own image in popular imagination. Invariably these campaigns have included works placed in popular culture by each branch's advocates, and these campaigns would make fruitful areas of study for future historians. No branch, however, has enjoyed the success air power advocates enjoyed after World War II. Not only did they successfully tap the power of America's faith in the airplane and use that power to help lead the air force to a premier position in national defense, they also helped convince average Americans, for a short time at least, that they should rely on that which they feared most—nuclear air power. This then is the ultimate testimony to the power of images to shape popular attitudes toward warfare. Fearing nuclear attack, Americans might have shunned nuclear weapons outright or put their faith in more direct forms of protection such as air defense. Instead, thanks in large part to the long parade of images advanced by air power advocates, they put inordinate faith in the very instrument that threatened their destruction, hoping desperately that Soviet fear would mirror their own and maintain the balance of terror. This bizarre situation is matched only by the bizarre images in popular culture that helped to shape that faith.

Notes

CHAPTER 1. INTRODUCTION

1. Joseph J. Corn, *Winged Gospel*; for another view of America's response to aviation see Michael Paris, *From the Wright Brothers to Top Gun*, particularly 108–14. Corn's pioneering work inspired similar studies of aviation's impact on popular culture in other industrialized nations. See, for example, Peter Fritzsche, *A Nation of Fliers*, Michael Paris, *Winged Warfare*, and Robert Wohl, *Passion for Wings*.

2. While several works dealing with the American public's response to human flight touch on the military uses of aviation, their primary focus is on aviation in general, not the development of air power. This is a good place to clarify the two terms. Aviation generally refers to civilian and commercial uses as opposed to military uses, and that is how it will be used in this study. While some air power advocates, especially in the period covered by this study, used the term "air power" to mean all things related to flying, including aircraft manufacturing and commercial airliners, today most people use "air power" to mean military uses of aviation. There is even some controversy surrounding the spelling of "air power." Some insist that it be spelled as one word; this was originally envisioned as a way to graphically reflect air power's revolutionary nature. Today this is confined primarily to the U.S. Air Force's Air University community and those influenced by it, though the practice has also spread to some degree to other nations' air forces. Unless otherwise indicated, for this study I will use the term "air power" to refer to the military applications of flying.

3. Michael S. Sherry, *Rise of American Air Power*.

4. Much has been written on the development of American air power, but the best overall works are Sherry, *Rise of American Air Power*; Robert Frank Futrell, *Ideas, Concepts, Doctrine*; and Walter Moody, *Building a Strategic Air Force*. Two exceptions to the lack of study of American air power and popular culture are Sherry, *Rise of American Air Power*, who explores popular culture themes up through World War II, and to a lesser extent, Corn, *Winged Gospel*, who gives only limited attention to military aviation; neither explores the full range of air power and popular culture, and each deals primarily with the period up to 1945.

5. Paris, *From the Wright Brothers to Top Gun,* 6–8, and especially chapters 5, 6, and 7; H. Bruce Franklin, *War Stars,* particularly chapter 2 for the air power popular culture campaign. Laurence Goldstein, *Flying Machine.*
6. Marshall Andrews, *Disaster through Air Power,* xi–xiii, 4, 7.
7. Corn, *Winged Gospel,* chapter 3.
8. Ibid., 138.

CHAPTER 2. IN THE BEGINNING

1. Quoted in Goldstein, *Flying Machine,* 24–30; quote, 30.
2. Benjamin Franklin to Jan Ingenhousz, Jan. 16, 1784, quoted in Franklin, *War Stars,* 81.
3. Simon Newcomb, *His Wisdom the Defender,* 5–11, 45–51, 59–64, 192–97, 295–98, 316–21, 326–29; Franklin, *War Stars,* 48.
4. S. W. Odell, *The Last War: Or, the Triumph of the English Tongue* (Chicago: Charles H. Kerr, 1898); for Odell's depiction of the long-term struggle between progressivism and reactionism symbolized by the showdown between the Anglo-American alliance and Russia see, for example, 66–75; for a depiction of airships and U.S. technology and ingenuity helping to turn the tide of the climactic battle see 151–53.
5. I. F. Clarke, *Voices Prophesying War,* 9–14, 59–61, 111–12.
6. H. G. Wells, *War in the Air,* 201–204, 205, 210–20, 238–41, 351, 376–79. H. G. Wells, *World Set Free,* 51–54, 171–74, 185–89, 196–97.
7. Many good works have examined the air war in World War I, but two excellent overviews are Lee Kennett, *First Air War,* and John Howard Morrow, *Great War in the Air.* The best work on how World War I as a whole affected Western culture is Paul Fussell, *Great War and Modern Memory.*
8. The best biography of Billy Mitchell, though dated, is still Alfred F. Hurley, *Billy Mitchell;* a more recent but narrower-focused treatment can be found in Douglas Waller, *A Question of Loyalty;* for another view on Mitchell's role in the air power debates see Sherry, *Rise of American Air Power,* particularly chapters 2 and 3.
9. Much has been written about the cult of the air ace; for concise, perceptive analyses see: Kennett, *First Air War,* especially chapter 9, and Goldstein, *Flying Machine,* chapter 5. Goldstein has also noted that when it comes to World War I literature, the great critics, most notably Paul Fussell, have completely ignored literature on the air war; see 75, 78–79.
10. Goldstein, *Flying Machine,* chapter 6; Corn, *Winged Gospel,* 18–25; Charles A. Lindbergh, *Spirit of St. Louis,* 503–30; Donald E. Keyhoe, "Seeing America With Lindbergh," *National Geographic Magazine,* January 1928.
11. Paris, *From the Wright Brothers to Top Gun,* 35.
12. Ibid., 37.

13. Stephen Pendo, *Aviation in the Cinema*, 85; James H. Farmer, *Celluloid Wings*, 47.

14. Pendo, *Aviation in the Cinema*, 97–99.

15. The evolution of air power theories and doctrine has received considerable scholarly investigation. A short list of good works includes: Sherry, *Rise of American Air Power*, particularly chapters 2 and 3; Kennett, *History of Strategic Bombing*; Thomas H. Greer, *Development of Air Doctrine*; and Futrell, *Ideas, Concepts, Doctrine*, particularly chapters 2 and 3.

16. Frank P. Donnini, "Douhet, Caproni, and Early Air Power," *Air Power Historian* (Summer 1990): 49; Giulio Douhet, *The Command of the Air*, vii–viii, 20–23.

17. Hurley, *Billy Mitchell*, 25–26; Kennett, *History of Strategic Bombing*, 51, 75–76; B. H. Liddell Hart, *Paris*; Greer, *Development of Air Doctrine*, 19–20.

18. Hurley, *Billy Mitchell*, 20–21, 22–25, 31–32, 75; for difficulty in determining the source and timing of Mitchell's ideas, see especially 168–69; Donnini, "Douhet, Caproni," 50; Greer, *Development of Air Doctrine*, 17.

19. Greer, *Development of Air Doctrine*, 44–45.

20. See particularly William Mitchell, "Aircraft Dominate Seacraft," *Saturday Evening Post*, Jan. 24, 1925, for details of bombing tests, and William Mitchell, "How Should We Organize Our National Air Power?" *Saturday Evening Post*, Mar. 14, 1925, 6, for conclusions.

21. William Mitchell, "Aeronautical Era," *Saturday Evening Post*, Dec. 20, 1924, 3–4; William Mitchell, *Winged Defense*, 126–27.

22. Hurley, *Billy Mitchell*, 101–105.

23. Ibid., 104–109; H. H. Arnold, *Global Mission*, 119–22.

24. Hurley, *Billy Mitchell*, 110–12; William Mitchell, "Look Out Below!" *Collier's*, Apr. 21, 1928, 8–9, 42.

25. Hurley, *Billy Mitchell*, 120, 123, 131–35; William Mitchell, *Skyways*.

26. Arnold, *Global Mission*, 120–22; Edgar F. Puryear, *Stars in Flight*, 18–19; Futrell, *Ideas, Concepts, Doctrine*, 51–53.

27. Futrell, *Ideas, Concepts, Doctrine*, 62.

28. Robert T. Finney, *History of the Air Corps Tactical School*, 8–9, 20–21, 46, 56–58, 102; Greer, *Development of Air Doctrine*, 47–49; Wesley Frank Craven and James Lea Cate, *The Army Air Forces in World War II*, vol. 1, *Plans and Early Operations, January 1939 to August 1942*, 45–46. One notable exception to this bomber emphasis in the ACTS is Claire Chennault's belief that fighters could stop any bombing attack; his views on bomber, as well as fighter, close air support, and interdiction strategy and doctrine were largely ignored; see Haywood S. Hansell Jr., *The Air Plan that Defeated Hitler*, 18–22, and Greer, *Development of Air Doctrine*, 36–38, 39–40, 60–67.

29. Finney, *History of the Air Corps Tactical School*, 42–43, 56–59, 115–20;

Hansell, *Air Plan that Defeated Hitler,* 16–18, 33–34, 40–41, 46; Hansell was one of the key architects developing daylight precision bombing before World War II and implementing it during the war, and this autobiographical work gives tremendous insight into the thinking and dynamics of those who developed the theory. As the title suggests, however, Hansell has a vested interest in garnering credit for "his" theory.

30. George H. Gallup, *The Gallup Poll: Public Opinion 1935–1971, Volume I, 1935–1948* (New York: Random House, 1972): 6–7, 84, 131–32, 189–90.

31. Sherry, *Rise of American Air Power,* xi.

32. The nature of World War II air power and public reaction to the air war are themes running throughout such works as Sherry, *Rise of American Air Power,* Ronald Schaffer, *Wings of Judgment,* Conrad C. Crane, *Bombs, Cities, and Civilians,* and to a lesser extent, John W. Dower, *War without Mercy.*

33. Sherry's photo montage between pages 146 and 147 includes several representative examples of such ads, but the full effect can only be gained by perusing the magazines themselves.

34. Gallup, *Gallup Poll,* 293, 346–47, 399.

35. One example of wartime air force efforts to exploit its success for the postwar environment is Perry McCoy Smith, *Air Force Plans for Peace.*

36. H. H. Arnold and Ira C. Eaker, *Winged Warfare,* 133–39.

37. Hansell, *Air Plan that Defeated Hitler,* chapter 4; Craven and Cate, *Army Air Forces,* 115–16, 146–50; Futrell, *Ideas, Concepts, Doctrine,* 108–112; and James C. Gaston, *Planning the American Air War* all give detailed accounts of the formulation and acceptance of AWPD-1.

38. Lawrence Howard Suid, ed., *Air Force,* 14–15, 17–20; this work is a reprint of the screenplay with an analytical and historical introduction.

39. Ibid., 158–60, 207–11, 214–16.

40. Phillip S. Meilinger, "Proselytiser and Prophet: Alexander P. de Seversky and American Airpower," in John Gooch, ed., *Airpower,* 9–12.

41. Ibid., 12–14.

42. Alexander P. de Seversky, *Victory Through Air Power,* see for example 335–38.

43. Ibid., 101–102, 120.

44. Meilinger, "Proselytiser," 20.

45. Walt Disney, prod., *Victory Through Air Power* (Hollywood: Walt Disney Pictures, 1943)

46. Meilinger, "Proselytiser," 20.

47. Russell E. Lee, "Impact of *Victory Through Air Power* Part I: The Army Air Forces' Response," *Air Power History* 40 (Summer 1993): 3–13, and Russell E. Lee, "Impact of *Victory Through Air Power* Part II: The Navy Response," *Air Power History* 40 (Fall 1993): 22, 28–29.

48. See, for example, Schaffer, *Wings of Judgment,* 69–70, 94, and 98–100.

49. A good illustration of how American popular passions favored brutal war measures is Dower, *War without Mercy*.

50. Sherry, *Rise of American Air Power*, "Bombing in the American Imagination: A Visual Essay," unpaginated photo montage between pages 146 and 147; David O. Woodbury, "Tokyo Calling Cards," *Collier's*, Apr. 14, 1945, 44, 58; Schaffer, *Wings of Judgment*, 154.

51. *The Saturday Evening Post Aviation Survey* (Philadelphia: Curtis Publishing, 1946): 14–15.

CHAPTER 3. THE AIR POWER REVOLUTION

1. Sarita Robinson, Bertha Joel, and Mary Keyes, eds., *Reader's Guide to Periodical Literature*, vol. 15, May 1945–April 1947 (New York: H. W. Wilson, 1947), 25.

2. The AAF reached a peak strength of 2,411,294 officers and enlisted members in 243 groups and 2,252 installations around the world during the war and purchased over 231,000 aircraft; Craven and Cate, *Army Air Forces in World War II*, vol. 7, *Services around the World*, 566, 569; Irving Brinton Holly Jr., *Buying Aircraft*, 548.

3. Many scholars have studied and debated the effectiveness of America's World War II strategic bombing campaign, but four works that span the spectrum of that debate are: Sherry, *Rise of American Air Power*; Schaffer, *Wings of Judgment*; Crane, *Bombs, Cities, and Civilians*; and David MacIsaac, *Strategic Bombing in World War Two*.

4. An excellent example of the effects of another transportation revolution is Wolfgang Schivelbusch, *Railway Journey*, which examines the cultural impact of railroads on U.S. and European society.

5. See, for example, Rhoda Hero Dunn, "The Aeronauts," *Atlantic Monthly*, May 1909, 617.

6. See, for example, Mitchell, "Look out Below!" 8–9, 41–42.

7. A good survey of "air-age globalism," its origins, and its impact on World War II is Alan K. Henrikson, "Maps, Globes, and the 'Cold War,'" *Special Libraries* (Oct./Nov. 1974): 445–54. See also his later expansions in "The Map as an 'Idea': The Role of Cartographic Imagery during the Second World War," *American Cartographer* 2, no. 1, 19–53, and "America's Changing Place in the World: From 'Periphery' to 'Centre,'" in *Centre and Periphery: Spatial Variation in Politics*, ed. Jean Gottman (London: Sage Publications, 1980).

8. Leonard O. Packard, Bruce Overton, and Ben D. Wood, *Our Air-Age World*, frontispiece, 9. The fact that an entire geography book would be written from the "air age" perspective is another indication of the wide acceptance of air power's "revolutionary world view."

9. William Bradford Huie, "How the Next War Will Be Fought," *American*

Mercury, Apr. 1946, 432–33; W. B. Courtney, "Will Russia Rule the Air?" *Collier's,* Jan. 25, 1947, 12–13, 61, and Feb. 1, 1947, 16, 67, 69.

10. Carl A. Spaatz, "Air Power in the Atomic Age," *Collier's,* Dec. 8, 1945, 11.

11. June 18, 1946, radio speech, Eaker Papers, Box II: 108, Speeches, 1946–49 folder, Library of Congress (hereafter LOC), emphasis in original.

12. Alexander P. de Seversky, "We're Preparing for the Wrong War," *Look,* Dec. 9, 1947; and Alexander P. de Seversky, *Air Power,* 307–13.

13. William V. Pratt, "Air Power in the Arctic: The Crux of Our Defense," *Newsweek,* Mar. 25, 1946, 39. For a good treatment of Pratt's career as an open-minded naval reformer see Gerald E. Wheeler, *Admiral William Veazie Pratt.*

14. John Kord Lagemann, "The Handwriting on the Ice," *Collier's,* Nov. 16, 1946, 18–19, 39–42, emphasis in original.

15. "War Can Come; Will We Be Ready?" *Life,* Feb. 27, 1950, 21–22.

16. Corn, *Winged Gospel,* see particularly chapter six.

17. Air Power League, *The Bulletin of the Air Power League,* Aug. 1945, unpaginated, last page; Air Power League, *Report to Members,* 4.

18. "Air-Age Babes in Toyland," *Collier's,* Aug. 27, 1949, 74; for National Air Council see memoranda, May 17, 1951, from James C. Evans to Mr. Lennartson and to Mr. Burden, and letter, undated, author unknown, to C. S. Jones, president, National Air Council, all in reel 33770, frames 239–43, Air Force Historical Research Agency, Maxwell AFB, Ala., hereafter cited as AFHRA.

19. H. H. Arnold, "If War Comes Again," *New York Times Magazine,* Nov. 18, 1945, 39; H. H. Arnold, "Air Power for Peace," *National Geographic Magazine,* Feb. 1946, 193; American Legion, *Keep America Strong in the Air,* unpaginated, fourth page; advertisement for North American Aviation, "How Do You Rate in the AIR-Q Test?" *Collier's,* Sept. 8, 1945, 54.

20. Much has been written on the interwar drive for an independent air force. The best place to start is Futrell, *Ideas, Concepts, Doctrine,* particularly chapters 2 and 3. A wide range of perspectives can be found in Greer, *Development of Air Doctrine;* Sherry, *Rise of American Air Power;* and Copp, *A Few Great Captains.*

21. Less has been written on the subject of postwar efforts to secure an independent air force. Futrell, *Ideas, Concepts, Doctrine,* and Herman S. Wolk, *Planning and Organizing the Postwar Air Force, 1943–1947* (Washington, D.C.: Office of Air Force History, 1984).

22. On the subject of military unification see Jeffery M. Dorwart, *Eberstadt and Forrestal,* Michael S. Sherry, *Preparing for the Next War,* and Demetrios Caraley, *Politics of Military Unification.*

23. Arnold, "If War Comes Again," 39.

24. Beirne Lay Jr., "Why Army, Navy and Air Must Combine at the Top,"

Reader's Digest, Nov. 1945, 29, 32, emphasis in original; for army position on military unification see Dorwart, *Eberstadt and Forrestal,* 72–77, and Caraley, *Politics of Military Unification,* 63–65.

25. Air Power League, *Report to Members,* inside front cover, 1. Very little has been written on the Air Power League. David Mets mentions it briefly, noting that Arnold and Spaatz knew of the League's early organizational efforts and worked behind the scenes in 1944 to find a suitable AAF officer, nearing retirement, who could help the committee with its work, but Mets mistakenly asserts that the group was a precursor to the Air Force Association. Two clear indications that this is not the case is that the Air Power League continued its activities as both the League and the National Air Council well after the AFA was founded, and one of the AFA's first corporate decisions was that they would not attempt to duplicate the efforts of the Air Power League. See David R. Mets, *Master of Airpower,* 292–93, and James H. Straubel, *Crusade for Airpower,* 33.

26. Air Power League, *Report to Members,* 2, 3, 10.

27. Air Power League, *Pros and Cons;* Air Power League, *"I Urge This as the Best Means of Keeping the Peace";* both can be found on reel A-1797, frames 2294–2315, AFHRA; Air Power League, *Report to the Members of the Air Power League,* 13; letter, Jacqueline Cochran to Ruth Groves dated Mar. 21, 1946, Mss. 628c, Jacqueline Cochran section, WASP [Women Airforce Service Pilots] Archival Collection, Texas Women's University Library.

28. Lay, "Why Army, Navy and Air Must Combine," 32.

29. William Bradford Huie, *Case against the Admirals,* see particularly 10–20. As with his earlier pro–air power book, *The Fight for Air Power,* this second work was written with considerable help from Hugh J. Knerr, who by this point was a major general in the AAF; see Barlow, *Revolt of the Admirals,* 48–49.

30. See, for example, Noel Francis Parrish, "Behind the Sheltering Bomb," Ph.D. diss., Rice University, 1968, 182, 185.

31. The definitive biography on Mitchell is Hurley, *Billy Mitchell;* for court martial see chapter 6. On Mitchell's guilt, see Arnold, *Global Mission,* 120.

32. De Seversky, *Victory Through Air Power,* iii and facing portrait of Mitchell; Emile Gauvreau and Lester Cohen, *Billy Mitchell,* and Isaac Don Levine, *Mitchell.*

33. Sample speech, Air Force Day—1946, reel A-1619, frame 0936, AFHRA; William Wister Haines, *Command Decision: A Play,* 30; William Wister Haines, *Command Decision,* 157.

34. W. B. Courtney, "Air Power—Today and Tomorrow," *Collier's,* Sept. 15, 1945, 11; Air Power League, *Peace through Air Power,* 13; Hurley, *Billy Mitchell,* 139.

35. Huie, *Case against the Admirals*, passim; William Bradford Huie, "The Struggle for American Air Power," *Reader's Digest*, Apr. 1949, 1; Arnold, *Global Mission*, 114.

36. Huie, *Case against the Admirals*, 12. For a depiction of the medal, as well as the authorizing bill, see reel A-1656, frames 871, 877, 881; the medal bears a likeness of Mitchell on the face and an inscription on the reverse: "For outstanding pioneer service and foresight in the field of American military aviation."

37. Hurley, *Billy Mitchell*, 140; Straubel, *Crusade for Airpower*, 104–106.

38. Letters, Dec. 23, 1941, Jack Warner to Arnold, Dec. 31, 1941, Arnold to Warner, and Jan. 6, 1942, Warner to Arnold, all in Arnold Papers, reel 28059, frames approximately 0425–28, AFHRA. Note: the frame numbers on this reel are extremely hard to read or, in most cases, nonexistent; therefore only a close approximation can be made.

39. Milton Sperling, prod., *The Court-Martial of Billy Mitchell* (Hollywood: Warner Brothers, 1955).

40. Hurley, *Billy Mitchell*, 101.

41. Carl Spaatz, "Strategic Air Power: Fulfillment of a Concept," *Foreign Affairs* (Apr. 1946): 388–89, 396.

42. Harry Borowski, *Hollow Threat*, 38–39, 106.

43. Social and cultural attitudes toward nuclear weapons in the Cold War era have received a great deal of scholarly attention; for a balanced yet wide-ranging introduction see Paul Boyer, *By the Bomb's Early Light*; Spencer R. Weart, *Nuclear Fear*; Charles Wolfe, "Nuclear Country: The Atomic Bomb in Country Music," *Journal of Country Music* (Jan. 1978): 4–21; and the documentary film, Kevin Rafferty, Jayne Loader, and Pierce Rafferty, prods., *The Atomic Cafe* (New York: Archives Project, 1982).

44. Arnold, "If War Comes Again," 5, 38–39; Spaatz, "Air Power in the Atomic Age," 11. For the same theme see also Huie, "How the Next War Will Be Fought," 431; Spaatz radio address, San Francisco, July 30, 1947, reel A-1618, frame 1059, AFHRA.

45. Courtney, "Air Power—Today and Tomorrow," Sept. 15, 1945, 30; Arnold, "If War Comes Again," 39; Francis Drake, "Let's Be Realistic about the Atom Bomb," *Reader's Digest*, Dec. 1945, 108–10, emphasis in original.

46. Arnold, "If War Comes Again," 39.

47. Air Power League, "Peace through Air Power," 30, back cover; Carl Spaatz, "Air Power Is Peace Power," CBS radio broadcast, Aug. 1, 1947, Spaatz Papers, Box I: 268, LOC; William Bradford Huie, "The Facts which *Must* Prevent War," *Reader's Digest*, Jan. 1949, 25. According to Noel Parrish, Spaatz's political advisor, Harvard professor Bruce Hopper suggested the slogan "Air Power Is Peace Power" and further advised him to keep all advocacy activities focused on air power not air force. Parrish, "Behind the Sheltering Bomb," 131, 154.

48. Carl Spaatz, "If We Should Have to Fight Again," *Life,* July 5, 1948, 35, 39; Carl Spaatz, "The Era of Air-Power Diplomacy," *Newsweek,* Sept. 20, 1948, 26; Huie, "How the Next War Will Be Fought," 434–35.

49. "Blueprint for a 30-Day War," *U.S. News and World Report,* Oct. 15, 1948, 15–16; Russell V. Ritchey, "What Would *You* Do?" *Collier's,* June 26, 1948, 28.

50. Stuart Chase, "The Two-Hour War," *New Republic,* May 8, 1929, 325–27. Chase was no fan of air power, but he had become so convinced that air power had the capability to swiftly bring national chaos and collapse with one raid on a nation's capital that he wrote this piece as a warning to try and curb the growth of air forces around the world.

51. De Seversky, *Air Power,* 61–63, 111–14, 146–50, 153–60, 182–98.

52. Ibid., see particularly chapter 12, quote from 185.

53. Borowski, *Hollow Threat,* 183, note 15.

54. Spaatz, "Strategic Air Power," 393, 396; Spaatz, "Era of Air-Power Diplomacy," 26; Carl Spaatz, "Strategic Air Power against Germany," *Newsweek,* Mar. 7, 1949, 28; Public Affairs Office Air Force Day Publicity Package, 1946, reel A-1619, frames 0933–34, AFHRA.

55. H. H. Arnold, radio address, Feb. 14, 1946, Philadelphia, reel A-1618, frame 0905, AFHRA; Courtney, "Air Power—Today and Tomorrow," Sept. 8, 1945, 11, and Sept. 15, 1945, 24; Air Power League, *Bulletin of the Air Power League,* 1; de Seversky, *Air Power,* 31, 43, 199–200.

56. The indispensable resource for understanding the USSBS is MacIsaac, *Strategic Bombing in World War Two;* for how the USSBS was used by all sides to support their positions, see Gian P Gentile, "A-bombs, Budgets, and Morality: Using the Strategic Bombing Survey," Air Power History (spring 1997): 18–31.

57. Spaatz, "Strategic Air Power against Germany," 28; James G. Stahlman, "The Strategic Bombing Myth," (privately published pamphlet, 1949), cover letter, 18–25, 36–52; Fletcher Pratt, "The Case for the Aircraft Carrier," *Reader's Digest,* May 1949, 54; Francis V. Drake, "The Case for Land-Based Air Power," *Reader's Digest,* May 1949, 61–62.

58. Beirne Lay Jr. and Sy Bartlett, *Twelve O'clock High!* 5–6, 11, 17–18.

59. "Top Grosses of 1950," *Variety,* Jan.3, 1951, 58; Steven Jay Rubin, *Combat Films,* 138–39; Darryl F. Zanuck, prod., *Twelve O'clock High* (Hollywood: Twentieth Century Fox, 1949).

60. For Lay's description of the Schweinfurt-Regensburg raid see Beirne Lay Jr., "I Saw Regensburg Destroyed," *Saturday Evening Post,* Nov. 6, 1943, 9–11, 85–88. For studies of the Schweinfurt-Regensburg raid see Thomas M. Coffey, *Decision over Schweinfurt: The U.S. 8th Air Force Battle for Daylight Bombing* (New York: Robert Hale, 1977) and Martin Middlebrook, *The Schweinfurt-Regensburg Mission* (New York: Charles Scribner's Sons, 1983).

61. Letter, Sept. 17, 1948, Zanuck to Vandenberg, Record Group 330, Entry 140, Box 677, Twelve O'clock High folder, National Archives (hereafter NA). Twentieth Century-Fox had earlier requested official air force support for the film and had been given a preliminary promise for assistance from the air force that was contingent upon final script approval and two changes in the projected plot; see letters, Nov. 3, 1947, Anthony Muto, Washington representative for Twentieth Century-Fox, to Donald E. Baruch, director of Air Information Division, and Nov. 17, 1947, William P. Nuckols, deputy director, Air Information Division, to Anthony Muto, Record Group 330, Entry 140, Box 677, Twelve O'clock High folder, NA; for King's relationship to Vandenberg see Rubin, *Combat Films*, 138–39; of this connection Rubin states that based on his friendship with King, "Vandenberg cheerfully gave the director carte blanche at Eglin," where much of the filming was done; for air force citation see memorandum, Feb. 13, 1950, William C. Lindley, chief, Staff Liaison Branch, Directorate of Public Relations, to Col. Roberts, executive to the chief of staff, Record Group 340, Entry 36, Box 4, Twelve O'clock High folder, NA.

62. Letter, Nov. 17, 1948, William Nuckols to Anthony Muto, Record Group 330, Entry 140, Box 677, Twelve O'clock High folder, NA; letter, May 25, 1951, H. O. Parsons to director of training, Headquarters Air Force, Record Group 330, Entry 140, Box 677, Twelve O'clock High folder, NA.

63. Clare D. Kinsman, ed., *Contemporary Authors: Permanent Series* (Detroit: Gale Research, 1967), 258–59; "Top Grossers of 1949," *Variety*, Jan. 4, 1950, 32.

64. Haines, *Command Decision: A Play*, 37–42; Haines, *Command Decision*, 63–69; Sidney Franklin, prod., *Command Decision* (Hollywood: Metro-Goldwyn-Mayer, 1949).

65. Haines, *Command Decision: A Play*, 43.

66. Ibid., 87–88.

67. Ibid., 98.

68. Ibid., 166.

69. Ibid., 130–34, 141–42; Haines, *Command Decision*, 163–64.

70. Haines, *Command Decision: A Play*, 134–36, 140–41; Haines, *Command Decision*, 232–36.

71. Haines, *Command Decision: A Play*, 5–9; Haines, *Command Decision*, 235–36.

72. Haines, *Command Decision: A Play*, 5–10, 152–54, 179–80; Haines, *Command Decision*, 236–40.

73. Letters, Mar. 12 and May 18, 1948, William Nuckols, director of air information, to Carter Barron, Washington, D.C., representative for M-G-M, Record Group 330, Entry 141, Box 702, Command Decision folder, NA; letters, July 10, 1947, Sidney Franklin, the film's producer, to Maj. Gen. Emmett O'Donnell, director of information, and Mar. 19, 1948, Carter

Barron to Joe Yovin, Pictorial Section, Air Information Division, both Record Group 330, Entry 141, Box 702, Command Decision folder, NA.

74. Letter, Apr. 9, 1948, LeMay to Bartlett, LeMay Papers, Container A-1, Bartlett folder, LOC; letters, Apr. 18, 1947, Parks to Carter Barron, and Mar. 2, 1948, O'Donnell to Sidney Franklin, both Record Group 330, Entry 141, Box 702, Command Decision folder, NA; message, Dec. 15, 1948, from Lieutenant Colonel Evans to a Captain Harris, and Memo for Record, Feb. 2, 1949, written by Joe Yovin and Donald Baruch, both Record Group 330, Entry 141, Box 702, Command Decision folder, NA; Farmer, *Celluloid Wings,* 261–62; letter, May 25, 1951, H. O. Parsons, deputy adjutant general of Air Training Command, to director of training, Headquarters Air Force, Record Group 330, Entry 140, Box 677, Twelve O'clock High folder, NA.

75. Gallup, *Gallup Poll,* 858–59, 1108, 1186, 1321, 1429.

CHAPTER 4. THE REVOLUTION UNDER FIRE

1. For treatments of the Revolt of the Admirals see Jeffery G. Barlow, *Revolt of the Admirals;* Michael T. Isenberg, *Shield of the Republic,* chapter seven; Moody, *Building a Strategic Air Force,* 300–307; and Futrell, *Ideas, Concepts, Doctrine,* 251–59.

2. Air Power League, *Peace through Air Power,* 4; Alexander P. de Seversky, "Navies Are Finished," *American Mercury,* Feb. 1946, 135–43, quotes from 136 and 137 respectively; William Bradford Huie, "The Backwardness of Navy Brass," *American Mercury,* June 1946, 647–53.

3. William Bradford Huie, "Navy Brass Imperils Our Defense," *American Mercury,* July 1948, 7–14; William Bradford Huie, "Shall We Abolish the Marine Corps?" *American Mercury,* Sept. 1948, 273–80; William Bradford Huie, "A Navy—Or an Air Force?" *Reader's Digest,* Dec. 1948, 62–67; Spaatz, "If We Should Have to Fight Again," 35; Carl Spaatz, "Gen. Spaatz on Atomic Warfare," *Life,* Aug. 16, 1948, 94, 99.

4. Barlow, *Revolt of the Admirals,* 197–200; Isenberg, *Shield of the Republic,* 146–47; Carl Spaatz, "Budgeting for Land-Sea-Air Power," *Newsweek,* Jan. 10, 1949, 24.

5. Alexander P. de Seversky, "Our Antiquated Defense Policy," *American Mercury,* Apr. 1949, 396–98; William Bradford Huie, "Why We Must Have the World's Best Air Force," *Reader's Digest,* Mar. 1949, 29, 31–32; Huie, "Struggle for American Air Power," 1–6, 124–30, quote from 1.

6. Barlow, *Revolt of the Admirals,* see particularly 206–209 for the "anonymous document"; Moody, *Building a Strategic Air Force,* 301–302; Futrell, *Ideas, Concepts, Doctrine,* 251–52; Richard G. Hubler, *SAC,* 86–88, 96–97; for a study of B-36 procurement see Michael E. Brown, *Flying Blind,* particularly chapter 4.

7. Stahlman, *Strategic Bombing Myth;* Pratt, "Case for the Aircraft Carrier," 53, 55, 57–58; Drake, "The Case for Land-Based Air Power," 59–66. The charges of bias were prompted by the fact that in the five-month period from December 1948 to April 1949 *Reader's Digest* ran three pro–air power articles, all by Huie.

8. D. V. Gallery, "An Admiral Talks Back to the Airmen," *Saturday Evening Post,* June 25, 1949, 25, 136–38; Barlow, *Revolt of the Admirals,* 117–21.

9. Richard Tregaskis, "We Need Carriers *and* the B-36," *Collier's,* Oct. 8, 1949, 16, 60–61.

10. Drake, "The Case for Land-Based Air Power," 61, 64–66.

11. Carl Spaatz, "Unify the Armed Forces," *Newsweek,* May 9, 1949, 26; Carl Spaatz, "Europe in Late Spring," *Newsweek,* May 30, 1949, 35.

12. Carl Spaatz, "Why We Need the B-36," *Newsweek,* July 11, 1949, 21; Carl Spaatz, "Our Diminishing Air Power," *Newsweek,* Aug. 8, 1949, 21. For a history of air force neglect of tactical air forces in late 1940s and early 1950s see Caroline Frieda Ziemke, "In the Shadow of the Giant."

13. H. H. Arnold, "Tradition *Can't Win* Wars," *Collier's,* 15 October 1949, 13, 65–66; Isenberg, *Shield of the Republic,* 158–61; Moody, *Building a Strategic Air Force,* 305–306; Futrell, *Ideas, Concepts, Doctrine,* 257–59.

14. William Bradford Huie, "The A-Bomb General of Our Air Force," *Coronet* (Oct. 1950): 87–91; William Bradford Huie, "Untold Facts in the Forrestal Case," *New American Mercury,* Dec. 1950, 643–52.

15. A number of scholars have examined reactions in the United States to the Soviet atomic bomb from several distinct perspectives; see for example Samuel R. Williamson Jr. and Steven L. Rearden, *Origins of U.S. Nuclear Strategy,* and Gregg Herken, *Counsels of War* for the military and political dimension; for the cultural and social dimension see Boyer, *By the Bomb's Early Light;* Weart, *Nuclear Fear;* and Elaine Tyler May, *Homeward Bound;* for a visual representation see Rafferty, Loader, and Rafferty, prods., *The Atomic Café.*

16. Boyer, *By the Bomb's Early Light,* 105–106, 336–40; Weart, *Nuclear Fear,* 124–27.

17. Sarita Robinson, Bertha Joel, and Mary Keyes, *Reader's Guide to Periodic Literature,* vol. 17, May 1949–March 1951 (New York: H. W. Wilson, 1951), 30–31; Sarita Robinson and Zada Limerick, *Reader's Guide to Periodic Literature,* vol. 23, March 1961–February 1963 (New York: H. W. Wilson, 1963), 30.

18. W. B. Courtney, "Will Russia Rule the Air?" Jan. 25, 1947, 12; American Legion, *What Is Happening to Our Air Power?* 4–5; W. B. Courtney, "Russia Reaches for the Sky," *Collier's,* Apr. 26, 1947, 97.

19. Spaatz, "Our Diminishing Air Power," 21; for other examples of Spaatz stressing the need for seventy groups see Spaatz, "Gen. Spaatz on Atomic Warfare," 99, and Spaatz, "Budgeting for Land-Sea-Air Power," 24; for an

account of how the seventy-group figure emerged see Sherry, *Preparing for the Next War,* 108–19, 226–32.

20. Wesley Price, "How Strong Is Stalin's Air Force?" *Saturday Evening Post,* Aug. 21, 1948, 26, 83; Frank Kluckhohn, "The Russian Knock on Alaska's Door," *Collier's,* Dec. 18, 1948, 13, 49, 54.

21. Kenneth Schaffel, *Emerging Shield,* 87–95; Ziemke, "In the Shadow of the Giant," 67–69.

22. Schaffel, *Emerging Shield,* 111–15, 143, 149–67.

23. Carl Spaatz, "Atomic Monopoly Ends," *Newsweek,* Oct. 3, 1949, 22; Carl Spaatz, "Gambling with U.S. Security," *Newsweek,* Dec. 5, 1949, 20.

24. Carl Spaatz, "Air Defense and Air Safety," *Newsweek,* Jan. 9, 1950, 22; Carl Spaatz, "Tomorrow's Weapons Won't Help Today," *Newsweek,* June 26, 1950, 19.

25. De Seversky, *Air Power,* 161–62; see also 66, 111–13, 198–99.

26. Hoyt S. Vandenberg, as told to Stanley Frank, "The Truth about Our Air Power," *Saturday Evening Post,* Feb. 17, 1951, 101–102.

27. Ibid.

28. Vannevar Bush, "In the Air, Bombers Will Find It Tough," *Life,* Nov. 14, 1949, 122–27; Vannevar Bush, "The Weapons We Need for Freedom," *Reader's Digest,* Jan. 1951, 48–49.

29. Joseph Alsop and Stewart Alsop, *Reporter's Trade,* 59–60; Robert W. Merry, *Taking on the World,* 244–46; Ralph E. Lapp and Stewart Alsop, "We Can Smash the Red A-Bombers," *Saturday Evening Post,* Mar. 21, 1953, 19–21, 82–83, 86.

30. Lapp and Alsop, "We Can Smash," 82, 86; Alsop and Alsop, *Reporter's Trade,* 59–63; Merry, *Taking on the World,* 244–45.

31. James R. Killian Jr. and A. G. Hill, "More Facts for a Continental Defense," *Atlantic Monthly,* Nov. 1953, 37–41.

32. Radio spot quoted in Schaffel, *Emerging Shield,* 159; Phil Gustafson, "Night Fighters over New York," *Saturday Evening Post,* Feb. 2, 1952, 32–33, 64–66; Schaffel, *Emerging Shield,* 173.

33. Henry Cabot Lodge Jr., "Let's Face It—We're in a Jam," *Saturday Evening Post,* July 28, 1951, 22 (quote), 23–66.

34. Carl Spaatz, "The Air-Power Odds against Us," *Reader's Digest,* June 1951, 13; Carl Spaatz, "The Only Hope for Peace," *Newsweek,* Mar. 5, 1951, 27; Carl Spaatz, "How Much Air Power?" *Newsweek,* Mar. 19, 1951, 29; Carl Spaatz, "The New Budget," *Newsweek,* Jan. 28, 1952, 23. In 1952 the air force began referring to groups as wings.

35. Editorial, *Life,* June 11, 1951, 28.

36. Harold H. Martin, "Could We Beat Back an Air Attack on the U.S.?" *Saturday Evening Post,* Nov. 4, 1950, 22–23, 146–50, quotes from 150.

37. Harold H. Martin, "Are Our Big Bombers Ready to Go?" *Saturday Evening Post,* Dec. 30, 1950, 18–19, 65–67, quotes from 65.

38. Milton Caniff, *Steve Canyon No. 21*, 61–73; quotes from 65, emphasis in original; Carl J. Horak, *A Steve Canyon Checklist, 1947–1988* (Calgary, Alberta: Remuda Publishing, 1990): 13; Milton Caniff, *Damma Exile*, 26–29, 66.

39. Greer, *Development of Air Doctrine*, 32–33, 66–67, 87–88, 121–23.

40. Ziemke, "In the Shadow of the Giant," 11–14, 67–69, 84–87, 128, 138–43; Futrell, *Ideas, Concepts, Doctrine*, 304–309, 373–79, 382–84; Robert Frank Futrell, *United States Air Force in Korea*, 469–70.

41. Roy E. Appleman, *South to the Naktong*, 123, 256–57, quotes from 476–77. Two good works on the air war in Korea that together describe the full range of air force, navy, and Marine Corps air operations are Futrell, *United States Air Force in Korea*, and Richard P. Hallion, *Naval Air War in Korea*. For a study of the close air support element of the air war see Allan R. Millett, "Korea, 1950–1953," in Benjamin Franklin Cooling, *Case Studies in the Development of Close Air Support* (Washington, D.C.: Office of Air Force History, 1990).

42. Joseph Alsop and Stewart Alsop, "Are American Weapons Good Enough?" *Reader's Digest*, May 1951, 102–103; Ziemke, "In the Shadow of the Giant," 175–79, 193; Futrell, *United States Air Force in Korea*, 469–70, 706–708.

43. Vandenberg, "Truth about Our Air Power," 21–100, 102.

44. Harold H. Martin, "How We Blasted the Enemy's Life Line to Russia," *Saturday Evening Post*, Aug. 26, 1950, 30, 105–106, quote from 106.

45. "The 'Wild Blue Yonder Boys' Snap into a Salute for GIs," *Life*, Aug. 28, 1950, 32–33.

46. Futrell, *United States Air Force in Korea*, 471–74.

47. Carl Spaatz, "How We Turned the Tables in Korea," *Newsweek*, Sept. 25, 1950, 28; Carl Spaatz, "Learning the Lessons of Korea," *Newsweek*, Oct. 16, 1950, 23; Lawrence Howard Suid, *Guts and Glory*, 113.

48. Edmund Grainger, prod., *One Minute to Zero* (Hollywood: RKO Pictures, 1952); Suid, *Guts and Glory*, 113–14.

49. Paris, *From the Wright Brothers to Top Gun*, 189; Pendo, *Aviation in the Cinema*, 231–32.

50. Fletcher Knebel, "Red Jets Can Rule the Skies," *Look*, Apr. 7, 1953, 31–35, quote from 31.

51. Francis Drake, "Give Our Troops in Europe a Chance," *Reader's Digest*, Sept. 1951, 5–9, quote from 6, emphasis in original; Spaatz, "Air-Power Odds against Us," 11–14, quote from 11.

52. Carl Spaatz, "Some Answers to Korean Questions," *Newsweek*, July 31, 1950, 19; Spaatz, "Air-Power Odds against Us," 12; Vandenberg, "Truth about Our Air Power," 100–101.

53. "Top Grossers of 1953," *Variety*, Jan. 13, 1954, 10; Melvin Frank and Norman Panama, prods., *Above and Beyond* (Hollywood: Metro-Goldwyn-

Mayer, 1952); letter, Jan. 11, 1951, Lay to LeMay, LeMay Papers, Box A-3, Lay folder, LOC; for air force assistance in the production of this film see Record Group 330, Entry 140, Box 689, Above and Beyond folder, and Record Group 340, Entry 36, Box 1, Above and Beyond folder, NA.

54. Wesley Price, "How Does Our Air Force Stack up against Stalin's?" *Saturday Evening Post,* Sept. 6, 1952, 25, 136–38.

55. Gallup, *Gallup Poll,* 1186.

CHAPTER 5. THE HEYDAY OF SAC

1. Much has been written about U.S. culture during the Cold War. For effects of the Red Scare see Stephen J. Whitfield, *The Culture of the Cold War,* especially chapter 2, and for the effects of possible nuclear war on American culture see Weart, *Nuclear Fear,* and Stephen Hilgartner, Richard C. Bell, and Rory O'Connor, *Nukespeak.* For the impact of the Cold War on family and home, see May, *Homeward Bound;* for a visual representation of U.S. fears of nuclear attack see Rafferty, Loader, and Rafferty, prods., *The Atomic Café.*

2. Phil Patton, "Dr. Strangelove's Children," *American Heritage,* Nov. 1998, 92.

3. Douglas Kinnard, *President Eisenhower and Strategy Management,* 7–11, 23–28; for other works examining Eisenhower defense policies and massive retaliation see John Lewis Gaddis, *Strategies of Containment,* Charles C. Alexander, *Holding the Line,* and on the larger question of nuclear strategy see Lawrence Freedman, *Evolution of Nuclear Strategy.*

4. "Remarks By General Eisenhower," Air Force Association Convention, Sept. 13, 1947, Reel A-1618, frames 1102–1106, AFHRA; Carl Spaatz, "Eisenhower and Air Power," *Newsweek,* June 16, 1952, 30.

5. Ziemke, "In the Shadow of the Giant," 316.

6. Kelsey-Hayes advertisement, *Newsweek,* Mar. 31, 1958, 66.

7. Martin, "Are Our Big Bombers Ready to Go?" 19, 65–66.

8. "SAC: The Strategic Air Command Has Its Big Planes Ready for Intercontinental War," *Life,* Aug. 21, 1951, 86–100, quotes from 87 and 95.

9. Francis Drake, "On Guard! The Day and Night Vigil of Our Atom-Bomber Combat Crews," *Reader's Digest,* Aug. 1953, 11–23, quotes from 12, 14–15.

10. Ibid., 24–25.

11. "Jet Age Man," *Life,* Dec. 6, 1954, 141–47, quotes from 141, 146, and 147.

12. Arthur Godfrey, as told to Peter Martin, "This Is My Story," *Saturday Evening Post,* Dec. 24, 1955, 21, 58, 59; Curtis E. LeMay, with MacKinlay Kantor, *Mission with LeMay,* 488–89; Thomas M. Coffey, *Iron Eagle,* 326.

13. Godfrey, "This Is My Story," 20–21, 58–61, quote from 59.

14. James A. Michener, "While Others Sleep: The Story of the Strategic Air Command," *Reader's Digest,* Oct. 1957, 68–75, 219–44, biographical sketch on 70, quote on 235.

15. Ibid., 219, 224, 226–28.

16. Clay Blair Jr., "Who Says Pilots Are Obsolete?" *Saturday Evening Post,* May 31, 1958, 31, 63–66, quotes from 64 and 66.

17. Philip Gustafson, "How We Would Strike Back," *Saturday Evening Post,* Aug. 30, 1958, 25, 53–56.

18. "SAC Alert," *Life,* June 23, 1961, 30–35, quotes from 31 and 34.

19. John G. Hubbell, "They Learn to Survive—the Hard Way," *Reader's Digest,* Dec. 1955, 43–51; John G. Hubbell, "Join Me in One of the New Jet Tankers," *Reader's Digest,* Aug. 1957, 50–54, quote from 54.

20. Corey Ford and James Perkins, "Our Key SAC Bases in Spain—and How We Got Them," *Reader's Digest,* Aug. 1958, 23–26; Corey Ford and James Perkins, "Boss of the Missilemen," *Saturday Evening Post,* Aug. 23, 1958, 30, 89–90, quotes from 89 and 90.

21. Corey Ford and James Perkins, "With the Men Who Fire the Atlas," *Reader's Digest,* Feb. 1960, 213–18, quotes from 213, 214, 215, 217, and 218.

22. LeMay, *Mission with LeMay,* 15, 41–47. LeMay's memoirs are supplemented by a biography, Coffey, *Iron Eagle,* 218–20, 222–23.

23. LeMay, *Mission with LeMay,* 220–23; Borowski, *Hollow Threat,* see particularly chapters 7 and 8.

24. See, for example, Drake, "On Guard!" 12; "SAC," *Life,* 87; and Martin, "Are Our Big Bombers Ready to Go?" 19, 65–66.

25. Huie, "A-Bomb General," 87–91, quotes from 87, 89, and 91.

26. Ernest Havemann, "Toughest Cop of the Western World," *Life,* June 14, 1954, 133, 134, 136, 142, 144–45; see also reprint as Ernest Havemann, "Air Guardian of the Western World," *Reader's Digest,* Sept. 1954, 57–62.

27. LeMay, *Mission with LeMay,* 489–94; "Helicopter Safari in Africa," *Life,* June 10, 1957, 80–93; "Off Hours of a Tough General," *Life,* Oct. 20, 1961, 145–50

28. See Jack Wilson, "Service Rivalries Aren't Likely to Ruffle the Air Force's Calm Nate Twining," *Look,* Feb. 23, 1954, 120; Roger Butterfield and Frank Gibney, "The Twining Tradition," *Life,* Aug. 26, 1957, 104–14, 119–22; and John G. Hubbell, "Tough Tommy Power—Our Deterrent-in-Chief," *Reader's Digest,* May 1964, 71–76.

29. See chapter 2.

30. See chapter 3.

31. See chapter 3.

32. Milton Sperling, prod., *The Court-Martial of Billy Mitchell* (Hollywood: Warner Brothers, 1955).

33. "Estimated Grosses of Past Year," *Variety,* Jan. 2, 1957, 4.

34. Letter, Oct. 13, 1952, Lay to LeMay, LeMay Papers, Box A-3, Lay folder, LOC; tie to *High Ramparts* is based on story outline, July 15, 1949, Lay to Sory Smith, director of air force public relations, Record Group 330, Entry 141, Box 706, High Ramparts folder, NA. The outline bears many similarities with *Strategic Air Command,* such as a reservist debating whether to stay in the air force or get out to earn higher pay, the reservist's decision to stay in because he is serving a higher purpose, and Lay's stated goal to convince the public and reservists that the air force needs the nation's best people willing to sacrifice personal success for the good of the nation.

35. Letters, Dec. 14, 1952, May 1, 1953, Oct. 20, 1953, and Nov. 6, 1953, Lay to LeMay, LeMay Papers, Box A-3, Lay folder, LOC.

36. Letter, Dec. 14, 1952, Lay to LeMay, LeMay Papers, Box A-3, Lay folder, LOC; Lay may have got the 80 percent figure from LeMay who told him that only 18 percent of SAC's officers were regulars; see letter, Oct. 21, 1952, LeMay to Lay.

37. Samuel J. Briskin, prod., *Strategic Air Command* (Hollywood: Paramount, 1955).

38. Letters, Oct. 21, 1952 (quote), Nov. 19, 1953, Mar. 15, 1954, and Apr. 7, 1954, LeMay to Lay, LeMay Papers, Box A-3, Lay folder, LOC.

39. For air force support see letters, Oct. 28, 1952, Sory Smith, director of public information, to Lay, and Mar. 16, 1953, and May 1, 1953, Lay to LeMay; on air force suggestions for script changes see letter, May 22, 1953, Lt. Col. Read Tilley, special assistant to LeMay, to Lay, and Memo, July 20, 1953, Col. Paul Carlton, aide to LeMay, to Tilley; for reaction to air force comments see letter, Mar. 4, 1954, Lay to LeMay, all in LeMay Papers, Box A-3, Lay folder, LOC.

40. Letter, Dec. 22, 1952, Lay to LeMay, and memo, May 19, 1954, Maj. C. E. Thomson, LeMay's deputy special assistant, to LeMay, LeMay Papers, Box A-3, Lay folder, LOC; Gerard Molyneaux, *James Stewart,* 121; Weart, *Nuclear Fear,* 218.

41. Letters, Mar. 21, 1955, Warner to LeMay, July 15, 1955, Nov. 16, 1955, and Apr. 23, 1956, Lay to LeMay; for LeMay's reaction to title *Flight Line* see letter, Aug. 23, 1955, LeMay to Lay, all in LeMay Papers, Box A-3, Lay folder, LOC; for letter identifying Lay as the producer see letter, July 21, 1955, George M. Dorsey at Warner Brothers to Donald Baruch, Chief Motion Picture Section, Record Group 330, Entry 1006, Box 32, Bombers B-52 folder, NA.

42. Richard Whorf, prod., *Bombers B-52* (Burbank, Calif.: Warner Brothers, 1957).

43. For military objections to high accident rate see memos, June 19, 1956, from Donald Baruch, and July 11, 1956, from Charles Hinkle, Air Force Office of Security Review, and letter, undated, no author, no recipient, titled "SAC

Comments on 'Flight Line' Script"; for reference to Boeing objections see memo, Sept. 24, 1956, from Donald Baruch, all in Record Group 330, Entry 1006, Box 32, Bombers B-52 folder, NA.

44. Memo, Oct. 3, 1956, from C. Gordon Furbish, chief, Pictorial Branch, Air Force Office of Information, and letter, Oct. 9, 1956, Baruch to George Dorsey, Warner Brothers; for objection to daughter's attitude, "SAC Comments on 'Flight Line' Script," all in Record Group 330, Entry 1006, Box 32, Bombers B-52 folder, NA.

45. Suid, *Guts and Glory*, 168–70; Pendo, *Aviation in the Cinema*, 265.

46. The base commander should not be confused with the wing commander. Prior to post–Cold War reorganization, the air force placed all base support facilities under a "base commander," who essentially ran the base for the "wing commander" who was in charge of the wing assigned to that base. The wing, which usually had an operational mission, was supported by the base, so the wing commander was supported by the base commander.

47. Sy Bartlett, prod., *A Gathering of Eagles* (Universal City, Calif.: Universal-International, 1963).

48. Suid, *Guts and Glory*, 167–70; 4126th Strategic Wing, Heavy, unit history, May and June 1962, K-WG-4126-HI, AFHRA; "Top Rental Features of 1963," *Variety*, Jan. 8, 1964, 71.

49. See for example, Pendo, *Aviation in the Cinema*, 220, 263–64; Suid, *Guts and Glory*, 169–70, 218; Paris, *From the Wright Brothers to Top Gun*, 184–87; Weart, *Nuclear Fear*, 149–51; and the at times patently absurd, Peter Biskind, *Seeing Is Believing*, 64–69.

50. For a study of cultural images stressing the paramount importance of family, especially traditional female roles within the family, during the Cold War see May, *Homeward Bound*, especially 109–13.

51. Ziemke, "In the Shadow of the Giant," chapter 5.

52. Frank Harvey, "Those Half-Pint A-Bombers!" *Saturday Evening Post*, Nov. 5, 1955, 32–33, 127, 130, quote from 127.

53. Henry Blanke, prod., *The McConnell Story* (Hollywood, Calif.: Warner Brothers, 1955); Ross Hunter, prod., *Battle Hymn* (Universal City, Calif.: Universal-International, 1956).

54. "The Air Age," *The March of Time* (New York: American Broadcasting Company, 1953). The Library of Congress holds a copy of this show in its Motion Picture and Television section.

55. Perry Wolff, prod., *Air Power* (New York: Columbia Broadcasting System, 1956–57).

56. Tim Brooks and Earle Marsh, *Complete Directory*, 53–55; Vincent Terrace, *Complete Encyclopedia*, 71–72.

57. Letters, Dec. 22, 1952, Godfrey to LeMay, July 29, 1953, Sept. 16, 1953, and Mar. 24, 1954, LeMay to Godfrey, and June 5, 1958, Ralph Cordiner, member of DoD Committee on Military Pay, to Godfrey, LeMay Papers,

Box A-3, Godfrey folder, LOC; Bill Davidson, "Arthur Godfrey and His Fan Mail," *Collier's*, May 2, 1953, 11–13.

58. Letter, July 3, 1958, Godfrey to Ralph Cordiner, LeMay Papers, Box A-3, Godfrey folder, LOC; Arthur J. Singer, *Arthur Godfrey*, 170.

59. Letters, Apr. 15, 1954, LeMay to Godfrey, and June 13, 1956, Reade Tilley, SAC chief of information, to Godfrey, LeMay Papers, Box A-3, Godfrey folder, LOC; Straubel, *Crusade for Airpower*, 110.

60. Massive retaliation critiques are many; see for example, Henry A. Kissinger, *Nuclear Weapons and Foreign Policy* (New York: Harper & Brothers, 1957), Maxwell D. Taylor, *The Uncertain Trumpet* (New York: Harper & Row, 1960), and Richard A. Aliano, *American Defense Policy*, chapter 1.

61. For the transition from Eisenhower's defense policies to the Kennedy administration's see Aliano, *American Defense Policy*; for a comparison of the two administrations within the context of the Cold War see Gaddis, *Strategies of Containment*, and Freedman, *The Evolution of Nuclear Strategy*; and for the formulation of defense policy in the Kennedy administration see Alain C. Enthoven and K. Wayne Smith, *How Much is Enough? Shaping the Defense Program, 1961–1969* (New York: Harper & Row, 1971).

CHAPTER 6. DISTURBING VISIONS

1. John Hersey, *Hiroshima*; Hermann Hagedorn, *The Bomb that Fell on America*; for information on the literary response to the atomic bomb and for Mumford's article see Boyer, *By the Bomb's Early Light*, 284–87; for response to *Hiroshima* see David Sanders, *John Hersey*, 14, 50.

2. Kennett, *History of Strategic Bombing*, chapter 4; Sherry, *Rise of American Air Power*, 33.

3. Weart, *Nuclear Fear*, 216–17, 241–42; Franklin, *War Stars*, 183.

4. "Jet Age Man," 141–53, see also editorials "Jet Age I: Advice to the Grounded," and "Jet Age II: Outlook for the Airman," same issue, 48; on June 18, 1956, *Life* devoted the entire issue to special "air age" features covering many topics of civil, commercial, and military aviation; for *Collier's* compare December 25, 1948, issue with December 18 and 25, 1953, issues.

5. For public reaction to the Soviet atomic bomb see chapter 5; *Reader's Digest* played a conspicuous role in extolling the missile effort, and some of the articles printed in their pages include George Barrett, "Visit to America's 'Earthstrip No.1'" *Reader's Digest*, Dec. 1957, 88–90; Corey Ford and James Perkins, "New Watch on the Rhine," *Reader's Digest*, Sept. 1958, 117–20; and Wolfgang Langewiesche, "Canaveral—From the Cape to the Stars," *Reader's Digest*, June 1959, 114–20.

6. For declining public fascination with the airplane in the fifties see Corn, *Winged Gospel*, 137–40.

7. Weart, *Nuclear Fear*, 263–64.

8. James Atwater, "How the Modern Minuteman Guards the Peace," *Saturday Evening Post*, Feb. 9, 1963, 65–69.

9. Ward Taylor, *Roll Back the Sky*, 53–55.

10. Ibid., 77–80, 111–17, 140.

11. Ibid., 141–42, 147–48, 244, 252.

12. Ibid., 150–52, 167–71.

13. Letter, Feb. 6, 1956, Ellen McDonnell, with Twentieth Century-Fox, to Donald Baruch, Record Group 330, Entry 1006, Box 26, The Hunters folder, NA; Paris, *From the Wright Brothers to Top Gun*, 190. Paris attributes the book, without comment, to James Horowitz. The name change was an attempt to preserve the author's anonymity from the air force and raised problems when the studio tried to purchase the film rights. Studio officials asked Baruch to write to the author, through his agent and publisher, promising that the air force would not try to determine his true identity.

14. James Salter, *The Hunters*.

15. Ibid., 5, 136–42, 229–37.

16. Ibid., 172–78.

17. Dick Powell, prod., *The Hunters* (Hollywood: Twentieth Century-Fox, 1958).

18. Letter, Feb. 1, 1956, Donald Baruch to Frank McCarthy, director of public relations at Twentieth Century-Fox, and Story Synopsis, dated Sept. 30, 1955, but which must be an error since the novel was not published until 1956, Record Group 330, Entry 1006, Box 26, The Hunters folder, NA.

19. Letter, Aug. 22, 1956, Baruch to Anthony Muto, with Twentieth Century-Fox, and memo, Mar. 6, 1957, Stockton B. Shaw, Air Force Pictorial Branch, to Baruch, both in Record Group 330, Entry 1006, Box 26, The Hunters folder, NA.

20. Message, Jan. 9, 1958, Major Thomson to chief, Air Force Office of Information Services, and memo, Feb. 5, 1958, Stockton Shaw to Baruch, both in Record Group 330, Entry 1006, Box 26, The Hunters folder, NA; memo, Feb. 13, 1958, Stockton Shaw to chief, Production Branch, Audio-Visual Division, DoD, and letter, June 23, 1958, Baruch to Frank McCarthy, Twentieth Century-Fox Director of Public Relations, both in Record Group 330, Entry 1006, Box 26, The Hunters folder, NA.

21. "Rental Potentials of 1960," *Variety*, Jan. 4, 1961, 47; Weart, *Nuclear Fear*, 217–19.

22. Nevil Shute, *On the Beach*, 12, 89–90; de Seversky, *Air Power*, 158–59; Shute, *On the Beach*, 93–95.

23. Shute, *On the Beach*, 94.

24. Stanley Kramer, prod., *On the Beach* (Hollywood: Metro-Goldwyn-Mayer, 1959).

25. Boyer, *By the Bomb's Early Light*, xvii; Weart, *Nuclear Fear*, 218, 320.

26. For literary views of this work see Sanders, *John Hersey*, 95–107, and Nancy L. Huse, *Survival Tales of John Hersey*, 101–10.

27. Goldstein, *Flying Machine*, 169; John Hersey, *The War Lover*, 67, 376, 82, 96, 381.

28. Huse, *Survival Tales of John Hersey*, 105.

29. Hersey, *The War Lover*, 230–31, 303–304.

30. Ibid., 156–57.

31. Ibid., 381–82, 75–76, 17, 32, 59, 71, 102, 188.

32. Arthur Hornblow Jr., prod., *The War Lover* (Burbank, Calif.: Columbia Pictures, 1962).

33. Gallup, *Gallup Poll*, 1552–53; Boyer, *By the Bomb's Early Light*, 352–56; Weart, *Nuclear Fear*, 184, 215–17, 241–50, 278, 301.

34. Franklin, *War Stars*, 119, 123; Suid, *Guts and Glory*, 270–73.

35. Joseph Heller, *Catch-22*, 63–66, 252–54, 301, 318–23.

36. Ibid., 88–91, 97–98, 119, 316, 438–43.

37. Franklin, *War Stars*, 123–27.

38. Heller, *Catch-22*, 426–30, quote from 430.

39. Ibid., 441–42.

40. Weart, *Nuclear Fear*, 275; Arthur S. Ragen, "The Image of the Military as Portrayed in Three Novels Made into Screenplays since 1958," 78; Eugene Burdick and Harvey Wheeler, *Fail-Safe*, 43–44, 279–80, 283–84.

41. Burdick and Wheeler, *Fail-Safe*, 154, 241–42, 251; Ragen, "The Image of the Military," 96–97.

42. Memo, Dec. 4, 1962, Arnhym to Power, reprinted in Ragen, "The Image of the Military," 89–94.

43. Donald Robinson, "How Safe Is Fail-Safe?" *Reader's Digest*, May 1963, 91–94; Bartlett, *A Gathering of Eagles*, see chapter 5 for a fuller discussion of this movie.

44. Suid, *Guts and Glory*, 195–201.

45. Weart, *Nuclear Fear*, 275–77; "Big Rental Pictures of 1964," *Variety*, Jan. 6, 1965, 39.

46. "Big Rental Pictures of 1964," *Variety*, Jan. 6, 1965, 39; Franklin, *War Stars*, 185; Suid, *Guts and Glory*, 190–91, 194.

47. Peter George, *Dr. Strangelove*, vii–x, the novel version of the film was first published in 1964, and this reprint edition includes an introductory analysis of the two novels and the film; for a study of the "future war" genre see chapter 2 and especially Clarke, *Voices Prophesying War*.

48. Peter George, *Red Alert*, 38–40, 87–95, 190.

49. Stanley Kubrick, prod., *Dr. Strangelove, Or: How I Learned to Stop Worrying and Love the Bomb* (Burbank, Calif.: Columbia, 1964).

50. Ragen, "The Image of the Military," 113–14, 129; Rubin, *Combat Films*, 195; Suid, *Guts and Glory*, 194–95.

51. William Bradford Huie, *Hiroshima Pilot*, 7–20, 23–25.

52. Ibid., 37–40, 50, 68–69, 71–76, 130–32.

53. William Bradford Huie, *In the Hours of Night;* Huie, "Facts which *Must* Prevent War," 25; *Contemporary Authors,* vol. 7, 238–39.

54. Fletcher Knebel and Charles W. Bailey II, *No High Ground.*

55. Fletcher Knebel and Charles W. Bailey II, *Seven Days in May,* 13, 33.

56. Edward Lewis and Kirk Douglas, prod., *Seven Days in May* (Hollywood: Paramount, 1964); "Big Rental Pictures of 1964," *Variety,* Jan. 6, 1965, 39; Suid, *Guts and Glory,* 202–205.

57. William Wister Haines, *Target,* 191, 289.

58. Ibid., 6, 27, 82.

59. Carl Spaatz, "The Case for the B-70 in an Age of Missiles," *Newsweek,* Apr. 17, 1961, 34; James Parton, *Air Force Spoken Here,* 473–76; for reference to actual number of papers carrying Eaker's column see list of questions, no date, Eaker Papers, Box II: 68, Tonight Show Appearance folder, LOC; the Eaker Papers contain copies of most of Eaker's columns in Boxes II: 89–91.

60. Letters, May 24, 1963, Godfrey to Eaker; May 28, 1963, Eaker to Godfrey; June 4, 1963, Eaker to Bruce Cooper, NBC; and list of questions, no date, all in Eaker Papers, Box II: 68, Tonight Show Appearance folder, LOC.

61. Singer, *Arthur Godfrey,* 174–75; for pay raise episode see chapter 5.

62. Nathan F. Twining, *Neither Liberty nor Safety,* xv, 195–96.

63. LeMay, *Mission with LeMay,* 565.

CHAPTER 7. CONCLUSION

1. For a perceptive study of why this claim is incorrect see Mark Clodfelter, *The Limits of Air Power;* for another look at air force mentality during the Vietnam War that reaches similar conclusions see Earl H. Tilford Jr., *Crosswinds.*

2. Harvey, "Those Half-Pint A-Bombers!" 127.

Bibliography

AIR FORCE ASSOCIATION. *Airpower Preparedness Symposium, Detroit, 1952.* Washington, D.C.: Air Force Association, 1952.

AIR POWER LEAGUE. *Bulletin of the Air Power League.* Vol. 1. New York: Air Power League, 1945.

———. *"I Urge This as the Best Means of Keeping the Peace."* New York: Air Power League, n.d.

———. *Industrial Preparedness—Education in Aviation: A Record of the Air Power League's Aviation Forum.* New York: Air Power League, 1946.

———. *Peace through Air Power.* New York: Air Power League, 1946.

———. *Pros and Cons: Unification of the Armed Forces.* New York: Air Power League, n.d.

———. *Report to the Members of the Air Power League.* New York: Air Power League, 1946.

ALBERS, LAWRENCE C. "Perry Wolff and *Air Power*: A Film Maker's Contribution to Historical Understanding." *Southern Quarterly,* no. 3 (1976): 231–35.

ALEXANDER, CHARLES C. *Holding the Line: The Eisenhower Era, 1952–1961.* Bloomington: Indiana University Press, 1975.

ALIANO, RICHARD A. *American Defense Policy from Eisenhower to Kennedy: The Politics of Changing Military Requirements, 1957–1961.* Athens: Ohio University Press, 1975.

ALSOP, JOSEPH W. *"I've Seen the Best of It": Memoirs.* With Adam Platt. New York: W. W. Norton, 1992.

ALSOP, JOSEPH, AND STEWART ALSOP. "Are American Weapons Good Enough?" *Reader's Digest,* May 1951, 98–103.

———. "The Race We Are Losing to Russia." *Reader's Digest,* August 1956, 127–30.

———. *The Reporter's Trade.* New York: Reynal & Company, 1958.

———. "Your Flesh Should Creep." *Reader's Digest,* September 1946, 5–8.

ALSOP, STEWART. *The Center: People and Power in Political Washington.* New York: Harper & Row, 1968.

————. "How Can We Catch Up?" *Saturday Evening Post*, December 14 1957, 26–27, 66–68.

AMERICAN LEGION. *Air Power in an Age of Peril*. Indianapolis: American Legion, 1954.

————. *Legion Air Review*. Vol. 1, no. 1. Indianapolis: American Legion, 1950.

————. *Legion Air Review*. Vol. 1, no. 2. Indianapolis: American Legion, 1950.

————. *Legion Air Review*. Vol. 3, no. 7. Indianapolis: American Legion, 1952.

————. *The Fifties: Decade of Air Decision*. Indianapolis: American Legion, 1949.

————. *Keep America Strong in the Air*. Indianapolis: American Legion, 1947.

————. *What Is Happening to Our Air Power?* Indianapolis: American Legion, 1947.

ANDREWS, MARSHALL. *Disaster through Air Power*. New York: Rinehart, 1950.

APPLEMAN, ROY E. *South to the Naktong, North to the Yalu*. Washington, D.C.: Center of Military History, 1986.

ARNOLD, H. H. "Air Power for Peace." *National Geographic Magazine*, February 1946, 136–93.

————. "Aviation's 8-Ball." *Collier's*, April 26, 1947, 117.

————. *Global Mission*. New York: Harper & Brothers, 1949.

————. "'Hap' Arnold Recollects." *Life*, September 12, 1949, 120–34.

————. "If War Comes Again." *New York Times Magazine*, November 18, 1945, 39

————. "Tradition *Can't Win* Wars." *Collier's*, October 15, 1949, 13, 65–66.

ARNOLD, H. H., and IRA C. EAKER. *Army Flyer*. New York: Harper & Brothers, 1942.

————. *Winged Warfare*. New York: Harper & Brothers, 1941.

ATWATER, JAMES. "How the Modern Minuteman Guards the Peace: Airmen and Missiles Go Underground." *Saturday Evening Post*, February 9, 1963, 65–69.

AVIATION DEVELOPMENT ADVISORY COMMITTEE. *America's Civil Air Power*. Washington, D.C.: Aviation Development Advisory Committee, 1950.

BALDWIN, HANSON W. "The Atom Bomb and Future War." *Life*, August 20, 1945, 17–32.

————. "Challenge of the MIG—And the Answer." *New York Times Magazine*, December 9, 1951, 9, 54–56.

————. *The Great Arms Race*. New York: Frederick A Praeger, 1958.

————. "The Myth of Security." *Foreign Affairs* (January 1948): 253–63.

———. *The Price of Power.* New York: Harper & Brothers, 1947.

———. "What Air Power Can—and Cannot—Do." *New York Times Magazine,* May 30, 1948, 5–7, 20–21.

———. "What Kind of War?" *Atlantic Monthly,* July 1949, 22–27.

———. "Why I Oppose Peacetime Conscription." *Reader's Digest,* July 1947, 103–107.

BARBEY, DANIEL E. "Let's Build This New Deterrent Force NOW." *Reader's Digest,* January 1958, 35–40.

BARLOW, JEFFREY G. *Revolt of the Admirals: The Fight for Naval Aviation, 1945–1950.* Washington: Naval Historical Center, 1994.

Barre Gazette. "Power Politics in National Security." Barre, Mass.: *The Barre Gazette,* 1961.

BARRETT, GEORGE. "Visit to America's 'Earthstrip No.1.'" *Reader's Digest,* December 1957, 88–90.

BARUCH, BERNARD M. "To Prevent War." *Reader's Digest,* February 1950, 33–36.

———. *Baruch: The Public Years.* New York: Holt, Rinehart, and Winston, 1960.

———. "World Atomic Control or Disaster." *Reader's Digest,* December 1946, 98–99.

BAUGHMAN, JAMES L. *Henry R. Luce and the Rise of the American News Media.* Boston: Twayne Publishers, 1987.

BISKIND, PETER. *Seeing Is Believing: How Hollywood Taught Us to Stop Worrying and Love the Fifties.* New York: Pantheon Books, 1983.

BLAIR, CLAY, JR. "The General Everybody Loves." *Saturday Evening Post,* August 17, 1957, 32–33, 65–67.

———. "Who Says Pilots Are Obsolete?" *Saturday Evening Post,* May 31, 1958, 31, 63–66.

———. "We Flew the 'Sharkbait' Mission." *Reader's Digest,* June 1957, 96–100.

BOAL, SAM. "Pilotless Fighter Plane of Tomorrow." *Collier's,* October 29, 1949, 26–27, 55.

BORGIASZ, WILLIAM S. *The Strategic Air Command: Evolution and Consolidation of Nuclear Forces, 1945–1955.* Westport, Conn.: Praeger, 1996.

BOROWSKI, HARRY R. *A Hollow Threat: Strategic Air Power and Containment before Korea.* Westport, Conn.: Greenwood Press, 1982.

BOYER, PAUL. *By The Bomb's Early Light: American Thought and Culture at the Dawn of the Atomic Age.* New York: Pantheon Books, 1985.

BRADLEY, OMAR, ET AL. *Effects of Air Power on Military Operations: Western Europe.* Wiesbaden, Germany: Air Effects Committee, Twelfth Army Group, 1945.

BROOKS, TIM, AND EARLE MARSH. *The Complete Directory to Prime*

Time Network TV Shows: 1946-Present. New York: Ballantine Books, 1979, 1981, 1985, 1988, 1992.

BROWN, MICHAEL E. *Flying Blind: The Politics of the U.S. Strategic Bomber Program*. Ithaca, N.Y.: Cornell University Press, 1992.

BURDICK, EUGENE, AND HARVEY WHEELER. *Fail-Safe*. New York: McGraw-Hill, 1962.

BURNHAM, FRANK A. *Hero Next Door*. Fallbrook, Calif.: Aero Publishers, 1974.

BUSH, PRESCOTT. "To Preserve Peace Let's *Show* the Russians How Strong We Are!" *Reader's Digest*, July 1959, 24–39.

BUSH, VANNEVAR. "The Atomic Bomb Is Not Absolute." *Life*, November 14, 1949, 128–30.

———. *Endless Horizons*. Washington, D.C.: Public Affairs Press, 1946.

———. "In the Air, Bombers Will Find It Tough." *Life*, November 14, 1949, 122–27.

———. *Modern Arms and the Free Men*. New York: Simon and Schuster, 1949.

———. "The Weapons We Need for Freedom." *Reader's Digest*, January 1951, 48–51.

BUTLER, IVAN. *The War Film*. New York: A. S. Barnes, 1974.

BUTTERFIELD, ROGER, AND FRANK GIBNEY. "The Twining Tradition." *Life*, August 26, 1957, 104–22.

BUXTON, FRANK, AND BILL OWEN. *Radio's Golden Age: The Programs and the Personalities*. New York: Easton Valley Press, 1966.

CANIFF, MILTON. *Damma Exile*. Princeton, Wis.: Kitchen Sink Press, 1956, 1957, 1991.

———. *In Formosa's Dire Straits*. Princeton, Wis.: Kitchen Sink Press, 1989.

———. "Steve Canyon and Me." *Collier's*, November 20, 1948, 36.

———. *Steve Canyon No. 21*. Princeton, Wis.: Kitchen Sink Press, 1988.

———. *Taps for 'Shanty' Town*. Princeton, Wis.: Kitchen Sink Press, 1989.

———. *War Games*. Princeton, Wis.: Kitchen Sink Press, 1957, 1958, 1992.

CARALEY, DEMETRIOS. *The Politics of Military Unification: A Study of Conflict and the Policy Process*. New York: Columbia University Press, 1966.

CHAMBERLAIN, CLARENCE D. "Shall We All Fly Soon?" *The North American Review* 226 (October 1928): 409–15.

CHASE, FRANCIS, JR. "World Changer." *Collier's*, March 9, 1946, 17, 59–61.

CHASE, STUART. "The Two-Hour War." *New Republic*, May 8, 1929, 325–27.

CHENNAULT, CLAIRE LEE. "The Flying Tigers Can Do It Again." As told to Edward B. Lockett. *Reader's Digest*, September 1954, 11–15.

———. *Way of a Fighter: The Memoirs of Claire Lee Chennault*. Edited by Robert Hotz. New York: G. P. Putnam's Sons, 1949.

CLARKE, I. F. *Voices Prophesying War: Future Wars 1763–3749*. Oxford and New York: Oxford University Press, 1992.

CLODFELTER, MARK. *The Limits of Air Power: The American Bombing of North Vietnam*. New York: Free Press, 1989.

COFFEY, THOMAS M. *Decision over Schweinfurt: The U.S. 8th Air Force Battle for Daylight Bombing*. New York: Robert Hale, 1977.

————. *Iron Eagle: The Turbulent Life of General Curtis LeMay*. New York: Crown Publishers, 1986.

Collier's. "Air-Age Babes in Toyland." August 27, 1949, 74.

————. "How Do You Rate in the AIR-Q Test?" September 8, 1945, 54.

————. "Mission Completed." June 21, 1947, 79.

————. "Our Aerial Arsenal." December 25, 1948, 34–35.

————. "Twelve Seconds that Shrank the Earth." December 25, 1948, 94.

COOKE, CHARLES M. "Soldiers Need Wings: The Development of Ground-Air Forces." *Foreign Affairs* (July 1949): 576–85.

COOPER, JOHN C. "Air Power and the Coming Peace Treaties." *Foreign Affairs* (April 1946): 441–52.

————. *The Fundamentals of Air Power*. Washington, D.C.: National Air Council, 1948.

————. *The Right to Fly*. New York: Henry Holt, 1947.

COPP, DEWITT S. *A Few Great Captains: The Men and Events that Shaped the Development of U.S. Air Power*. McLean, Va.: EPM Publications, 1980.

CORN, JOSEPH J. *The Winged Gospel: America's Romance with Aviation, 1900–1950*. New York: Oxford University Press, 1983.

CORT, DAVID. *The Sin of Henry R. Luce: An Anatomy of Journalism*. Secaucus, N.J.: Lyle Stuart, 1974.

COTTRELL, LEONARD S., JR., AND SYLVIA EBERHART. *American Opinion on World Affairs in the Atomic Age*. Princeton, N.J.: Princeton University Press, 1948.

COURTNEY, W. B. "Air Power—Today and Tomorrow." *Collier's*, September 8, 1945, 11–12, 37; September 15, 1945, 24, 28–30.

————. "Power and Glory on Wings." *Collier's*, March 27, 1948, 25, 61–66.

————. "Russia Reaches for the Sky." *Collier's*, April 26, 1947, 18, 95–99.

————. "Will Russia Rule The Air?" *Collier's*, January 25, 1947, 12–13, 59–61, and February 1, 1947, 16, 67–69.

COZZENS, JAMES GOULD. *Guard of Honor*. New York: Harcourt, Brace, 1948.

CRANE, CONRAD C. *Bombs, Cities, and Civilians: American Airpower Strategy in World War II, Modern War Studies Series*. Lawrence: University Press of Kansas, 1993.

CRAVEN, WESLEY FRANK, AND JAMES LEA CATE, EDS. *The Army Air*

Forces in World War II. Chicago: University of Chicago Press, 1948–58; reprint, Washington, D.C.: Office of Air Force History, 1983.

CROUCH, TOM D. *A Dream of Wings: Americans and the Airplane, 1875–1905*. New York: W. W. Norton, 1981.

DAVIDSON, BILL. "Arthur Godfrey and His Fan Mail." *Collier's*, May 2, 1953, 11–15.

———. "Mr. Charm, of Washington." *Collier's*, June 15, 1946, 20, 24–26.

DE ROOS, ROBERT. "Safety Gadgets: Do They Kill Our Fighter Pilots?" *Collier's*, March 21, 1953, 15–18.

DE SEVERSKY, ALEXANDER P. *Air Power: Key to Survival*. New York: Simon and Schuster, 1950.

———. *America: Too Young To Die!* New York: McGraw-Hill, 1961.

———. "Atomic Bomb Hysteria." *Reader's Digest*, February 1946, 121–24.

———. "Korea Proves Our Need for a Dominant Air Force." *Reader's Digest*, October 1950, 6–10.

———. "The Military Key to Survival." *Reader's Digest*, September 1950, 1–9, 163–80.

———. "Navies Are Finished." *American Mercury*, February 1946, 135–43.

———. "The Only Way to Rearm Europe." *American Mercury*, March 1949, 263–72.

———. "Our Antiquated Defense Policy." *American Mercury*, April 1949, 389–99.

———. "Peace through Air Power." *Reader's Digest*, February 1949, 18–26.

———. *Victory Through Air Power*. New York: Simon and Schuster, 1942.

———. "Walt Disney: An Airman in His Heart." *Aerospace Historian* (Spring 1967): 5–8.

———. "We're Preparing for the Wrong War." *Look*, December 9, 1947. 21–25.

———. "World War III and How to Win It." *Coronet*, January 1955, 116–21.

DE VORE, ROBERT. "What the Atomic Bomb Really Did." *Collier's*, March 2, 1946, 19, 36–38.

DEWEY, DONALD. *James Stewart: A Biography*. Atlanta: Turner Publishing, 1996.

DOHERTY, THOMAS. *Projections of War: Hollywood, American Culture, and World War II*. New York: Columbia University Press, 1993.

DONNINI, FRANK P. "Douhet, Caproni and Early Air Power." *Air Power History* (Summer 1990): 45–52.

DONOGHUE, DENNIS JOSEPH. "Military Interest Groups: The Political Attitudes of the Service Associations." Ph.D. diss., Miami University, 1972.

DOOLITTLE, JAMES H. "Safety Gadgets: They're Helping Our Fighter Pilots" *Collier's*, May 30, 1953, 14–17.

DORWART, JEFFREY M. *Eberstadt and Forrestal: A National Security*

Partnership, 1909–1949. College Station: Texas A& M University Press, 1991.

DOUHET, GIULIO. *The Command of the Air.* Translated by Dino Ferrari. New York: Coward-McCann, 1942; reprint, Washington, D.C.: Office of Air Force History, 1983.

DOWER, JOHN W. *War without Mercy: Race and Power in the Pacific War.* New York: Pantheon Books, 1986.

DRAKE, FRANCIS. "The Case for Land-Based Air Power." *Reader's Digest,* May 1949, 61–62.

————. "Give Our Troops in Europe a Chance." *Reader's Digest,* September 1951, 5–9.

————. "Let's Be Realistic about the Atom Bomb." *Reader's Digest,* December 1945, 108–12.

————. "On Guard! The Day and Night Vigil of Our Atom-Bomber Combat Crews." *Reader's Digest,* August 1953, 11–25.

————. "A Realistic Plan for National Survival." *Reader's Digest,* February 1958, 43–48.

————. "SAC Is Ready!" *Reader's Digest,* August 1961, 63–68.

DRAKE, FRANCIS, AND KATHERINE DRAKE. "Biggest News yet in Jet Flying." *Reader's Digest,* July 1953, 20–24.

————. "Do We Want the Second-Best Air Force?" *Reader's Digest,* May 1956, 17–24.

————. "High Drama in the Desert." *Reader's Digest,* January 1957, 13–20.

————. "How We Could Have Better National Defense—For Less Money." *Reader's Digest,* February 1957, 73–78.

————. "Our Next Pearl Harbor?" *Atlantic Monthly,* October 1947, 21–26.

————. "Threat to the Air Force." *Reader's Digest,* July 1954, 15–21.

EARLE, EDWARD MEAD. "The Influence of Air Power upon History." *Yale Review* 35 (June 1946): 577–93.

ELIOT, GEORGE FIELDING. *Bombs Bursting in Air: The Influence of Air Power on International Relations.* New York: Reynal & Hitchcock, 1939.

————. *Hour of Triumph.* New York: Reynal & Hitchcock, 1944.

————. *If Russia Strikes.* New York: Bobbs-Merrill, 1949.

————. *The Ramparts We Watch: A Study of the Problems of American National Defense.* New York: Reynal & Hitchcock, 1938.

————. *Victory without War: 1958–1961.* Annapolis, Md.: U.S. Naval Institute, 1958.

ENGELHARDT, TOM. *The End of Victory Culture: Cold War America and the Disillusioning of a Generation.* New York: Basic Books, 1995.

FARMER, JAMES H. *Celluloid Wings: The Impact of Movies on Aviation.* Blue Ridge Summit, Penn.: Tab Books, 1984.

FELLERS, BONNER. "Britain Turns to Air Power." *Reader's Digest*, October 1953, 57–59.

———. *Wings for Peace: A Primer for a New Defense.* Chicago: Henry Regnery, 1953.

FINLETTER, THOMAS K. *Power and Policy: U.S. Foreign Policy and Military Power in the Hydrogen Age.* New York: Harcourt, Brace, 1954.

———. "Should the Navy and the Air Force Merge?" *Collier's*, May 9, 1953, 13–15.

———. "The Strength to Win." *Atlantic*, October 1954, 48–53.

———. "When Russia Is Ready." *Atlantic*, September 1954, 29–34.

FINNEY, ROBERT T. *History of the Air Corps Tactical School, 1920–1940.* Maxwell Air Force Base, Ala.: Research Studies Institute, USAF Historical Division, Air University, 1955; reprint, Washington, D.C.: Center for Air Force History, 1992.

FISHGALL, GARY. *Pieces of Time: The Life of James Stewart.* New York: Scribner, 1997.

FORD, COREY. "The Truth about the 'Sonic Boom.'" *Reader's Digest*, February 1955, 67–69.

FORD, COREY, AND JAMES PERKINS. "Boss of the Missilemen." *Saturday Evening Post*, August 23, 1958, 88–90.

———. "The New Watch on the Rhine." *Reader's Digest*, September 1958, 117–20.

———. "Our Key SAC Bases in Spain—and How We Got Them." *Reader's Digest*, August 1958, 23–26.

———. "With the Men Who Fire the Atlas." *Reader's Digest*, February 1960, 213–17.

FOULOIS, BENJAMIN D. *From the Wright Brothers to the Astronauts: The Memoirs of Major General Benjamin D. Foulois.* New York: McGraw-Hill, 1968.

FRANKLIN, H. BRUCE. *War Stars: The Superweapon and the American Imagination.* New York: Oxford University Press, 1988.

FREEDMAN, LAWRENCE. *The Evolution of Nuclear Strategy.* 2nd ed. New York: St. Martin's Press, 1981, 1989.

FRISBEE, JOHN L., ED. *Makers of the United States Air Force.* Washington, D.C.: Office of Air Force History, 1987.

FRITZSCHE, PETER. *A Nation of Fliers: German Aviation and the Popular Imagination.* Cambridge, Mass.: Harvard University Press, 1992.

FUSSELL, PAUL. *The Great War and Modern Memory.* New York: Oxford University Press, 1975.

FUTRELL, ROBERT FRANK. *Ideas, Concepts, Doctrine: Basic Thinking in the United States Air Force.* Vol. 1, *1907–1960.* Maxwell Air Force Base,

Ala.: Air University, 1971; reprint, Maxwell Air Force Base, Ala.: Air University Press, 1989.

———. *The United States Air Force in Korea, 1950–1953.* Rev. ed., Washington, D.C.: Office of Air Force History, 1983.

GADDIS, JOHN LEWIS. *Strategies of Containment: A Critical Appraisal of Postwar American National Security Policy.* New York: Oxford University Press, 1982.

GALLAGHER, JAMES. "My Hop around the World." *Collier's*, April 16, 1949, 14–15,66–71.

GALLERY, D. V. "An Admiral Talks Back to the Airmen." *Saturday Evening Post*, June 25, 1949, 25, 136–38.

———. "Sea Power—Keystone of Air Power." *Reader's Digest*, May 1953, 29–35.

GARDNER, LESTER D. "The World the Kitty Hawk Made." *Collier's*, December 25, 1948, 36, 65–66.

GASTON, JAMES C. *Planning the American Air War: Four Men and Nine Days in 1941.* Washington, D.C.: National Defense University Press, 1982.

GAUVREAU, EMILE, AND LESTER COHEN. *Billy Mitchell, Founder of Our Air Force and Prophet without Honor.* New York: E. P. Dutton, 1942.

GAYN, MARK. "Terror in Japan." *Collier's*, June 16, 1945, 11–12, 59.

GEORGE, PETER. *Dr. Strangelove.* Boston, Mass.: Gregg Press, 1979.

———. *Red Alert.* New York: Ace Books, 1958.

GODFREY, ARTHUR, AS TOLD TO PETER MARTIN. "This Is My Story." *Saturday Evening Post*, December 24, 1955, 21, 58, 59.

GOLDSTEIN, LAURENCE. *The Flying Machine and Modern Literature.* Bloomington: Indiana University Press, 1986.

GRAY, JUSTIN. *The Inside Story of the Legion.* With Victor H. Bernstein. New York: Boni & Gaer, 1948.

GREER, THOMAS H. *The Development of Air Doctrine in the Army Air Arm, 1917–1941.* Maxwell Air Force Base, Ala.: USAF Historical Division, Research Studies Institute, Air University, 1955; reprint, Washington, D.C.: Office of Air Force History, 1985.

GUSTAFSON, PHILIP. "How We Would Strike Back." *Saturday Evening Post*, August 30, 1958, 25, 53–56.

———. "Night Fighters over New York." *Saturday Evening Post*, February 2, 1952, 32–33, 64–66.

HAGEDORN, HERMANN. *The Bomb that Fell on America.* New York: Association Press, 1951.

HAGGERTY, JAMES J. "The Atom-Liner." *Collier's*, May 23, 1953, 40–55.

———. "How Much Can We Count on Guided Missiles?" *Collier's*, December 11, 1953, 98–101.

HAINES, WILLIAM WISTER. *Command Decision.* New York: Dodd, Mead, 1946, 1947, 1973, 1974.

———. *Command Decision: A Play.* New York: Random House, 1947, 1948.

———. *Target.* Boston: Little, Brown: 1964.

HALLION, RICHARD P. *The Naval Air War in Korea.* Baltimore, Md.: Nautical & Aviation Publishing Co. of America, 1986.

HANSELL, HAYWOOD S., JR. *The Air Plan that Defeated Hitler.* Atlanta: Higgins-McArthur/Longino & Porter, 1972.

HART, MOSS. *Winged Victory: The Air Force Play.* New York: Random House, 1943.

HARVEY, FRANK. "Those Half-Pint A-Bombers!" *Saturday Evening Post,* November 5, 1955, 32–33, 127, 130.

HARVEY, HOLMAN. "Weekend Warriors." *Reader's Digest,* February 1951, 47–49.

HAVEMANN, ERNEST. "Air Guardian of the Western World." *Reader's Digest,* September 1954, 57–62.

———. "Toughest Cop of the Western World." *Life,* June 14, 1954, 132–47.

HEIDENRY, JOHN. *Theirs Was the Kingdom: Lila and DeWitt Wallace and the Story of the Reader's Digest.* New York: W. W. Norton, 1993.

HELLER, JOSEPH. *Catch-22.* New York: Simon and Schuster, 1961.

HENRIKSON, ALAN K. "America's Changing Place in the World: From 'Periphery' to 'Centre.'" In *Centre and Periphery: Spatial Variation in Politics,* ed. Jean Gottman. (London: Sage Publications, 1980).

———. "The Map as an 'Idea': The Role of Cartographic Imagery during the Second World War," *American Cartographer* 2, no. 1, 19–53.

———. "Maps, Globes, and the 'Cold War,'" *Special Libraries* (October/November 1974): 445–54.

HERKEN, GREGG. *Counsels of War.* New York: Alfred A. Knopf, 1985.

HERSEY, JOHN. *Hiroshima.* New York: Alfred A. Knopf, 1946, 1985.

———. *The War Lover.* New York: Alfred A Knopf, 1959.

HERZSTEIN, ROBERT E. *Henry R. Luce: A Political Portrait of the Man Who Created the American Century.* New York: Charles Scribner's Sons, 1994.

HILGARTNER, STEPHEN, RICHARD C. BELL, and RORY O'CONNOR. *Nukespeak: The Selling of Nuclear Technology in America.* New York: Penguin Books, 1982.

HOLLY, IRVING BRINTON, JR. *Buying Aircraft: Matériel Procurement for the Army Air Forces.* United States Army in World War II. Washington, D.C.: Center of Military History, 1989.

HOOPES, ROY. *When the Stars Went to War: Hollywood and World War II.* New York: Random House, 1994.

———. "When the Stars Went to War: Hollywood and World War II." *Prologue* (Spring 1996): 35–43.

HOOVER, HERBERT. "The Effective Military Policy for Us." *Reader's Digest*, May 1952, 40–44.

HORAK, CARL J. *A Steve Canyon Checklist, 1947–1988*. Calgary, Alberta: Remuda Publishing, 1990.

HUBBELL, JOHN G. "How a Pilot Learns Discipline." *Reader's Digest*, November 1953, 1–10.

———. "Join Me in One of the New Jet Tankers." *Reader's Digest*, July 1957, 50–54.

———. "Men against the Sky." *Reader's Digest*, February 1957, 47–52.

———. "They Learn to Survive—the Hard Way." *Reader's Digest*, December 1955, 43–51.

———. "Tireless Sentinel for North America." *Reader's Digest*, October 1960, 108–14.

———. "Tough Tommy Power—Our Deterrent-in-Chief." *Reader's Digest*, May 1964, 71–76.

HUBLER, RICHARD G. *SAC: The Strategic Air Command*. New York: Duell, Sloan and Pearce, 1958.

HUIE, WILLIAM BRADFORD. "The A-Bomb General of Our Air Force." *Coronet* (October 25, 1950): 87–91.

———. "The Backwardness of Navy Brass." *American Mercury*, June 1946, 647–53.

———. *The Case against the Admirals: Why We Must Have a Unified Command*. New York: E. P. Dutton, 1946.

———. "The Facts which Must Prevent War." *Reader's Digest*, January 1949, 23–30.

———. *The Fight for Air Power*. New York: L. B. Fischer, 1942.

———. *The Hiroshima Pilot*. New York: G. P. Putnam's Sons, 1964.

———. "How the Next War Will Be Fought." *American Mercury*, April 1946, 432–37.

———. *In the Hours of Night*. New York: Delacorte Press, 1975.

———. "A Navy—Or an Air Force." *Reader's Digest*, December 1948, 62–67.

———. "Navy Brass Imperils Our Defense." *American Mercury*, July 1948, 7–14.

———. "Shall We Abolish the Marine Corps?" *American Mercury*, September 1948, 273–80.

———. "The Struggle for American Air Power." *Reader's Digest*, April 1949, 1–6, 124–30.

———. "Untold Facts in the Forrestal Case." *New American Mercury*, December 1950, 643–52.

———. "Why We Must Have the World's Best Air Force." *Reader's Digest*, March 1949, 27–34.

HURLEY, ALFRED F. *Billy Mitchell: Crusader for Air Power*. New York: Franklin Watts, 1964.

HUSE, NANCY. *The Survival Tales of John Hersey.* Troy, N.Y.: Whitson Publishing, 1983.

ISENBERG, MICHAEL T. *Shield of the Republic: The United States Navy in an Era of Cold War and Violent Peace.* New York: St. Martin's Press, 1993.

JONES, ERNEST. "The Show Goes On." *Collier's,* September 28, 1946, 97.

KAGAN, NORMAN. *The War Film.* New York: Pyramid Publications, 1974.

KENNETT, LEE. *The First Air War, 1914–1918.* New York: Free Press, 1991.

———. *A History of Strategic Bombing.* New York: Charles Scribner's Sons, 1982.

KENNEY, GEORGE C., AND BERNARD BRODIE. "Our Air Force under Attack." *Saturday Review* (February 18, 1950): 14–15.

KEYHOE, DONALD E. "Seeing America with Lindbergh." *National Geographic,* January 1928, 1–46.

KILLIAN, JAMES R., JR., AND A. G. HILL. "More Facts for a Continental Defense." *Atlantic* (November 1953): 37–41.

KINNARD, DOUGLAS. *President Eisenhower and Strategy Management: A Study in Defense Politics.* Lexington: University Press of Kentucky, 1977.

KLUCKHOHN, FRANK. "The Russian Knock on Alaska's Door." *Collier's,* December 18, 1948, 13, 49–54.

KNEBEL, FLETCHER. "Red Jets Can Rule the Skies." *Look,* April 7, 1953, 31–35.

———. "Remote Control War: Are We Ready for It?" *Look,* November 21, 1950, 33–37.

KNEBEL, FLETCHER, AND CHARLES W. BAILEY II. *No High Ground.* New York: Harper & Brothers, 1960.

———. *Seven Days in May.* New York: Harper & Brothers, 1962.

KOZOL, WENDY. *Life's America: Family and Nation in Postwar Photojournalism.* Philadelphia: Temple University Press, 1994.

LAGEMANN, JOHN KORD. "The Handwriting on the Ice." *Collier's,* November 16, 1946, 18–19, 39–41.

LANGEWIESCHE, WOLFGANG. "Canaveral—From the Cape to the Stars." *Reader's Digest,* June 1959, 114–20.

———. "The Skyrocketing Cost of Air Power." *Reader's Digest,* June 1953, 29–34.

———. "Soon You'll Be Flying the Polar Path." *Reader's Digest,* December 1956, 64–69.

LAPP, RALPH E., AND STEWART ALSOP. "We Can Smash the Red A-Bombers." *Saturday Evening Post,* March 21, 1953, 19–21, 82–86.

LAURENCE, WILLIAM L. "How Hellish Is the H Bomb?" *Look,* April 21, 1953.

———. "Why There Can Not Be Another War." *Reader's Digest,* November 1956, 98–100.

LAY, BEIRNE, JR. "I Saw Regensburg Destroyed." *Saturday Evening Post,* November 6, 1943, 9–11, 85–88.

———. *I Wanted Wings.* New York: Harper & Brothers, 1937.

———. *I've Had It: The Survival of a Bomb Group Commander* (also published as *Presumed Dead*). New York: Harper & Brothers, 1945.

———. "Why Army, Navy, and Air Must Combine at the Top." *Reader's Digest,* November 1945, 29–32.

LAY, BEIRNE, JR., AND SY BARTLETT. *Twelve O'clock High!* New York: Dodd, Mead, 1948.

LEE, RUSSELL E. "Impact of *Victory Through Air Power* Part I: The Army Air Forces' Reaction." *Air Power History* (Summer 1993): 3–13.

———. "Impact of *Victory Through Air Power* Part II: The Navy Response." *Air Power History* (Fall 1993): 20–30.

LEMAY, CURTIS E., AND MACKINLAY KANTOR. *Mission with LeMay: My Story.* Garden City, N.Y.: Doubleday, 1965.

LEVIERO, ANTHONY. "Air War across the Pole." *New York Times Magazine,* December 14, 1947, 10–11, 61–65.

LEVINE, ISAAC DON. *Mitchell: Pioneer of Air Power.* Cleveland: World Publishing, 1943.

LIDDELL HART, B. H. *Paris; or, The Future of War.* New York: E. P. Dutton, 1925.

Life. "Aerial Gunnery Meet." May 8, 1950.

———. "Aerial Protector around the World." December 23, 1957, 41–45.

———. "Air Age: Man's New Way of Life in World Reshaped by Conquest of Skies." June 18, 1956, 14–25, 67–82, 99–104, 109–14, 135–52, 154–61.

———. "Air Defense of the U.S." January 22, 1951, 77–89.

———. "Air Force Knocks Our Navy's Super Carrier." May 2, 1949, 46–47.

———. "The Air Force's New Command Team." November 1, 1948, 87–90.

———. "An Air Show with Live Bombs." January 3, 1949, 64–69.

———. "The Armed Services Battle It Out." June 16, 1949, 41–47.

———. "The Atomic Age." August 20, 1945, 32.

———. "Atomic Control." October 10, 1949, 38–39.

———. "Atomic Warfare." August 16, 1948, 91–104.

———. "Barnstorming Take-Off for Jet Fighter." November 23, 1959.

———. "Can Russia Deliver the Bomb?" October 10, 1949, 44–45.

———. "52s Shrink a World: a Historic Show of U.S. Power." January 28, 1957, 21–27.

———. "From Continent to Continent." March 7, 1955, 28–31.

———. "Helicopter Safari in Africa." June 10, 1957, 80–93.

———. "How Could Soviet Attack Come?" February 27, 1950, 21–23.

———. "Jet Age Man." December 6, 1954, 48, 141–58.

———. "Jets over Germany." October 11, 1948, 101–105.

————. "Off Hours of a Tough General." October 29, 1961, 147–50.

————. "P-80's." December 9, 1946, 98–105.

————. "Plane Makers Turn It On." August 28, 1950, 45–48.

————. "Red Air Force in Close-Up." July 9, 1956, 90–96.

————. "A Report on Air Policy." January 26, 1948, 35–37.

————. "SAC Alert." June 23, 1961, 30–35.

————. "SAC: The Strategic Air Command Has Its Big Planes Ready for Intercontinental War." August 21, 1951, 86–100.

————. "A Shoestring Is Not Enough." June 11, 1951, 28.

————. "The Struggle for Aerial Supremacy." April 28, 1952, 28–29.

————. "Test for a B-52 Crew." June 9, 1958.

————. "The 36-Hour War." November 19, 1945, 27–35.

————. "Twelve O'clock High." February 20, 1950, 55–58.

————. "The U.S. Arms for Peace." May 17, 1948, 33–39.

————. "Victory through Air Power." July 19, 1943, 50–52.

————. "War Can Come; Will We Be Ready?" February 27, 1950, 21–22.

————. "The War End." August 20, 1945, 25–31.

————. "Who Fights Brush-Fire Wars?" January 13, 1961, 43.

————. "The 'Wild Blue Yonder Boys' Snap into a Salute for G.I.s." August 28, 1950, 32–33.

LINDBERGH, CHARLES A. *The Spirit of St. Louis*. New York: Charles Scribner's Sons, 1953.

LIPPMANN, WALTER. "The Russian-American War." *Atlantic* (July 1949): 17–21.

————. "Why We Are Disarming Ourselves." *Reader's Digest*, November 1946, 1–4.

Literary Digest, The. "Deeds of Captain Rickenbacker Whose Middle Name Is 'Victor.'" 61 (April 5, 1919): 64–66.

————. "'Strafing' New York from the Clouds." 101 (June 8, 1929): 60–66.

LITTELL, ROBERT. "What the Atom Bomb Would Do to Us." *Reader's Digest*, May 1946, 125–28.

Look. "Test for Combat." June 30, 1953, 80–83.

MANCHESTER, HARLAND. "Green Light for Air Power—From Borax." *Reader's Digest*, January 1958, 87–89.

MARTIN, HAROLD H. "Are Our Big Bombers Ready to Go?" *Saturday Evening Post*, December 30, 1950, 63–67.

MASON, GEORGE. "Lobster Line." *Colliers*, January 25, 1945, 85.

MAY, ELAINE TYLER. *Homeward Bound: American Families in the Cold War Era*. New York: Basic Books, 1988, 1999.

MACDONALD, CHARLES B. "Novels of World War II: The First Round." *Military Affairs* (October 10, 1950): 42–46.

MCEVOY, J. P. "'Hold 'Em! Harass 'Em! Hamstring 'Em!' The Chennault Plan." *Reader's Digest*, October 1949, 25–28.

MACISAAC, DAVID. *Strategic Bombing in World War Two: The Story of the United States Strategic Bombing Survey.* New York: Garland Publishing, 1976.

MCFARLAND, STEPHEN L. *America's Pursuit of Precision Bombing, 1910–1945.* Washington, D.C.: Smithsonian Institution Press, 1995.

MEILINGER, PHILIP S. *Hoyt S. Vandenberg: The Life of a General.* Bloomington: Indiana University Press, 1989.

———. "Proselytiser and Prophet: Alexander P. de Seversky and American Airpower." In *Airpower: Theory and Practice.* Edited by John Gooch. London: Frank Cass, 1995.

MERRY, ROBERT W. *Taking on the World: Joseph and Stewart Alsop—Guardians of the American Culture.* New York: Viking, 1996.

MERYMAN, RICHARD S., JR. "The Guardians." *Harper's Magazine,* October 1955, 37–44.

METS, DAVID R. *Master of Airpower: General Carl A. Spaatz.* Novato, Calif.: Presidio Press, 1988.

MEYEROWITZ, JOANNE, ED. *Not June Cleaver: Women and Gender in Postwar America, 1945–1960.* Philadelphia: Temple University Press, 1994.

MICHENER, JAMES A. *The Bridges at Toko-Ri.* New York: Random House, 1953.

———. "While Others Sleep: The Story of the Strategic Air Command." *Reader's Digest,* October 1957, 69–75, 219–44.

MICHIE, ALLAN A. "Germany Was Bombed to Defeat." *Reader's Digest,* August 1945, 77–81.

MIDDLEBROOK, MARTIN. *The Schweinfurt-Regensburg Mission.* New York: Charles Scribner's Sons, 1983.

MILLER, KAREN. "'Air Power Is Peace Power:' The Aircraft Industry's Campaign for Public and Political Support, 1943–1949." *Business History Review* (Autumn 1996): 297–327.

MILLETT, ALLAN R. "Korea, 1950–1953." In Benjamin Franklin Cooling, *Case Studies in the Development of Close Air Support.* Washington, D.C.: Office of Air Force History, 1990.

MITCHELL, RUTH. "The Saga of General Billy Mitchell." *Reader's Digest,* May 1954, 163–80.

MITCHELL, WILLIAM. "Aëronautical Era." *Saturday Evening Post,* December 20, 1924, 3–4, 99, 101–102.

———. "Aircraft Dominate Seacraft." *Saturday Evening Post,* January 24, 1925, 22–23, 72, 77–78.

———. "Airplanes in National Defense." *Annals of the American Academy of Political and Social Science* 131 (May 1927): 38–42.

———. "American Leadership in Aëronautics." *Saturday Evening Post,* January 10, 1925, 18–19, 148, 153.

————. "Civil and Commercial Aviation." *Saturday Evening Post,* February 7, 1925, 14, 169–70, 173.

————. "How Should We Organize Our National Air Power?" *Saturday Evening Post,* March 14, 1925, 6–7, 214, 216–18.

————. "Look Out Below!" *Collier's,* April 21, 1928, 8–9, 41–42.

————. *Memoirs of World War I: From Start to Finish of Our Greatest War.* New York: Random House, 1928, 1956, 1960.

————. *Skyways: A Book on Modern Aeronautics.* Philadelphia: J. B. Lippincott, 1930.

————. *Winged Defense: The Development and Possibilities of Modern Air Power—Economic and Military.* Port Washington, N.Y.: Kennikat Press, 1925, 1971.

MOLYNEAUX, GERARD. *James Stewart: A Bio-Bibliography.* New York: Greenwood Press, 1992.

MOODY, WALTON S. *Building a Strategic Air Force.* Washington, D.C.: Air Force History and Museums Program, 1996.

MOORE, SAMUEL TAYLOR. "A Bargain in Preparedness." *Harper's Magazine,* May 1924, 826–33.

MORROW, JOHN HOWARD. *The Great War in the Air.* Washington, D.C.: Smithsonian Institution Press, 1993.

MURPHY, CHARLES J. V. "The State of the Armed Forces." *Life,* September 2, 1946, 96–108.

Nation, The. "The Challenge of the Airplane." May 16, 1923, 561–62.

————. "The Next War." May 9, 1923, 535.

NEELY, FREDERICK R. "The Collier Trophy." *Collier's,* December 25, 1948, 30–31.

————. "The Winner of the Collier's Trophy." *Collier's,* December 22, 1945, 24, 80.

NEWCOMB, SIMON. *His Wisdom the Defender.* New York: Harper & Brothers, 1900; reprint, New York: Arno Press, 1974.

NEWLON, CLARKE. "There They Were! Jet Hop to Europe." *Collier's,* August 6, 1949, 24–25, 32.

OGBURN, WILLIAM FIELDING. *The Social Effects of Aviation.* Boston: Houghton Mifflin, 1946.

O'NEILL, JOHN J. "The Blasts that Shook the World." *Reader's Digest,* October 1945, 8–12.

ORRISS, BRUCE W. *When Hollywood Ruled the Skies.* Hawthorne, Calif.: Aero Associates, 1984.

PACKARD, LEONARD O., BRUCE OVERTON, AND BEN D. WOOD. *Our Air-Age World: A Textbook in Global Geography.* New York: Macmillan, 1944.

PALMER, PAUL. "Soviet Union vs. U.S.A.—What Are the Facts?" *Reader's Digest,* April 1958, 41–46.

PALTOCK, ROBERT. *The Life and Adventures of Peter Wilkins*. New York: Oxford University Press, 1973.

PARIS, MICHAEL. *From the Wright Brothers to Top Gun*. New York: Manchester University Press, 1995.

————. *Winged Warfare: The Literature and Theory of Aerial Warfare in Britain, 1859–1917*. Manchester: Manchester University Press, 1992.

PARKER, DAVID B. "Mist of Death over New York." *Reader's Digest*, April 1947, 7–10.

PARRISH, NOEL FRANCIS. "Behind the Sheltering Bomb: Military Indecision from Alamogordo to Korea." Ph.D. diss., Rice University, 1968.

PARTON, JAMES. *"Air Force Spoken Here": General Ira Eaker and the Command of the Air*. Bethesda, Md.: Adler & Adler, 1986.

PATTON, PHIL. "Dr. Strangelove's Children." *American Heritage*, November 1998, 92–101.

PENDO, STEPHEN. *Aviation in the Cinema*. Metuchen, N.J.: Scarecrow Press, 1985.

PERRET, GEOFFREY. *Winged Victory: The Army Air Forces in World War II*. New York: Random House, 1993.

POSSONY, STEFAN T. *Strategic Air Power: The Pattern of Dynamic Security*. Washington, D.C.: Infantry Journal Press, 1949.

POWER, THOMAS S., AND ALBERT A. ARNHYM. *Design for Survival*. New York: Coward-McCann, 1964, 1965.

PRATT, FLETCHER. "The Case for the Aircraft Carrier." *Reader's Digest*, May 1949, 53–66.

PRATT, WILLIAM V. "Air Power in the Arctic: The Crux of Our Defense." *Newsweek*, March 25, 1946, 39.

PRICE, WESLEY. "How Does Our Air Force Stack up against Stalin's?" *Saturday Evening Post*, September 6, 1952, 25, 136–38.

————. "How Strong Is Stalin's Air Force?" *Saturday Evening Post*, August 21, 1948, 26, 83.

PURYEAR, EDGAR F. *Stars in Flight: A Study in Air Force Character and Leadership*. Novato, Calif.: Presidio Press, 1981.

QUESADA, ELWOOD R. "How to Make Peace at the Pentagon." *Reader's Digest*, October 1956, 125–28.

RAGEN, ARTHUR S. "The Image of the Military as Portrayed in Three Novels Made into Screenplays since 1958: *Seven Days in May, Fail-Safe, Red Alert*." M.S., Boston University, 1964.

RANKIN, ALLEN. "One of Our Airplanes Is Missing—Again." *Reader's Digest*, June 1959, 39–44.

Reader's Digest. "The Facts about A-Bomb 'Fall-Out.'" June 1955, 22–24.

————. "Fastest Man on Earth." December 1955, 86–90.

————. "Man of the Missiles." June 1957, 47–51.

————. "New Facts about the Atomic Bomb." July 1949, 16–18.

————. "Our Triple-Threat Atomic Weapons." April 1951, 29–30.

————. "Why Russia Will Not Attack This Year." April 1951, 101–102.

REYNOLDS, QUENTIN. "The Battle Hymn of Dean Hess." *Reader's Digest,* February 1957, 199–206.

RICHARDSON, ROBERT S. "Rocket Blitz from the Moon." *Collier's,* October 23, 1948, 24–25, 44–46.

RITCHEY, RUSSELL. "What Would *You* Do?" *Collier's,* June 26, 1948, 28.

ROBINSON, DONALD. "How Safe Is Fail-Safe?" *Reader's Digest,* May 1963, 91–94.

ROSS, ANDREW. *No Respect: Intellectuals and Popular Culture.* New York: Routledge, 1989.

ROYSE, M. W. "The Next War in the Air." *Nation,* May 9, 1923, 537–39; May 16, 1923, 566–68.

RUBIN, STEVEN JAY. *Combat Films: American Realism, 1945–1970.* Jefferson, N.C.: McFarland, 1981.

SALTER, JAMES. *Burning the Days.* New York: Random House, 1997.

————. *The Hunters.* New York: Harper and Brothers, 1956.

SANDERS, DAVID. *John Hersey.* New York: Twayne Publishing, 1967.

SCHAFFEL, KENNETH. *The Emerging Shield: The Air Force and the Evolution of Continental Air Defense, 1945–1960.* Washington, D.C.: Office of Air Force History, 1991.

SCHAFFER, RONALD. *Wings of Judgment: American Bombing in World War II.* New York: Oxford University Press, 1985.

SCHIVELBUSCH, WOLFGANG. *The Railway Journey.* Berkeley: University of California Press, 1986.

SCHUBERT, PAUL. "Circles of Our Defense." *Collier's,* June 5, 1948, 18–19, 86–90.

————. "How America Will Defend Herself." *Collier's,* May 22, 1948, 16–17, 64–65.

SCHWARTZ, ROBERT. "Atomic Bomb Away." *Reader's Digest,* January 1950, 107–10.

SHAHEEN, JACK G., ed. *Nuclear War Films.* Carbondale: Southern Illinois University Press, 1978.

SHAIN, RUSSELL EARL. *An Analysis of Motion Pictures about War Released by the American Film Industry 1930–1970.* New York: Arno Press, 1976.

SHALETT, SIDNEY. "The Deadliest War." *Reader's Digest,* August 1946, 29–32.

SHERRY, MICHAEL S. *In the Shadow of War.* New Haven: Yale University Press, 1995.

————. *Preparing for the Next War: American Plans for Postwar Defense, 1941–45.* New Haven: Yale University Press, 1977.

————. *The Rise of American Air Power: The Creation of Armageddon.* New Haven: Yale University Press, 1987.

SHERWOOD, JOHN DARRELL. *Officers in Flight Suits: The Story of American Air Force Fighter Pilots in the Korean War.* New York: New York University Press, 1996.

SHINDLER, COLIN. *Hollywood Goes to War: Films and American Society 1939–1952.* Boston: Routledge & Kegan Paul, 1979.

SHUTE, NEVIL. *On the Beach.* New York: William Morrow, 1957.

SIGAUD, LOUIS A. *Air Power and Unification: Douhet's Principles of Warfare and Their Application to the United States.* Harrisburg, Penn.: Military Service Publishing, 1949.

SIKORSKY, IGOR. "What Can Aircraft Do in the Next War?" *Independent* (November 7, 1925): 521–23.

SIMONS, DAVID G., WITH DON SCHANCHE. "The Incredible Survival of Demi McClure." *Reader's Digest,* August 1960, 29–35.

———. "My 32 Hours at the Edge of Space." *Reader's Digest,* November 1957, 37–43.

SINGER, ARTHUR J. *Arthur Godfrey: The Adventures of an American Broadcaster.* Jefferson, N.C.: McFarland, 2000.

SKOGSBERG, BERTIL. *Wings on the Screen: A Pictorial History of Air Movies.* New York: A. S. Barnes, 1981.

SLESSOR, SIR JOHN. *The Great Deterrent: A Collection of Lectures, Articles, and Broadcasts on the Development of Strategic Policy in the Nuclear Age.* New York: Frederick A. Praeger, 1957.

SMALL, COLLIE. "The Biggest Blast of Them All and the Untold Secrets behind It." *Collier's,* August 6, 1949, 18–19, 40–41; August 13, 1949, 26–27, 34–35.

SMITH, PERRY MCCOY. *The Air Force Plans for Peace, 1943–1945.* Baltimore, Md.: Johns Hopkins Press, 1970.

SPAATZ, CARL A. "Air Defense and Air Safety." *Newsweek,* January 9, 1950, 22.

———. "Air Power in the Atomic Age." *Collier's,* December 8, 1945, 11–12, 83–85.

———. "The Air Power Odds against Us." *Reader's Digest,* June 1951, 11–14.

———. "Atomic Monopoly Ends." *Newsweek,* October 3, 1949, 22.

———. "Eisenhower and Air Power." *Newsweek,* June 16, 1952, 30.

———. "Europe in Late Spring," *Newsweek,* May 30, 1949, 35.

———. "Gambling with U.S. Security." *Newsweek,* December 5, 1949, 20.

———. "How Much Air Power?" *Newsweek,* March 19, 1951, 29.

———. "How We Turned the Tables in Korea." *Newsweek,* September 25, 1950, 28.

———. "If We Should Have to Fight Again." *Life,* July 5, 1948, 35–44.

———. "Learning the Lessons of Korea." *Newsweek,* October 16, 1950, 23.

———. "The New Budget." *Newsweek,* January 28, 1952, 23.

———. "The Only Hope for Peace." *Newsweek*, March 5, 1951, 27.

———. "Our Diminishing Air Power." *Newsweek*, August 8, 1949, 21.

———. "Some Answers to Korean Questions." *Newsweek*, July 31, 1950, 19.

———. "Strategic Air Power: Fulfillment of a Concept." *Foreign Affairs* (April 1946): 383–96.

———. "Tomorrow's Weapons Won't Help Today." *Newsweek*, June 26, 1950, 19.

———. "The Truth about Your Air Force." *Coronet* (September 1947): 10–16.

———. "Unify the Armed Forces." *Newsweek*, May 9, 1949, 26.

———. "Why We Need the B-36." *Newsweek*, July 11, 1949, 21.

SPAIGHT, J. M. *Air Power Can Disarm: A Sequel To Air Power and the Cities, 1930*. London: Air League of the British Empire, 1948.

STAHLMAN, JAMES G. "The Strategic Bombing Myth." Privately published pamphlet, 1949.

STAPLETON, BILL. "We Bombed America." *Collier's*, April 25, 1953, 15–18.

STOKESBURY, JAMES L. *A Short History of Air Power*. New York: William Morrow, 1986.

STOUT, WESLEY W. "This Aviation Business." *Saturday Evening Post*, March 21, 1925, 6–7, 104, 107, 111, 114.

STRAUBEL, JAMES H. *Crusade for Airpower: The Story of the Air Force Association*. Washington, D.C.: Aerospace Education Foundation, 1982.

STUART, JOHN. *Wings over America*. New York: Public Affairs Committee, 1946.

SUID, LAWRENCE HOWARD. *Air Force*. Madison: University of Wisconsin Press, 1983.

———. *Guts and Glory: Great American War Movies*. Reading, Mass.: Addison-Wesley, 1978.

SUSMAN, WARREN I. *Culture as History: The Transformation of American Society in the Twentieth Century*. New York: Pantheon Books, 1984.

TANGYE, NIGEL. "Flying Bombs and Rockets." *Foreign Affairs* (October 1945): 40–49.

TAYLOR, WARD. *Roll Back the Sky*. New York: Henry Holt, 1956.

TERRACE, VINCENT. *The Complete Encyclopedia of Television Programs, 1947–1979*. New York: A. S. Barnes, 1979.

THORN, BLISS K. "A Ride through the Sound Barrier." *Reader's Digest*, January 1954, 115–17.

TILFORD, EARL H., JR. *Crosswinds: the Air Force's Setup in Vietnam*. College Station: Texas A&M University Press, 1993.

TRAIN, ARTHUR, AND ROBERT WILLIAMS WOOD. *The Man Who Rocked the Earth*. New York: Doubleday, Page, 1915.

TREGASKIS, RICHARD. "We Need Carriers *and* the B-36—Without Fighters Our Bombers Are Sitting Ducks." *Collier's*, October 8, 1949, 16–17, 60–61.

TUPPER, HARMON. "The Exciting Search for the First Space Man." *Reader's Digest*, May 1959, 42–47.

TWINING, NATHAN F. *Neither Liberty nor Safety: A Hard Look at U.S. Military Policy and Strategy.* New York: Holt, Rinehart and Winston, 1966.

ULMAN, WILLIAM A. "Russian Planes Are Raiding Canadian Skies." *Collier's*, October 16, 1953, 32–34, 36, 39–45.

VANDENBERG, HOYT S., AS TOLD TO STANLEY FRANK. "The Truth about Our Air Power." *Saturday Evening Post*, February 17, 1951, 101–102.

VINSON, CARL. "For a 'West Point' of the Air." *New York Times Magazine*, June 22, 1952, 13, 35.

WALLER, DOUGLAS. *A Question of Loyalty: Gen. Billy Mitchell and the Court-Martial that Gripped the Nation.* New York: Harper Collins, 2004.

WARD, J. CARLTON. *The Economic Consequences of Air Power.* Washington, D.C.: National Air Council, 1949.

WATSON, GEORGE M., JR. *The Office of the Secretary of the Air Force: 1947–1965.* Washington, D.C.: Center for Air Force History, 1992.

WATTS, BARRY D. *The Foundations of U.S. Air Doctrine: The Problem of Friction in War.* Maxwell Air Force Base, Ala.: Air University Press, 1984.

WEART, SPENCER R. *Nuclear Fear: A History of Images.* Cambridge, Mass.: Harvard University Press, 1988.

WECHSBERG, JOSEPH. "Target: Hollywood." *Collier's*, April 5, 1947, 13, 47–49.

WELLS, H. G. *The War in the Air.* London: George Bell and Sons, 1908.

———. *The Shape of Things to Come.* New York: Macmillan, 1933.

———. *The World Set Free.* New York: E. P. Dutton, 1914.

WERMUTH, ANTHONY L. "Twelve Myths about Airpower." *Harper's Magazine*, July 1956, 78–82.

WHEELER, GERALD E. *Admiral William Veazie Pratt, U.S. Navy: A Sailor's Life.* Washington, D.C.: Naval History Division, 1974.

WHITE, STEPHEN. "Will Our Cities Survive?" *Look*, June 30, 1953, 35–37, 80–84.

WHITE, WILLIAM L. "The Little Tot Dog: The Story of an Air Mission." *Reader's Digest*, July 1962, 107–11,217–40.

WHITEHEAD, ENNIS C. "Our Airpower Can Enforce Peace." *Saturday Evening Post*, May 22, 1954, 22–24,149–50.

WHITELEY, JOHN F. "Alexander DeSeversky." *Aerospace Historian*, September 1977, 155–57.

WHITFIELD, STEPHEN J. *The Culture of the Cold War.* Baltimore: John Hopkins University Press, 1991, 1996.

WILLIAMSON, SAMUEL R., JR., AND STEVEN L. REARDEN, *The Origins of U.S. Nuclear Strategy, 1945–1953.* New York: St. Martin's Press, 1993.

WILSON, EUGENE E. *Air Power for Peace.* New York: McGraw-Hill, 1945.

———. *Wings of the Dawn: A Study of Air Power as a Contribution to Civilization.* Hartford: Connecticut Printers, 1955.

WILSON, JACK. "Service Rivalries Aren't Likely to Ruffle the Air Force's Calm Nate Twining." *Look,* February 23, 1954, 120.

WOHL, ROBERT. *A Passion for Wings: Aviation and the Western Imagination 1908–1918.* New Haven: Yale University Press, 1994.

WOLFE, CHARLES. "Nuclear Country: The Atomic Bomb in Country Music." *Journal of Country Music* (January 1978): 4–21.

WOOD, JAMES PLAYSTED. *Of Lasting Interest: The Story of the Reader's Digest.* New York: Doubleday, 1967.

WOODBURY, DAVID O. "Tokyo Calling Cards." *Collier's,* April 14, 1945, 44, 58.

YARMOLINSKY, ADAM. *The Military Establishment: Its Impacts on American Society.* New York: Harper & Row, 1971.

YARNOLD, K. W. *Lessons on Morale to Be Drawn from Effects of Strategic Bombing on Germany with Special Reference to Psychological Warfare.* Washington, D.C.: Operations Research Office, 1949.

YODER, EDWIN M., JR. *Joe Alsop's Cold War: A Study of Journalistic Influence and Intrigue.* Chapel Hill: University of North Carolina Press, 1995.

ZIEMKE, CAROLINE FRIEDA. "In the Shadow of the Giant: USAF Tactical Air Command in the Era of Strategic Bombing, 1945–1955." Ph.D. diss., Ohio State University, 1989.

ZIFF, WILLIAM B. *Two Worlds: A Realistic Approach to the Problem of Keeping the Peace.* New York: Harper & Brothers, 1946.

Index

Italicized page numbers refer to illustration captions.

Printed in the United States
149574LV00005B/22/P